FOUNDATIONAL CRISES IN SOUTH AND SOUTHEAST ASIA BANGLADESH, INDONESIA AND MALAYSIA

FOUNDATIONAL CRISES IN SOUTH AND SOUTHEAST ASIA BANGLADESH, INDONESIA AND MALAYSIA

Abu Nasar Saied Ahmed

AKANSHA PUBLISHING HOUSE
NEW DELHI • GUWAHATI • VISAKHAPATNAM

AKANSHA PUBLISHING HOUSE
4649-B/21, Ansari Road
Daryaganj, New Delhi-110002
Phones: 23268193, 09435116718
Email: ektabooks@yahoo.com
visit us: www.akanshapublishinghouse.com

Foundational Crises in South and Southeast Asia
Bangladesh, Indonesia and Malaysia

First Published 2011

ISBN 978-81-8370-247-8

PRINTED IN INDIA

Published by Akansha Publishing House, New Delhi-110002 and printed at Harmain Offset Press, Delhi.

In Memory
of
My Two Brothers
HASAN AND SHAWAL

CONTENTS

PREFACE

It is fascinating to see the diversity in the Muslim majority countries of South and Southeast Asia, such as Bangladesh, Indonesia and Malaysia, where ethnicity and religion interplay to create the foundation of the nation-states. My fascination to understand the problematic scenario in these three countries started in 2004 when I prepared a paper on what I assumed to be foundation crises in South and Southeast Asia to be presented in an international seminar. As I frequented the Library of Jawaharlal Nehru University, New Delhi, in search of data on the ethnicity, religion and politics in these countries, I felt it necessary to make a field trip to these countries. With the enormous support from the Ministry of External Affairs, Government of India, I could make it. My stay in Bangladesh for more than three weeks in November 2006 followed by a sojourn of two months in Indonesia, Malaysia and Singapore in 2008 generously supported by the Ministry made it possible to produce the present work in written form. In other words, it is the result of a sustained academic endeavour lasting for more than four years.

My friend Aris Ananta at Institute of Southeast Asian Studies, Singapore, while sharing many of the issues facing the Muslim world in our lunch-time on April 15, 2008 on the campus of National University of Singapore, told me, "I am a Chinese by race, Indonesian by nationality and Muslim by religion. I do not have any problem in adjusting my three identities. Likewise there cannot be a problem in the case of a nation, which might have more than one identity. It will be huge problematic if we drag these identities to political domain for short-term political gain." This is a classical comment, which I have found in many parts of the world. Long back in 1981-82, while spending academically rewarding time at University of Illinois at Urbana-Champaign as a Fulbright Visiting Fellow, I used to interact with a number of Asian and American friends working and staying on the University campus on issues of ethnicity, religion and politics. My Bangladeshi friend Zaffar, who had applied for American citizenship at that point of time and used to discuss with me the issues of religion and ethnicity, said to me almost in a similar language about his three identities. Linda, another friend of mine in the United States once told me "I am an Armenian-origin American. In my family life I am Armenian. I follow all the Armenian customs and traditions. I speak Armenian language. Like any American I speak English fluently. It is my second mother tongue. At the same time, I am an American by birth. I am Christian by religion. There is perfect harmony of my three identities." Almost identical view was expressed when I interacted with Radha Binod Misra, head priest of Shri Saitenya Dev Mandir at Gopalganj in Sylhet district of Dhaka on October 6, 2008. He is proud to be a Hindu and also a Bangladeshi national, at the same time, does not suffer from any contradiction whatsoever. Long back one of India's highly respected nationalists, Maulana Abul Kalam Azad wrote in *India Wins Freedom*: "I am a Muslim and I am proud of it. I am an Indian I am proud of it." Trouble takes place when we try to thrust upon certain super-imposed values on one of these identities and fight for a larger and dominant public space for it. A politically mature nation learns through experience the transcendental fulfillment in accommodating, adjusting and assimilating diverse identities. The readiness to learn from experience is the basis of the future of all diverse nations in the world. And there is no nation-state, which is not diverse.

This book is the result of my enduring consultation of literature available in the libraries of both India and abroad. I had the unique opportunities to meet a number of scholars, journalists, students, diplomats, and common individuals with whom I had free interactions. I had the privilege of presenting my research topic on which I had been working over the years before scholarly assemblies in Bangladesh, Indonesia, Malaysia and Singapore. The interactive sessions following my presentation helped articulate my thoughts and views in what I hold to be concrete manner. Consequently, it makes me feel happy that I got the benefit of the wisdom of a number of persons to whom I owe a lot. While many wanted to remain anonymous, others figure in the following section.

At the outset, I must express my profound gratitude to the Policy Planning and Research Division of the Ministry of External Affairs, Government of India, for being generous to me in providing fund to make my field trip to Bangladesh, Indonesia, Malaysia and Singapore in pursuit of my study. Without this enormous financial support the present work would not have seen the light of reality. A number of important functionaries of the Ministry were extremely helpful to whom I owe a lot, and they are Jaimini Bhagwati, currently Indian Ambassador to European Union, who had happened to be Additional Secretary to Ministry at the time of my preparation for the field trip, Amrit Lugun, currently Joint Secretary to the Ministry, Anup Singh, Director, Policy Planning and Research Division in the Ministry. I am particularly indebted to Bhagwati who facilitated the transshipment of several thousand pages of xeroxed materials, and more than hundred books and documents from Kuala Lumpur, Jakarta and Singapore to my place of residence. I am grateful to N.K. Saxena, Deputy High Commissioner of India at Kuala Lumpur, Mukhtesh Pardesi, Charge de Affaire, Troilokya Bora, First Secretary and Manika Jain, Counsellor at Indian Embassy, Jakarta, for giving me time to discuss many issues relating to the political developments in Indonesia and Malaysia.

It is difficult for me to find appropriate words to thank a number of persons who gave me institutional affiliation to pursue my studies. They are Sirajul Islam, President of Asiatic Society of Bangladesh, Muhamad Hisyam, Director of Centre for Social and Cultural Studies at LIPI (Indonesian Institute of Sciences) and, Hadi Soesastro, Director, Centre for Strategic and International Studies at Jakarta, Salleh Hassan, Director of Institute for Social Science Studies at Universiti Putra Malaysia, and K. Kesavapany, Director of Institute of Southeast Asian Studies, Singapore. They also gave me wonderful opportunity present my work and view points before an intellectual assembly at their respective premises, which helped me crystallize my ideas and ward off my unfounded misgivings. I had the opportunity to interact with a number of scholars. To name some of them are, Harun Or Rashid, Sonia Amin, Dil Rowshan Zinnat Ara Nazneen, Shaheen Ahmed, Nazmunnessa Mahtab of University of Dhaka, Anupam Sen, Vice-Chancellor of Premier University, Chittagong, Aminur Rashid, Executive Director of Shamol Bangla Media, Masud Mannan of National Defence College and Director General, Ministry of Foreign Affairs, Dhaka, Mohammed Sadique, Joint Secretary to the Government of Bangladesh, Hasanuzzaman Chowdhury and Iftekhar Uddin Chowdhury of Chittagong University, Herman Hidayat of LIPI, Jakarta, Abdul Rahman Embong, University Kebangsaan Malaysia, Fatimah Mohamed Arshad, Zaid Ahmad, Asmawati Suhid and Musa Abu Hassan of Universiti Putra Malaysia, Abdul Rashid Moten of International Islamic University Malaysia, Hussin Mutalib, M.C. Recklifs and Syed Farid Alatas of Singapore National University, Barry Wain, Aris Ananta, Daljit Singh, Bernhard Platzasch, Y.L. Lee, Ch'ng Mim See and Junainah Sariman of Institute of Southeast Asian Studies, Singapore. My relative Mainu Syed and her husband Syed Mahmoodulla who have settled in Singapore, deserve special thanks for receiving us at Changi airport and offering hospitality on the first day of stay in Singapore for three weeks. I had a long discussion with Ahmad Zahid Hamidi, Deputy Information Minister of Federal Government of Malaysia on various issues, such as, role of

Islam in the political process in Malaysia, the ethnic and racial issues, secularism, affirmative action and the elections of March 8, 2008. He was extremely courteous to my wife and me, offered sweets and tea besides presenting us a few valuable items as souvenir gifts. I record his gesture with profound gratitude. I will be failing my duties if I do not acknowledge with thanks three young persons who worked with me on this project, collected books for me and remained attached to me and the project whole-heartedly during my stay in their respective countries. They are Sahidul in Dhaka, Mohamad Azmi at UPM and Azam Mannan in Jakarta. I fondly remember Intan at ISSS for her helping hand in so many matters during my stay on the UPM campus. I cannot forget Zamri Bahrin, a driver of ISSS, who used to take me in UPM vehicle provided by Salleh Hassan from one place to another, from University to University, from bookstore to supermarket. He is an extremely informative person, who has a precise answer to all my small queries whether anthropological or geographical, religious or sociological. My experience with this wonderful man during my three-week stay in Malaysia will remain evergreen. His young wife Noor was very generous and courteous to us and offered us beautiful gifts.

I am particularly indebted to my teacher Anuradha Dutta for her constant inspiration and encouragement. I am grateful to Faruq-sad-uddin Ahmed of Gauhati University for going through the initial draft of the book and for offering critical comments. I thank Gautam Barua, Director of Indian Institute of Technology Guwahati and Archana Barua, Head, Department of Humanities and Social Sciences at IIT Guwahati, for extending infrastructural support. Rustam Ali deserves thanks for his technical support. My wife Ruby accompanied me to all these three countries with her supportive zeal and helped me in my library works besides offering critical comments on my somewhat whimsical conclusions. My children Sazhiv and Rosa are always infinite source of inspiration. They deserve my sincere thanks.

While I owe a great to all mentioned above for the support and cooperation, which enabled me to complete the study, I alone remain accountable for any inadvertent factual and interpretative errors that might have crept in the text of the report.

I dedicate the work to the memory of my two brothers, Hasan and Shawal, who left for their heavenly abode at a very tender age without getting a single dose of medicine. Poverty and remoteness of the place of residence took away these two creative, intelligent and innovative little geniuses.

Abu Nasar Saied Ahmed

ABBREVIATIONS

ABIM	Angkatan Belia Islam Malaysia (Islamic Youth Movement of Malaysia
BDR	Bangladesh Rifles
BA	Barisan Alternatif
BN	Barisan Nasional
BNP	Bangladesh National Party
CHT	Chittagong Hills Tract
DAP	Democratic Action Party
DDII	Dewan Dakwah Islamiyah Indonesia (Council of Indonesia for Propagation of Islam)
DPR	Dewan Perwakilan Rakyat (People's Representative Council)
GDP	Gross Domestic Product
GNP	Gross National Product
HINDRAF	Hindu Rights Action Force
HuJI	Harkat-ul Jihad-al-Islam
ICMI	Ikatan Cendekiawan Muslim *Indonesia* (Association of Indonesian Muslim Intellectuals)
JI	Jemmah Islamiyah
JMB	Jamaat-ul-Mujahideen Bangladesh
JMJB	Jagrata Muslim Janata Bangladesh

KISDI	Komite Indonesia untuk Solidaitas Dunia Islam (Indonesian Committee for Solidarity with Islamic World)
LDP	Liberal Democratic Party
MATA	Majlis Agama Tertinggi Malaya (Malayan Supreme Religious Council)
MCA	Malaysian Chinese Association
MCP	Malaysian Communist Party
MIC	Malaysian Indian Congress
MPR	Majelis Permusyawartan Rakyat (People's Consultative Assembly)
MUI	Majelis Ulema Indonesian (Council of Indonesian Religious Scholars)
NII	Negara Islam Indonesia (Indonesian Islamic State)
NEP	New Economic Policy
NPI	National Party of Indonesia
NU	Nahdlatul Ulama (Awakening of Ulema, scholars)
OIC	Organization of Islamic Countries
PAN	Partai Amanat Nasional (National Mandate Party)
PAS	Parti Islam SeMalaysia (Pan Malaysia Islamic Party)
PBB	Partai Bulan Bintang (Crescent Moon and Star Party)
PDI-P	Partai Demokrasi Indonesia-Perjuangani (Indonesian Democratic Party-Struggle)
PGR	Parti Gerakan Rakyat (People's Movement Party)

PKB	Partai Kebangkitan Bangsa (National Awakening Party)
PKI	Partai Komunis Indonesia (Communist Party of Indonesia)
PKR	Parti Keadilan Rakyat (People's Justice Party)
PKS	Partai Keadilan Serjaterah (Prosperous Justice Party)
PNU	Partai Nehdlatul Ummat (Community Awakening Party)
PBB	Parti Pesaka Bhumiputera
PPP	Partai Persatuan Pembangunan (United Development Party)
PPP	Parti Progresif Penduduk (People's Progressive Party)
PBRS	Parti Bersatu Rakyat Sabah
PBS	Parti Bersatu Sabah
SPDP	Sarawak Progressive Democratic Party
SUPP	Sarawak United People's Party
UMNO	United Malay National Organization
UPKO	United Pasokmomogun Kadazandusum Murut Organization
VOC	Verenigde Oostindische Compagnie (Dutch East India Company)

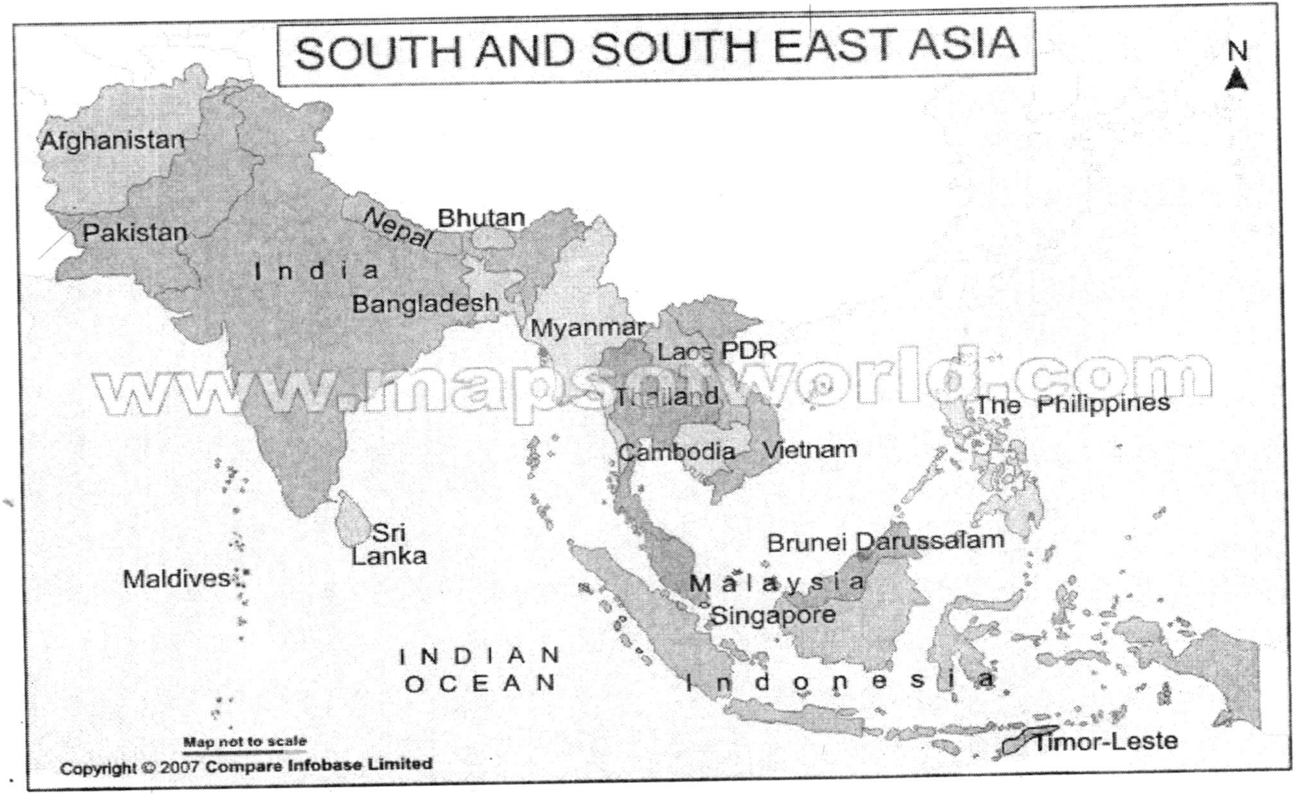
SOUTH AND SOUTH EAST ASIA
N
Afghanistan
Pakistan
Nepal
Bhutan
India
Bangladesh
Myanmar
Laos PDR
Thailand
The Philippines
Cambodia
Vietnam
Sri Lanka
Maldives
Brunei Darussalam
Malaysia
Singapore
INDIAN OCEAN
Indonesia
Timor-Leste
Map not to scale
Copyright © 2007 Compare Infobase Limited
www.mapsofworld.com

1

INTRODUCTION

The Islamic world is not alike all over. It is not a monolithic and atomized entity. It has a uniform prescription to the followers for adhering to the formal methodology of worship. It has five pillars of faith. The concept of monotheism, which is the guiding principle of Muslims' way of life, and the ways and means of keeping oneself physically purified to enable them to go for five-time daily prayer present a monolithic sacerdotal image of Islam. Beyond that the civic life is divergent. The Qur'an is eloquent on the diversity of humankind. There are several references in the Holy Book that the philosophy of life is divergent. What could be more exotic an expression to celebrate diversity than the following oft-quoted verses in the Qur'an:

> If Allah had so willed,
> He would have made you
> A single People, but (His
> Plan is) to test you in what
> He hath give you; so strive
> As a race in all virtues.
> (Qur'an 5:48 Abdullah Yusuf Ali translation)

To cite another eloquent verse:

> And among His signs
> Is the creation of the heavens
> And the earth, and the variations
> In your languages
> And your colours; verily

In that are Signs
For those who know.[1]
(Qur'an 32:22)

That mankind with enormous diversity was created from the union of two persons is also stated in the Qur'an:

O' Mankind! We created
You from a single (pair)
Of a male and a female,
And made you into
Nations and tribes, that
Ye may know each other.
(Qur'an 49:13)

The philosophy of creation is diversity, which has to be maintained and celebrated to ensure peace. The Qur'an enjoins obligation on the Muslims towards attainment of peace. Sura 36:58 says:

"Peace!" – a word
(Of salutation) from a Lord
Most Merciful.[2]

One more verse to supplement the holy spirit of the Qur'an:

...if anyone slew
A person – unless it be
For murder or for spreading
Mischief in the land –
It would be as if
He slew the whole people:
And if anyone saved a life,
It would be as if he saved
The life of the whole people.
(Sura 5: 32)

The discourse on diversity as the core of creation is not a new exercise. Ibn Khaldun (d. 1406), the 14th century scholar was emphatic in arguing that Islamic world is diverse and colourful. The diversity was there during the lifetime of the Prophet Muhammad. The diversity has grown all the more and is both pronounced and profound. Islam spread after the death of the Prophet, not entirely through military invasion and coercion to execute forced conversion, but largely and essentially owing to the missionary activities of the Sufi saints. Consequently, Islam rooted deeply in folk and cultural tradition of the local land, which is different from the other. That is why Islamic society in Muslim majority countries, as in the case of Bangladesh, Indonesia and Malaysia, is quite different from those in the Middle East, where Islam originated.

In the recent times, diversity is threatened by the call of a section of the Muslims intending to create a monolithic Islamic world by brutal force. The call is a threat-driven expression. How valid is this threat? Estimated over 1.3 billion Muslim community in the world which spreads over more than forty-seven Muslim majority countries extended from Algeria to Indonesia and substantially in many other countries such as India which has a Muslim population over 15 million, is a matter of renewed academic interests in the recent years in view of violent manifestation of anger and threat of certain section of the Muslim society. The religion of the Muslims, Islam, is one of the youngest faiths, born in the seventh century AD in the desert land of Arabia and propagated by Prophet Muhammad is a fast growing one. It is a matter of 14 centuries only during which a small community has engulfed not only Arabia but also spread in an epic proportion to cover the countries in Africa and Asia, and then moved to occupy a distinctive space in Europe and North America, and thus, to become one of the world's most populous religions. The Muslims are known to be the children of Abraham, the common Prophet of the Christians, the Jews and the Muslims, yet they differ substantially from the other two prophetic traditions. Islam is an uncompromising monolithic faith and to that extent represents an atomized sacerdotal-dominant and unifying force. Beyond that lie divergent social, political and other ways of life, which make the Islamic world fascinating and interesting. At the same time, the issues of religion are entrenched more or less deeply in secular aspects of life of all the Muslims, making them sometime indistinguishable from each other. In this way, Islam today is a prominent ideological force in the Muslim world encompassing wide ranges of human activities such as education, finance and banking, social service, health sector and undoubtedly politics.[3] The pronounced divergence and multi-faceted expression of Islamic society all over the world are sources of strength and not weakness. Viewed from that perspective, the threat-driven expression of a violent section of Muslims does not rest on any solid foundation. How can the Islamic world of 1.3 billion population having glorious history, literature, architecture, culture and tradition be so fragile to collapse in the face of perceived threats?

The Islamic world captured the imagination of political practitioners, scholars, policy makers and leaders of other faiths ever since the fall of Reza Shah Pehlavi of Iran and the eventual rise of 'puritan' Islam under the leadership of Ayatullah Khomeini in February 1979, when resurrection of political Islam had taken an all-pervasive form. From Algeria, Sudan, Afghanistan, Middle East, down to South and Southeast Asia, Islamic movements have emerged to install an alternative puritan socio-political paradigm. Such movements have been mostly violent taking toll of innocent civilians. The objectives are also varied ranging from toppling the democratically elected governments or traditionally installed monarchies to hitting hard the West's economic interests. The most glaring is the attack on the twin towers on September 11, 2001 which changed dramatically the non-Muslims' perception of the Islamic political world. Islam is often identified as a religion of the terrorists. The Prophet Muhammad is also not spared from the insinuation. The erroneous painting of Islam is based on a wrong understanding of the religion and socio-political dynamics of the Muslim community spreading over the world. It obviously leads to question – is Islamic world a monolithic and also violent?

In a recent publication of John L. Esposito and Dalia Mogahed entitled *Who Speaks for Islam*,[4] it has been suggested that the strait-jacketed perception of Islam representing the world of Arabia is inherently wrong. Beyond the sectarian cleavages of Shia and Sunni traditions, there is a vast Muslim world in other parts too, which is culturally, linguistically, socially and politically different from the Middle East, traditionally known to be the representative of the Islamic world. South and Southeast Asia is one such Muslim world, which has a huge population (Table 1.1) and at the same time different from others in the Islamic *Ummah* (community).

Table 1.1
Muslim population in South and Southeast Asia

SL No.	*Country*	*Total population*	*% of Muslim population*	*Muslim total*
1	Afghanistan	31,889,923	99.00	31,571,023
2	Bangladesh	150,448,339	89.7	134,952,160
3	Bhutan	2,327,859	0.5	11,639
4	India	1,129,866,154	13.4	151,402,065
5	Indonesia	234,693,997	88.20	199,959,285
6	Malaysia	24,821,286	60.4	14,992,057
7	Maldives	369,031	99.41	366,853
8	Nepal	28,901,790	4.00	1,156,072
9	Pakistan	164,741,924	97.00	158,152,247
10	Singapore	4,553,009	15.00	682,951
11	Sri Lanka	20,926,315	7.00	1,464,842
	Total	1,794,539,627	38.71	694,711,203

Being a fast growing religion, Islam has a long and continuous record of its expansion in the non-Arab region of South and Southeast Asia, not only in demographic terms, but also in cultivating a sustainable interface with local and indigenous culture, tradition and social practices. Like all other Muslims, the followers of the faith generally consider Islam as a self-contained system, which embodies beliefs and concepts of creativity, practicability and guidance for man in his relationship with his Creator and his fellow citizens, state and society. That is why the impact of Islam as a religion on socio-political life is pervasive and encompassing. The faith of the Muslims in their religion serves as an instrument of promoting not only spiritual enlightenment but also temporal aspects of social and political life. Therefore, John L. Esposito argues: "The traditional Islamic world view provided a holistic approach to life, a life in which religion was intimately and organically related to politics, law and society".[5] The all-pervading and omnipresence of God and his commands expressed through the verses of the Holy Qur'an provide the right and moral attitude for human action, both at individual and collective levels of society and the state.[6] A vast majority of Muslims believe that Islam is a total way of life and yet would like to remain unaffected by political manipulation and mechanization. However, many of them would go a step further to assert that Islam is an integrated totality that offers a solution to all problems of life.[7] It encompasses the three 'Ds' - *din*, religion; *dunya*, life; and *dawla*, the state. They argue that establishment of an Islamic state is the ultimate goal of the Muslims and towards the achievement of this ultimate goal, the Muslims need to create socio-economic, cultural and political life based exclusively on the fundamental principles of Islam.[8] It is pertinent to note that there is no reference in the Qur'an about the nature of the state, the rulers and the institutions of governance.

At the same time, there is no monolithic character of Islam. Two shades of ideas have always dominated the Muslim discourse of temporal life – strict adherence to Sharia law and Islamic ways of life as commanded in the Qur'an and the Hadith, and secular political life making religion as a private affair having least role to play in political life of a state. Around these two broad notions there revolves many other perceptions and ideas which tell about divergent and multi-faceted contours of the Muslim world.

Like other parts of the Islamic world, the Muslim community in this broad region of South and Southeast Asia continues to display its dynamism and diversity in various forms of expression, be it in the matter of language, tradition or social practices, dress and food habit[9], which have nominal association with the faith. To take three Muslim majority countries in the region – Bangladesh (89.7%), Indonesia (88.2%) and Malaysia (60.4%) – to score a point in the discourse, both religion and ethnicity have played a role in the national reconstruction in the colonial and post-colonial era. The interplay of religion and ethnicity has consequential bearing on the political processes of these countries. Bangladesh was born out of Bengali nationalism, which superseded the religious binding of the two geographically separated entities of Pakistan. A new-born country, deeply swayed by ethnic affiliation to language and culture, eventually faced Islamic resurgence at the behest of military dictatorship as well as popularly elected government, and thus, found itself embroiled in the foundational crisis of identity – Bengali first or Muslim first.[10] Neither religion nor linguistic nationalism could provide a canopied structure for the nearly homogeneous population of Bangladesh.[11] The attempt to supplant 'Bengali nationalism' by so-called 'Bangladeshi nationalism' during the military regime of Ziaur Rahman is yet to make headway owing to the inherent infirmities and confusions reflected in the very outline of the concept. This paves the way for the resurgence of Islamic groups to present an alternative paradigm for a massively Muslim dominated country.

Like Bangladesh, Indonesia is also a hugely Muslim majority country (88.2 per cent). It has also the largest Muslim population. Unlike Bangladesh it is not ethnically homogeneous. It is the home of around 300 ethnic groups spread over 13,000 large and small inhabited islands. While the Javanese constitute the largest segment of the population (42 per cent)[12], others remain in the periphery. In this largest Muslim inhabited country, the Muslims too are not homogeneous, as eloquently narrated by Clifford Geertz, and are broadly divided into three distinct categories – *abangan* (nominal), *santri* (devout) and *priyayi* (aristocratic/ bureaucratic).[13] In other words the Muslims in Indonesia are neither monolithic ethnically nor atomized religiously.[14] Geographically diverse because of its multiple and separated entities create a broad canvas of the archipelago, Indonesian political geography centering round Java, Sumatra, Sulawesi and Kalimantan provides both regional and ethnic dimensions. Consequently, politics in Indonesia has dynamics of ethnic and regional base compounded further by fragmented affiliations to the aforesaid three sectarian denominations. For all these inherently built-in considerations, Islam has remained at the periphery of political process in Indonesia. Indonesia has not officially used Islam as the cornerstone in the domestic and international politics. At the same time, despite its overall secular credentials, politics in that country is too complex to be comprehended easily.

Close to Indonesia and a part of the archipelago, Malaysia presents a different scenario. Known as a land of multiculturalism and home of four distinct communities – Malay, Chinese, Indian and Orang Asli (aboriginal people), Malaysia has been ethnically compartmentalized and constitutionally sanctified. Like Bangladesh, Islam is its state religion and other religions may be practiced in peace and harmony (Article 3).[15] The constitutional provisions in favour of affirmative action to safeguard and promote the interest of the Malay[16] and the natives of Sarawak and Sabah, known as Bumiputera (Article 153) preordain the interlay of Islam and Malay ethnicity in the political domains of the country. Politics in the Malay Peninsula, which occupied the center stage of national political scenario, is, thus, full of complexities.

The Muslim community is ethnically homogeneous with one Malay denomination, but at the same time politically divided to prove which segment is more Islamic. The attempt to have an inclusive image of national political system, both Barisan Nasional and Barisan Alternatif seem to have been preparing ground in that direction, and therefore, it has brightened the prospects of multi-culturalism in Malaysia. Nonetheless, the continued state sponsorship to promote the Malay-Islamic majority segment has sparked off agitation spearheaded by the HINDRAF in December 2007 and alienation of the Chinese origin Malaysian, leading thereby the erosion of the support base of the Barisan Nasional. The result of the alarming rate of erosion has been reflected in the March 2008 general elections in the country. The latest electoral developments is an early warning to the dominant political elite that unless multiculturalism in the real sense of the term is respected and allowed to flourish, Malaysia, might face many more unmitigated racial problems in the near future.

The panoramic contour of the three Muslim majority countries will be further elaborated and analyzed to make a core point loud and clear that all these countries are yet to form a consensus towards building either ethnic or religious based national foundation, or a combination of the both. The tendency towards modernization not in the western classical definition but in terms of better access to education, health, human security, gender equality and sensitization through secular and democratic means and movements are gaining ground in all these three countries. While trying to understand the current political scenario in these countries where the interplay of religion and ethnicity is profusely seen in the political process, it is imperative to have a close look at certain definitional issues such as Islam, political Islam and its resurgence in the recent time, and closely associated terminology of militant Islam, the question of ethnicity and interplay of religion and ethnicity in the political domains of a country.

A simple question as to "What is Islam?" is fraught with difficulties and controversies. The Holy Qur'an has often presents it as "Peace" which is a chosen word of God. For a dispassionate student of social sciences and humanities, the answer lies in the historical and textual roots of belief, customs, tradition and discourses on Islam. For an ethnographer, Islam is what Muslims understand it to be. Muslims differ even on theological definition. In a theological sense Islam means a religion of those who "submits to Allah". One who does not is outside the religion. This exclusiveness in the definition is also a matter of controversy. To brand some one as "non-Muslim" or "nominally Muslim" (abangan for example) sparks difference of opinion.[17] To quote John L. Esposito:

> The term *Islam* is derived from the Arabic root s-l-m, which means "submission" or "peace". Muslims are those who surrender to God's will or law, rendering them at peace with themselves and with God. To embrace Islam is to become a member of a worldwide faith community (ummah). Thus believers have a religious identity that is both individual and corporate as well as a responsibility or duty to obey and implement God's will in their personal and social lives.[18]

Thus, Islam and its followers, the Muslims, offer a broad canvas leaving enormous scope for wide variety of interpretations carrying potentiality of arousing political conflict of various forms among the members of the community. The political overtones of differences of opinion and controversies shape what the world today find it to be political Islam in which the causes and dynamics of conflict between the state and Islamic organizations could be located. There are occasions when both tend to hold contradictory positions on issues of religious doctrines, socio-political reality and ideology and political economy. There lies the fertile ground for the growth of political Islam. The attempt to create a space for Islam in public and political domain could be viewed as political Islam. That means that political Islam finds expression when issues that concern Islam and its faithful adherents are articulated and raised in public spheres with political objectives, ranging from policy formulation to capturing political power. There is a section of the Muslim society who believes that Islam as a body of faith has something to do with politics, society and economy integrating religion with state; they deny the validity of their separation by advocating the concept of "Islam *din*, *dunya* and *dawla*", (Islam is religion, life and state). The protagonists of political Islam reject the idea of multiculturalism and secularism saying that Islam has a sacerdotal face only. To them, Islam encompasses everything in human life, including the political, for its adherents living in any part of the world, and therefore, it has a unifying international image. They tend to attach the concept as a part of the faith of the Muslims. This approach to Islam, with an all-pervasive spectrum, provides the foundation of what is today understood as political Islam, which has originated in the form of a movement against authoritarian regimes, capricious government policies, corruption and moral degradation of ruling classes. It originated in the writings of Taqi al-Din Ahmad Ibn Taymiyyah (d.1328), a Syrian theological jurist of Hanbali tradition who tied Islam to politics and state formation. It has descended down to Islamic schools of thought better known as school of Islamic Brotherhood of Egypt in the 20th century. Eventually, political Islam found fullest expression in Algeria, Iran, Sudan and Middle East.[19]

A section of the protagonists of political Islam have taken an extreme position in the pursuit of creating an Islamic state of totalitarian character by violent means, where Sharia law would be enforced and a monolithic state structure would be created, in which non-Muslims would be treated well and protected as second class citizens. That resulted in the rise of militant or radical Islam.[20] One might like to use the term 'Islamist' or 'Islamism' to denote the violent approach taken by the militant Muslims to realize political objectives. It cannot be equated with political Islam just as it cannot always be equated with Islamic fundamentalism, which rejects copying of Western methods, affirming instead the comprehensive and effective notion of the Islamic message by going back to the basics laid in the Qur'an, Hadith and teachings of Prophet Muhammad. At the same time, fundamentalism in the name of religion might lead to extremism, i.e. radical or militant Islam. All violent movements, such as, resurgence of radical Islamic movements in Bangladesh during 2001-2006, Indonesia in 2000-2003 and Malaysia in early 1980s were manifestation of militant Islamic movements.

For the purpose of articulation of the role of Islam in three Muslim majority countries in the region, these terms have been carefully used to so as to leave no scope for loose interpretation or understanding of the basic thrust of the work.

Islam came to South and Southeast Asia through trade. Then followed the Sufi missionary activities, which led to widespread conversion to Islam. Unlike present Bangladesh[21], which witnessed military expeditions too that facilitated spread of Islam by both coercive means and Sufi influence, the spread of Islam in Indonesia-Malaysian archipelago was accomplished through Sufi intervention, which was essentially a non-military missionary enterprise.[22] While the Sufi tradition of Hanafi was active in the Indian sub-continent, the Shafi tradition played its part in Indonesia-Malaysian archipelago in spreading Islam. Sufis belong to the Sunni Islam and have two other traditions known as Hanbali and Maliki.[23] Sufis represent mysticism and are associated with "internationalization and intensification of Islamic faith and practice".[24] They preach about the omnipresence of all-pervading God, and also about the direct divine-human relationship which could be promoted and enriched through prayer and contemplation. They value spiritual development, enrichment of soul, emotional imagination and integration with God. Founded on equality and humane approach to life, Sufism believes in universal brotherhood, and therefore, has nothing to do with the Sunni-Shia schism, social or class, gender, territorial divisions, family connections and various schools of jurisprudence. That is why it could attract millions to Islam and could accomplish the mammoth task of speedy conversion in various parts of the world.[25] It is dear to both conservative and liberal Islam. Sufism is a common referral point in the process of massive Islamization in South and Southeast Asia. The most striking feature in this process is that Sufism, which represents a tolerant and liberal face of Islam, allows the retention of language, culture, and social practices even after conversion to Islam, for, the issue of faith in the monolithic concept of God and five pillars of Islam are pivotal, other aspects are secondary. Consequently, in all these three Muslim majority countries of South and Southeast Asia, the Muslims have retained and are proud of their culture, language and social practices shaped by Hindu and Buddhist traditions, which are so different from that of the original world of Islam.

At the same time, the evidence of religiosity among the Muslims of these three countries - Bangladesh, Indonesia and Malaysia – is as strong as those living in other parts of the world including the Middle East.

Despite divergence in social and cultural life of Islam, religion has a role to play in a society where Muslims constitute a substantial percentage of the population. Their group behaviour manifests in several ways. To cite precisely, some of the known expressions of experience could be a worthwhile exercise to illustrate how monolithic and yet diverse the Islamic world is. (i) Local issues and conditions encompassing economic, linguistic and cultural life affecting the common masses shape their social and political activities and responses. (ii) Various Islamic movements, both violent and peaceful, often defined as resurgence, have impact on all parts of the world were Muslims' presence is distinctly felt. Such movements could be either in relation to the West and non-Muslim world, or in the context of Muslims' search for an alternative political paradigm, based on classical Islamic tradition and implementation of Islamic laws. The contemporary Islamic experience in democratization and modernization, understood in terms of western model, is not so happy, since a substantial section of the Muslims considers the western methodology a threat to the puritan version of Islam. On the other hand, there are countries, such as Malaysia, which pleads for modernization and development of scientific temper. Such divergent discourses keep the Islamic world absorbed with common issues that transcend national boundaries. (iii) Revival of Islam through militant means is an alarming and most discussed issue. The militant Islamic groups with their terrible agenda of violence and destruction of innocent lives manifest another disturbing face of Islam, despite the fact that the religion has no role to play in supporting, promoting and prescribing violence of any form. Militant activism spearheaded by some limited section of Muslims has been considered as one feature of Islamic resurgence in responding to issues of modernization and globalization of Islam.[26] All these patterns of behaviour could be seen in the Islamic world, and therefore, South and Southeast Asia could not stand apart as exceptions. Politically, Islam as the religion of the majority in these countries played the most crucial role in formation of the respective nation-states. This is more or less evident in almost all the Muslim majority states in the world.[27] Taking the Islamic foundation of the state, the revivalist or radical Islamic forces have been trying to enforce Islamic way of life through enactment and enforcement of Sharia laws, either by ballots or by bullets. The recent growth of militant Islam is an offshoot of the extreme form of political Islam, i.e. militant Islam, which has been trying to take over the political system in different Muslim majority countries. The ideals of democracy, diversity, liberalism, secularism, equality, gender equality and more importantly humanism have become the causalities of intolerant surge of militant Islam.

It has been found that while ethnic issues having religious and political implications remain localized, the search for an alternative Islamic paradigm in the matter of governance and the resurgence of Islamic revivalism transcend national boundaries to make the Islamic movement a global one. The latter affects not only the Muslim world but also others. That makes the interplay of religion and politics, to put precisely as political Islam, difficult and contentious. What is political Islam? Is it different from militant Islam or Islamic fundamentalism, an expression, which is often contested with strong narrations? There is no universally acceptable definition of these terms. When Islamic symbols and beliefs become a matter of public issue and debate leading to mobilization of people belonging to the faith, a dialectical relationship takes place between individuals and groups on one hand and the state on the other. It produces political groups, which try to garner support of the masses with the ultimate objective of capturing power.[28] The entire process of using religious issues and symbols for political mileage could be precisely termed as political Islam. Such attempts continue to dominate the social and political map of the Middle East and the North Africa. At the same time, political Islam is different from 'fundamentalism', an overused expression of Islamic resurgence, which puts Qur'an at the central place in the religion. Just as "Christianity is the religion of and about Jesus, Islam is the religion of the Qur'an".[29] It is imperative that all Muslims go by the commandments of the Qur'an and to that extent all Muslims could be classified as "fundamentalist". The term goes beyond that. Fundamentalism "involves an effort to purify or reform adherents' beliefs and practices in accord with self-defined fundamentals of faith, and a self-conscious effort to avoid compromise, adaptation, or critical reinterpretation of basic texts and sources of belief". It is a movement that rejects "copying of Western methods, affirming instead the comprehensive and effective Islamic message."[30] Essentially a religious movement to confront a perilous situation in the Muslim world, fundamentalism turned into politically motivated one, when anti-modern and anti-West emotions gathered storm, at first in Iran, to topple the regime of Reza Shah Pahlavi and then spread all over, to capture the imagination of grassroots organizations to oust existing political systems in Muslim majority countries and to supplant them with Islamic regimes. The first political victory for political Islam could be traced to Iranian revolution of February 1979 followed by the imposition of military dictatorship in Sudan in 1989, which enforced Sharia law under the guidance of a fundamentalist movement called National Islamic Front. Immediately, it had impacted the Islamic movement in Algeria under the leadership of Front Islamic du Salut, FIS. The movement further expanded to Afghanistan in which the Taliban captured power soon after the Soviet withdrawal of troops. Bangladesh and Pakistan in South Asia, and Indonesia and Malaysia in Southeast Asia too have experienced similar movements in a varied degree and intensity, which were however not too strong to capture political power.

In this way Islam has proven to be in the significant force in public life of not only about 47 Muslim majority countries but also in the rest of world where the Muslims constitute a notable demographic segment. Besides, the contentious issue of demands raised by the Islamists for implementation of the Sharia law in the Muslim majority countries which has garnered a substantial support base of the both political and militant Muslims, the developments in the certain parts of world had far-reaching bearing on the Islamic world in terms of growth of the Islamists. The 1967 six-day War in the Middle East, which led to disastrous defeat of the Arab forces at the hands of Israel and huge loss of Arab territories such as Sinai desert, Golan Height, West Bank, Gaza Strip and Jerusalem to Israel, was the starting point of Muslim disillusionment and frustration, leading to a quest for an alternative political paradigm, now understood in the framework of Islamic fundamentalism, political and militant Islam. The pent up anger and frustration were reinforced by the subsequent developments, such as, another war in the Middle East in 1973, Soviet invasion of Afghanistan and occupation in 1979, US-led invasion of Iraq in 1991 and 2003, the Palestinian issue, the Russian onslaught on Chechnya and Serbian atrocities on the Muslims of Bosnia. All these not only inspired anti-west movements in different parts of the world but also raised a volley of questions as to why the Muslim society and governments are "impotent, authoritarian, poor, illiterate, and corrupt" and too weak to face West's anti-Muslim stance, and subsequently, led to self-criticism and a quest for identity along with a surge for capturing political power to set things right. An appeal for Islamic alternative within the framework of religious ideals and Sharia laws became the core of Islamic movements in different parts of the world.[31]

Bangladesh experienced such resurgence in the post-Mujib era, at the behest of both military and popularly elected governments. Various militant groups emerged with the objective of transforming the country into Islamic one in which so called Islamic way of governance would take place within the framework of Sharia laws. While the extremists indulged in indiscriminate violence targeting liberal political parties and leaders, intellectuals, media persons, judges and social activists who opposed their agenda, the political wings such as the Jamaat-i-Islami became a partner of coalition government with the objective of pursuing Islamic agenda through constitutional means. However, the Islamic movements – both political and militant – could neither capture power through electoral processes nor could score a military victory. At one point of time during 2001-2006 the militant groups surfaced at an alarming proportion, but the harsh measures adopted by the caretaker government headed by President Iajuddin Ahmed in the post-Begum Khaleda Zia period of two years have broken the backbone of the militants.[32] Coinciding the developments in Bangladesh, in

Indonesia, the Jemaah Islamiyah's terror tactics in the pursuit of Islamization led to the Bali bombing on October 10, 2002 killing 202 persons and its similar subsequent attacks indicated the rise of militant Islamic forces in the archipelago. But these terror tactics could not overwhelm the political will of the country to remain democratic and secular. The attempts made by similar militant outfits in Malaysia did not succeed much for reasons spelt out in the relevant Chapter.

It is difficult to find the dividing line between militant and political Islam when both attempt to turn religious issues to take political shape and colour, and eventually transform these as the basis of waging a violent course of action against their opponents and adversaries. Politics understood in terms of power capturing and sharing constitutes the core of all movements undertaken in the name of the religion. But religion, as such, is not a monolithic entity, which can command allegiance of one and all. Even in a comparatively homogeneous country like Bangladesh, where religion has a space in public life, it cannot unite all under one political banner. Ethnicity, religion, party affiliations, political ideologies, cultural diversities keep people divided, though not in mutually extremely hostile camps. In multi-racial countries like Indonesia and Malaysia where ethnic divisions are sharp, and so are political lineups, none can provide a canopied structure for one and all to assemble under. This is a basic parameter of human behaviour, which one could hardly wish away. That is why, there is a process of interplay of religion, ethnicity and politics in these three Muslim majority countries under the present study.

The study has been organized in order to make a country-wise presentation thematically and comparatively, so that the totality is not missed. The foci centrally seen in the three Muslim majority countries in South and Southeast Asia is that there is an interface of ethnicity and religion in the political process of these countries, notwithstanding the fact that just a single aspect cannot override the others for multifarious reasons. The most striking feature is that religion has not provided the foundation of these three countries, despite the fact that religion occupies demographically preeminent place. All these countries have a respective individual identity to be recognized and respected, even if religion is taken away from the national scene, because of long and rich ethnic heritage. These three countries, as their names tell, are known to the rest of the world not by their religion but by their ethnic and geographical identities. There would be no vacuum in the spirit of nationalism, even if religion is done away with. There could be internal contradictions as to which component, religion or politics, is pivotal and the all-pervading national symbol of these countries, but ethnic nationalism supersedes all other forms of affiliation.

NOTES AND REFERENCES

1. Abdullah Yusuf Ali interprets the idea of variations or diversities: "The variations in language and colours may be viewed from the geographical aspect or from the aspect of periods of time. All mankind was created of a single pair of parents; yet they have spread to different countries and climates and developed different languages and different shades of complexions. And yet their basic unity remains unaltered. They feel in the same way, and are all equally under Allah's care. Then there are the variations of time. Old languages die out and new ones are evolved. New conditions of life and thought are constantly evolving new words and expressions, new syntactical structures, and new modes of pronunciation. Even old races die, and new races are born." See *The Holy Qur'an: Text, Translation and Commentary*, Revised Edition, Abdullah Yusuf Ali translation (Brentwood, Maryland, Amana Corporation, 1989), p. 1013, fn. 3527.

2. Abdullah Yusuf Ali comments: "... we reach the highest grade of bliss, the mystic salutation 'Peace! from Allah Most Merciful. The word sums up the attainment of the final Goal. For it explains the nature of the Most High – He is not only a Lord and Cherisher, but Whose supreme glory is Mercy, Peace and Harmony." See *ibid*, p. 1129, fn. 4004.

3. John L. Esposito (ed), *The Oxford History of Islam* (New York: Oxford University Press, 1999), p. x.
4. John L. Esposito and Dalia Mogahed, *Who Speaks for Islam?: What a Billion Muslims Really Think* (New York: Gallup Press, 2007).
5. John L. Esposito (ed), *Voices of Resurgent Islam* (New York: Oxford University Press, 1983), p. 5.
6. Fazlur Rahman, *Islam* (New York: Holt, Rinehart, and Winston, 1966), p. 241
7. Nazih Ayubi, *Political Islam: Religion and Politics in the Arab World* (London: Routledge, 1991), pp. 63-64.
8. Mohammad Arkoun, "The Concept of Authority in Islamic Thought' in Klauss Ferdinand *et al.,* (eds), *Islam: State and Society* (London: Curzon Press, 1988), pp. 70-71.
9. Halal food is a non-negotiable mandatory concept for the Muslims all over, but instances of non-adherence could be found in some places, where some Muslims differ from one another in various types of Halal food.
10. Abu Nasar Saied Ahmed, *Fundamentalism in Bangladesh: Its Impact on India* (New Delhi: Akansha Publishing House, 2008).
11. Bangladesh is predominantly a Muslim country (89.6 per cent). The other segments of the society such as Buddhists (0.6%) Hindus (9.0%) and others constitute a small minority. Bengali is the official and most spoken language which transcends other primordial boundaries, and thus, the Bengali speaking population constitute (98%) of the total population.
12. Other segments of ethnic landscape are Sundanese, Madurese and Malays.
13. Clifford Geertz, *The Religion of Java* (Chicago: University of Chicago Press, 1976).
14. Bachtiar Effendi, *Islam and the State of Indonesia* (Singapore: Institute of Southeast Asian Studies, 2004).
15. Almost identical narration could be found in Article 2A (Eighth Amendment, 1988) of the Constitution of Bangladesh which reads, "Islam is the state religion. All other religions can be practiced freely in peace and harmony".

16. Article 160 defines: "Malay" means a person who professes the religion of Islam, habitually speaks the Malay language, conforms to Malay customs".
17. John R. Bowen, *Muslims Through Discourse* (Princeton: Princeton University Press, 1993), pp. 18-38.
18. John L. Esposito (ed), *The Oxford Dictionary of Islam* (New York: Oxford University Press, 2003), p. 144.
19. For a detailed discussion on political Islam see special issue of *The Annals of The American Academy of Political and Social Science*, Vol. 524, November 1992.
20. John L. Esposito (ed), *Political Islam: Revolution, Radicalism or Reform* (London: Boulder, 1977).
21. Present Bangladesh was known as Vanga since 5th century and then as East Bengal till the partition of India in 1947, when it came to be known as East Pakistan. It emerged as a free and sovereign country, renamed as Bangladesh in 1971 after a terrible civil war followed by India's military intervention to stop the acts of genocide.
22. Hussin Mutalib, *Islam in Southeast Asia* (Singapore: Institute of Southeast Asian Studies, 2008), Chapter I.
23. For some details see Francis Robinson, *Atlas of Islamic World since 1500* (Oxford: Phaidon Press, 1982), p. 29.
24. John L. Esposito (ed), *The Oxford Dictionary of Islam*, n. 18, p. 302. For details on Sufism in Bengal see Abu Nasar Saied Ahmed, *Fundamentalism in Bangladesh*, n. 10.
25. For some details on conversion and the role of the Sufi saints, see Nehemia Levtzion (ed), *Conversion to Islam* (New York: Holmes and Meier Publishers, 1979), Chapter 1.
26. John Obert Voll, *Islam: Continuity and Change in the Modern World* (Syracuse, New York: Syracuse University Press, 1994), p. 5.
27. Peter G. Mandaville, *Global Political Islam* (London: Routledge, 2007), Chapter 3.
28. For some discussion on political Islam see Dale F. Eckelman and James Piscatori, *Muslim Politics* (Princeton, New Jersey: Princeton University Press, 1996).

29. Frederick M. Denny, *An Introduction to Islam* (London: Macmillan, 1994), p. 345.
30. John L. Esposito, *The Oxford Dictionary of Islam*, n. 14, p.88. It is noteworthy that there are large number of publications which provide a more or less accepted idea as to what Islamic fundamentalism stands for.
31. For some perceptive assessment see John L. Esposito (ed), *Political Islam: Revolution, Radicalism, or Reform?* (London: Boulder, 1997), Introduction Chapter.
32. See Abu Nasar Saied Ahmed, *Fundamentalism in Bangladesh*, n. 10, Chapter 4.

BANGLADESH
Political Map
N
INDIA
Ruhera
Thakurgaon
Saidpur
Nilphamari
Rangpur
Dinajpur
Chilkamari
Hilli
Gaibanda
Phulchari
Jhanjail
Sunamganj
Sylhet
Naogaon
Bogra
Rohanpur
Santahar
Mohanganj
Mymensingh
Rajshahi
Rajshahi
Sirajganj
Dhaka
Shaistaganj
Ishurdi
Tangail
Pabna
Bhairab Bazar
Brahmanbaria
Kushtia
Manikganj
Meherpur
Akhaura
DHAKA
Magura
Comilla
INDIA
Jessore
Madripur
Laksharn
Gopalganj
Maijdi
Chittagong
Khulna
Khulna
Rangamati
Barisal
Bagherhat
Bhola
Naz Hat
Patuakhali
Chittagong
Dohazari
Kutubdia Island
LEGEND
International Boundary
State (Bundesland) Boundary
National Capital
State Capital
Other Cities
Mouth of the Ganges
Maiskhal Island
Cox's Bazar
Bay of Bengal
0 20 Km
MYANMAR (BURMA)
Copyright © 2007 Compare Infobase Limited

2

BANGLADESH: BENGALI FIRST OR MUSLIM FIRST

Situated between 20.34^0 and 26.38^0 North latitudes and 88.01^0 and 92.41^0 East longitudes, present People's Republic of Bangladesh, previously known as East Bengal during colonial era and East Pakistan from 1947 to 1971, is an almost plain landmass, with the exception of the Chittagong Hill Tracts, surrounded by a 4053 km long frontier with India. This deltaic country looks "Flat like a map" crisscrossed by countless rivers, which flow down from the Himalayas towards the Bay of Bengal.[1] A country with an estimated population of 147,365,352[2], Bangladesh is the 8th most populous country in the world with the highest density of population of over 1000 per square km. Taking the current growth rate of population at 1.48, the country will have a massive population of 192 million in 2051.

Table 2.1
Human and economic development in Bangladesh

Literacy rate	*47.5*
Population growth	2.2 %
GDP per capita	US$2053
Life expectancy	62
Annual growth rate	2.9%
GDP in US$	60.0 billion

Source: UNDP, *Human Development Report, 2007/2008*

Bangladesh is one of least developed countries. The UNDP report, 2008, puts it at 140 HDI rank among 177 countries in the world. Table 2.1 presents a general profile of its economic and human development.

Bangladesh had been passing through a difficult phase in the recent times. At the end of the five-year tenure of Begum Khaleda Zia's coalition government in October 2006, a caretaker government headed by President Iajuddin Ahmed had ran the country under the provisions of Article 58(b) of the Constitution. The general election for the Jatiyo Sansad (National Parliament), scheduled for February 2007, was indefinitely postponed after a nation-wide agitation launched by the 14-party alliance, headed by the Awami League, that virtually crippled the country. The agitation was spearheaded with demands to scrap the much disputed voters' list which was alleged to have contained more than 12 million fake voters, to remove the then Chief Election Commissioner, M.A. Aziz, who was a proven supporter of the Bangladesh National Party (BNP) headed by Begum Khaleda Zia, and to do away with the dual position of the President as the Chief Adviser to the caretaker government. The two former Prime Ministers, Begum Khaleda Zia and Sheikh Hasina Wajed, were put behind bars on graft charges. Under the circumstances, the economy failed to show any sign of improvement; in fact economic growth percentage was predicted to fall from 6.5 in the fiscal year 2006-07 to 5.7 per cent in 2007-2008, along with a fall in the export from 11.4 to 4.4 per cent during the same interval.[3] A gloomy picture continued till the installation of a new elected government headed by Sheikh Hasina Wajed in January 2009, after an emphatic victory in the elections held on December 29, 2008.

Bangladesh is yet to stand solidly on a constitutional democratic system. Its political history since 1972, i.e. after the liberation of the country and release of Sheikh Mujib from Pakistani jail, is yet to show political stability. Its history is marred by assassinations, military rule, uncompromising hostility between the two main political parties, and a long span of rule by the caretaker government backed by military. All these have a bearing in the reconstruction of national identity. Consequently, the country has not been able to resolve which way it should move – whether towards a liberal and ethnicity based, and democratic nation-state or towards a theocratic Islamic state governed by Sharia laws, as demanded by the Islamists for the last several years since 2001.

Bangladesh is preeminently a Muslim majority country (89.6 per cent). Most of the Muslims adhere to Sunni tradition. Although at the formative period of the country it pursued a policy of secularism till 1978, Islam was till 2010 a state religion. Through a constitutional amendment the basic structure of the polity was altered. Recently, the Supreme Court has restored the secular credentials of the country. Other religious groups have insignificant presence (Table 2.1).

Table 2.1
Percentage of religious communities in Bangladesh

Year	*Muslim*	*Hindu*	*Buddhist*	*Christian*	*Others*
1941	70.3	28.0	-	0.1	1.6
1951	76.9	22.0	0.7	0.3	0.1
1961	80.4	18.5	0.7	0.3	0.1
1971	85.4	13.5	0.6	0.3	0.2
1981	86.7	12.1	0.6	0.3	0.3
1991	88.3	10.5	0.6	0.3	0.3
2001	89.6	9.2	0.6	0.3	0.3

Source: Census 1991 and 2001

Ethnically Bangladesh is a Bengali nation-state. Its Bengali population constitutes 98 per cent of the total population. The rest are Urdu speaking Biharis and others. Two aspects of demographic composition have a role to play, as we shall find subsequently – ethnicity and religion. Apparently, these two are independent variables. At the same time, one is both Bengali and also a Muslim. Yet, there has been clash of identity which leads one to pose a question – whether Bengali first or Muslim first. Which one is the driving force in determining the identity of an individual and for that matter the identity of a nation-state in a comparatively homogeneous country? Bangladesh has experimented with the both at certain historic points of time. There had been popular movements in search of and in fixing identity around either of the two. At one point of time, it appeared that the people have laid the foundation of the nation-state with religion, but later on it was rejected as the basis to be replaced by ethnic identity. Then again, a determined section, quite sizeable in absolute terms and negligible in percentage, came out with a motivated campaign towards restoration of the past identity as an Islamic nation state. The victory of the Awami League in the December 2008 elections and the complete rout of the Jamaat indicate that the masses are asserting with the ethnic based national identity and they are not prepared to revert to Islamic identity of pre-1971. At the same time, it is too early to say whether Bangladesh has found a solution to its foundational crisis. Hence the question is Bangladeshi first or Muslim first. This Chapter tries to understand the matrix of the question that has been disturbing Bangladesh for quite some time.

Understanding that there has been a negative growth in the Hindu population due to continuous persecution and violence against this religious minority, which has been discussed elsewhere,[4] the above question is undoubtedly a social issue, but it carries a huge politically surcharged and contentious dimension. Bangladesh has not been able to find a precise answer to this question. There lies the foundational crisis in that country. Which of the two parameters is paramount in the articulation of national identity? Such uncomfortable questions lead to enormous politicking in most of the newly emergent countries in the world. The issue of national identity is a volatile one in all multi-ethnic states; some have resolved it, while others are still struggling. The present state of Pakistan took more than two decades to resolve the issue under the canopy of religion. To quote lengthy consensus about Islam deeply rooted in this country would be relevant:

> ...the wish to see the kingdom of God established in a Muslim territory...was the moving idea behind the demand for Pakistan, the cornerstone of the movement, the ideology of the people, and the raison d'etre of the new nation-state...if we let go the ideology of Islam, we cannot hold together as a nation by any means...If the Arabs, the Turks, the Iranians, God forbid, give up Islam, the Arabs remain Arabs, the Turks remain Turks, the Iranians remain Iranians, but what do we remain if we give up Islam?[5]

The rationale behind the creation of Pakistan through partition was an expression of the ideological commitment of the dominant Muslims of undivided India. It was a quest for Muslim homeland where the hegemonic class aspired to rule. Pakistan became a reality in the midst of an unrealistic situation not only in the geographic context, but also in other contexts of multi-racial, multi-ethnic and multi-religious nation-state formation. The East wing of Pakistan had a different story to tell at different stages of its history with religion taken as the initial foundational issue.

Islam came to the present geographical entity now called Bangladesh by means of military conquest of Muslim rulers in India. Islam arrived here in the 13th century when Ikhtiaruddin Muhammad Bakhtiar Khilji entered Nadia, the capital city of Lakhnauti ruled by a Hindu king Lakhmana Sena and conquered it in 1203-1204. Khilji created a small principality, which gradually started expanding into a Muslim kingdom by the latter part of the 14th century. By the next century, the whole of Bengal came under Muslim rule.

Simultaneously, there was massive immigration and settlement that contributed to the steady rise of the Muslim population in Bengal.[6]

Along with this invasion-related immigration and settlement there was massive missionary activities of the Sufi preachers of Hanafi tradition.[7] As in the case of most of the South and Southeast Asian countries, the Muslims landed in the geographic area identified by pre-colonial and colonial nomenclature, Vanga or Banga and East Bengal respectively, with seafaring traders from Arabia establishing a small colony at Chittagong port. [8] Along with them, a few Sufi preachers from Mecca, Yemen, Ghazni and Delhi came to the port city, to engage themselves in missionary activities. This is how Islam started to grow in a small way.[9] The conversion of Hindus and Buddhists, initiated by the Sufis, received a tremendous boost in the 13th century when Ikhatiaruddin Muhammad Bakhtiar Khilji invaded and occupied Lakhanuti. As already stated, it was followed by immigration and settlement of Muslims coming from other parts of India. Several factors, including conversion, led to transformation of Bengal into a Muslim majority region within a period of about three centuries.[10] In other words, the transformation of Bengal into a Muslim majority area was a resultant of a combination of three mutually supplementary elements – invasion, immigration and missionary activities of Sufi preachers. Among these elements, the role played by the Sufi saints was most striking. The occupation of Bengal by a general from the Khilji dynasty, was only a facilitatory starting point from where the other two clements took over in a massive way.

The transformation of the religious landscape of Bengal had, however, no impact on the social and traditional practices of the new converts, who retained their language, culture, rituals, festivals and names, making Bengali Muslims almost indistinguishable from their Hindu counterparts. It is also interesting to see that the overwhelming majority of the Muslims were poor peasants, virtually ruled by the Hindu zamindars (landlords). These Bengali Muslims were quite different from the Muslims in other parts of Northern India in terms of culture, tradition, language and social practices. They remained totally attached to pre-Islamic Buddhist and Hindu traditions. In this way, the Bengali Muslims became a social category quite different from the Muslims elsewhere. Their identity was essentially based on Bengali ethnicity and not on religion.

Emergence of Muslim consciousness

Being alarmed at the persistence of the Hindu face of the Bengali Muslims, who were essentially rural and known as *atraps*, quite different from immigrant, urban and aristocratic *ashrafs*, a revivalist movement started in the nineteenth century under the banner of the Fariadi movement led by Haji Shariatullah (1781-1840) to reduce Hindu influence and instill Arab-oriented version of Islamic culture.[11] It was followed by the Wahhabi movement, which aimed at supplanting the indigenous and folk oriented Bengali Muslim culture and way of life with a puritan tradition of Arab mould. The participation of rural Bengali Muslims under the leadership of Tutu Mir (1782-1831) and his son Dadu Mian (1819-1862) in 'jihad' in the North West Frontier Province during the first half of the 19th century[12] ignited the Muslim consciousness among the Bengali Muslims in Bengal. It was followed by an Islamic revivalist movement called Tariq-i-Muhammadiya, better known as Wahhabi movement, also aimed against the British in different parts of India, inspired by a call to 'fight for Islam'.[13] These two movements stirred the Muslim consciousness in Bengal but had only nominal impact on rural Bengali Muslims who constitute the bulk of the population. Fighting for the cause of Islam was an issue on which the Bengali Muslims of that period would have agreed. But to abandon the language, the tradition and culture shaped by several centuries in order to accept an alien Arab culture, tradition, dress, food habit and language was an altogether different matter in which they not prepared to give in. That is why these Islamic movements failed to make a breakthrough, despite the efforts to make the Muslims present themselves as puritan adherents of the Arab mould.

Although the reformers advocating puritanism among the Bengali Muslims failed to transform the socio-religious landscape of Bengal, they succeeded in another front, though that was not their principal objective. The nineteenth century reformers' attempt to import extra-territorial Islamic culture and plant it in Bengal generated social discourses on the distinctiveness of the Muslims as a community, encouraged greater degree of social mobility and provided emerging organizational structure which eventually enabled the Muslim League to grow at a rapid speed throughout this geographical territory. Although Islam as a religion and Muslims as a community found a solid space, the communal identity could not cut off the local root, which is indigenous and not external. The Bengali linguistic identity "could not be banished from the Muslim society of Bengal as it was the only language spoken by members of the society, but it could be Islamicized".[14] The concerted efforts to use Urdu and Arabic words in Bengali language during the nineteenth century led to the development of a new format of the language, known as "Musalmani Bangla". A syncretistic tradition secured infallible grounding which eventually helped crystallize the Bengali ethnic identity.

It was a somewhat confused state of affairs as to which direction the Muslims of East Bengal during the colonial era had been moving. Did they incline to Islamization or remain steadfast in their local roots, but at the same time upholding the Islamic values and symbols? They tried to strike a balance between Islam and Bengali character, for, it was impossible for them to be uprooted totally from the cultural, linguistic and traditional life of the place where they were born. At the same they could not sideline their religious faith.

The political dynamics of the Muslim community in the 19th century Bengal had something to do with the demographic component. The phenomenal growth of Muslim population to reach a staggering 48 per cent of the total population in undivided Bengal remained unnoticed till the publication of the first census conducted in 1872, which reported that Bengal had already become a Muslim majority province of British India.[15] The census report made the Muslim elite of Bengal conscious of their demographic strength as well as their profound weakness in taking socio-administrative responsibilities owing to backwardness in all fronts in comparison with their Hindu counterpart. This prompted them to take to western education, which eventually led to the formation of a Bengali Muslim middle class, capable of articulating their interests and identity, resulting in the partition of Bengal in 1905. This historic event provided territoriality to Bengali Muslims, more on religious foundation than anything else, including linguistic identity.

The sense of separate identity on religious count inspired the Muslims of East Bengal to join the chorus demanding partition of India. The background of Muslim separatism in an otherwise communally harmonious East Bengal started with the foundation of the All-India Muslim League in Dhaka in 1906 as an exclusive Muslim body, separate electorate and reservation of seats for the Muslims since 1909 onwards, simultaneously, the anti-partition movement of Bengal in 1905-1911 and the fear of Hindu domination among the Muslims consolidated their religious separatism.[16] At that historic point of anti-colonial movement, the Muslims of Bengal had the pronounced agenda of asserting their Islamic identity to the extent of taking recourse to massacre of the Hindu minority, in total disregard of other common identities of language, race, tradition and culture. There was virtually for no reason for the Bengali Muslim to join Pakistan except the putative fear of Hindu domination in politics. A fractured political and geographical territory was carved to satisfy the resurgence of religion as a basis for a nation-state in South Asia, without foreseeing the consequences of a geographically fragmented country with ethno-culturally opposite nationalities. A contested Pakistani nationality was too weak a concept to hold the country together for a long time.

Where has gone Islamic fraternity?

History is a reservoir of ironical events of adjustment, change, partition, reunification, nullification of popular concepts and theories, and countless political and geographical dispensations. No historian or political analyst could suggest in 1947 that a hasty and costly partition of the great Indian sub-continent on religious line would prove to be an exercise in futility, for, one of its wings was going to secede sooner or later. A number of scholars found Pakistan an unrealistic proposition with two wings separated by Indian territory over 1700 kilometers wide. Except for religion, which was the basis of partition of the undivided Indian sub-continent, within the framework of "two-nation theory", nothing was common and shared. The bizarre geographical layout of Pakistan has always been questioned by scholars.[17] The unusual geo-political scenario prompted Rupert Emerson to comment: "...by the accepted criteria of nationhood there was in fact no such a thing as a Pakistani nation".[18] It took a quarter of a century only, a small slice of time in the history of a nation, to see the edifice of a false nationhood founded on Islam got dismantled. When deep-rooted distrust and contradictions of nationhood overwhelm apparently constructed religious coherence of a nation and when the hegemonic ruling elite, stationed far away from the grassroots, dictates all political terms to be accepted by others who suffer injustice and discrimination, the nation based on false premises is bound to fall apart. Yet no one could predict how the unrealistic arrangement would fall apart till March 1971, when People's Republic of Bangladesh was proclaimed, rejecting totally the religious foundation of that part of Pakistan, created twenty-four years back.

The symptoms of the collapse of Islamic fraternity and nationhood of Pakistan surfaced, and the euphoria of founding an Islamic country disappeared soon after 1947. The geographic separation of the two wings was then a historical reality, which could not be altered; but the human areas of discomfiture and the pandemic sense of relative deprivation among the masses in East Pakistan, was too strong and unaddressed to be solaced by religious appeal alone.

Among all the issues of politically volatile nature, such as, economic and educational backwardness, and uneven allocation of resources, the clear denigration of Bengali culture and language by the rulers in West Pakistan planted the seeds of massive rebellion in 1971, which finally led to the birth of a new nation out of Pakistan. Bengali nationalism that grew out of the linguistic pride and national fervor found expression soon after the creation of Pakistan. East Pakistan was a land of Bengali speaking people who constituted 80% of the total population. It was more homogeneous than the other part, West Pakistan, which is a multi-lingual region with Urdu, Punjabi, Sindhi and Pushtu speaking people who have separate ethnic identities. Soon after the creation of Pakistan, the Urdu-speaking leaders of Pakistan decided to recognize their own language as the only official language for the entire country, with utter disregard to the social and linguistic composition of East Pakistan where Urdu was not a language of the vast multitude of the people. Therefore, the Bengali Muslims demanded that Bengali should be one of the official languages. Reacting to it Mohammad Ali Jinnah declared, while delivering the convocation address at the Dhaka University on March 21, 1948, that the Bengalis demand for their language as one the national languages was inimical to the interest of Pakistan His statement cited below was a turning point in the history of East Pakistan. It marked the beginning of resurgence of Bengali nationalism and rejection of religion as the foundation of a nation, separated from the other wing not merely by geography but by differences of grave magnitude. To quote Jinnah:

> Let me restate my view on the question of a state language for Pakistan. For official use in [East Pakistan] the people

> of the province can choose any language they wish. The question will be decided solely in accordance with the wishes of the people of this province alone, as freely expressed through their accredited representatives at the appropriate time and after full and dispassionate consideration. There can, however, be one lingua franca – that is the language for intercommunication between various provinces of the state – and that language should be Urdu and cannot be other.

He went further to place Urdu at the national status. He said that Urdu

> has been nurtured by a hundred million of this sub-continent, [it is] a language understood throughout the length and breath of Pakistan and above all a language which is more than any other provincial language, embodies the best that is in Islamic culture and Muslim tradition and is nearest to the language used in other countries.[19]

The idea of putting Urdu above all languages including Bengali language was counter-productive. For Bengali speaking Muslims, the language was rooted in their heart, and therefore, more important than a language of a distant place. Jinnah's claim that Urdu is closer to Islam was unconvincing. Urdu is one of the languages, which had originated in India in a process of admixture of three languages – Arabic, Persian and Hindustani. Its closeness to Islamic culture in the sub-continent did not appeal to the Bengalis for whom it was an alien language. The successors of Jinnah continued to impose Urdu on the Bengali Muslims; when they failed to do so, they tried to Urduize the Bengali script. The recommendation of the Central Advisory Committee for Education in favour of making Urdu as the only national language "in the interest of national unity and solidarity and the rapid advancement of general education in Pakistan" was unacceptable to the people of East Pakistan.[20] One of the comments coming from responsible quarters in this regard was provocative and insulting for any one who is deeply attached to a language of national identity. To quote Pakistan's Education Minister:

> Not only Bengali literature, even the Bengali alphabet is full of idolatry. East Bengali letter is associated with this or that god or goddesses of Hindu pantheon ... Pakistan and Devanagari script cannot co-exist. It looks like defending the frontier of Pakistan with Bharati soldiers! To assure a bright and great future for Bengali language it must be linked with the Holy Quran. Hence the necessity and importance of Arabic script.[21]

Even the Prime Minister of Pakistan, Liaquat Ali Khan, who was expected to take a more rational position on the language issue, considering the territorial separation and cultural diversity of the two wings of the new born country and its fragility in the process of nation-building, gave a religious orientation to the issue in 1949 when he said: "the defence of Bengali language in front of Urdu is against laws of Islam".[22] It was not difficult for Bengali Muslims to argue that the Islam has not prescribed any language to its adherents.

The imposition of Urdu as the only official language of Pakistan and the proposal to Urduize the Bengali script were hegemonic acts designed to centralize the cultural content of both wings of Pakistan and to marginalize in the name of Islam the Bengali population who constituted the vast majority in East Pakistan. While Urdu was symbolized with Islam, Bengali was looked down upon as an inferior language and not compatible with Islamic culture and tradition. It is obvious for a linguistically prominent community, who are proud of their language that has attained maturity through a long process of development spanning several centuries, to rise in protest against any attempt towards its displacement from its legitimate space in the national life. This is how linguistic solidarity and ethnic affiliation shaped the Bengali nationalism superseding the religious boundaries of a Muslim country. The first symptom of political orientation of Bengali nationalism surfaced in the formation of Awami Muslim League in 1949, under the leadership of Maulana Abdul Hamid Khan Bhasani, Hussain Shaheed Suhrawardy, Samsul Haq, Ataur Rehman and Sheikh Mujibur Rehman. The formation of the new party was a serious challenge to the Muslim League, under whose banner the movement for Pakistan was spearheaded. It proved in unmistakable terms that Islam was too fragile a component to hold Pakistani nationalism together.

The fragility of religion as the basis of nation-building appeared to be problematic since the birth of Pakistan, as its ruling and dominant elite gave the impression to the people living in the eastern wing that their culture and language were not compatible with Islam. They needed to be good 'Muslims' and mould their social practices in conformity with Islam and Urduize their language. The leaders of East Pakistan were opposed to all such notions including even the nomenclature of Pakistan.[23] Although later on Bengali became one of the national languages, the pressure to Urduize Bengali language continued.

Close on the heels of these developments, the West Pakistani leaders, who had been suffering from some kind of superiority complex, made demeaning observations about Bengali culture, language and tradition. Some of them such as Rabindra Sangeet (songs composed by Nobel laureate Rabindranath Tagore), wearing *sarees* and putting *bindis* on the forehead by women, speaking Bengali language, observing certain local festivals and social practices were looked down upon by the West Pakistani rulers with disdain, and therefore, they considered the Bengali Muslims some what lesser than their counterparts in West Pakistan. Such contemptuous attitude towards the Bengali Muslims were evident in the comments and writings of the Urdu speaking political elite; a representative is that of Ayub Khan, President of Pakistan (1956-1969), who wrote in his autobiography:

> East Bengalis...probably belong to the very original Indian races. It would be no exaggeration to say that up to the

> creation of Pakistan, they had not known any real freedom or sovereignty. They have been in turn ruled either by caste Hindus, Moghals, Pathans, or the British. In addition they have been and still are under considerable Hindu cultural and linguistic influence. As such they have all the inhibitions of down-trodden races and have not found it possible to adjust psychologically to the requirements of the new born freedom. Their popular complexes, exclusiveness, suspicion and a sort of defensive aggressiveness probably emerge from this historical background. Prudence, therefore, demands that these factors should be recognized and catered for and they be helped so as to feel equal and prove an asset".[24]

Contrary to this demeaning and unhistorical assessment of the Bengalis born to be ruled, Ayub was all praise for the people of his part of the world. To quote him in the same context, would be more appropriate:

> The population in West Pakistan, on the other hand, is probably the greatest mixture of races found anywhere in the world. Lying on the gateways to the Indian subcontinent, it was inevitable that each successive conquering race should have left its races here. Consequently, this forced mixture of races has brought fusion of ideas, outlook and culture, despite the linguistic variety that obtained.

Ayub went a step further in 1967. In order to cleanse away 'Hindu influence' he banned playing Rabindra Sangeet in East Pakistan, a step that the people of this part of Pakistan was not going to tolerate in view of the fact that Rabindranath Tagore was close to the heart of the Bengalis, irrespective of their religious affiliation. Tagore's songs were part of Bengali nationalism. One of such songs "Amar sonar Bangla ami tomae Bhalobashi" (My golden Bengal I love you) became a symbol of Bengali nationalism and eventually became the national anthem of Bangladesh in 1971. The Bengali nationalism is deeply rooted in every walk of the life in Bengal, be it culture, tradition, social behaviour, language and even territorial perspective and distinctiveness.[25] The Bengali people constitute the world's second largest

Muslim ethnic group after the Arabs.[26] In the South Asian context, the Bengalis constitute one of the major ethno-linguistic groups numbering around 220 million, 67 per cent of whom are Muslims. Despite the politico-geographic division and dispensation caused by partition, the ethno-linguistic bond among the Bengali people was strong enough to transcend the international boundaries. That gives a unique characteristic of the Bengali people, who under no circumstances would tolerate any abuse directed to their ethnicity. The tendency on the part of the political elite located in the West Pakistan to undermine the ground reality was a colossal misunderstanding of the composition of Pakistan nationhood, which proved in two decades of its existence to be too costly.

Added to this, the people of East Pakistan found that the economic and political balance heavily favoured West Pakistan. A sense of relative deprivation was prominently visible in almost all walks of life in the eastern part such as in GDP growth rate, investment, allocation of resources, industrialization, urbanization, connectivity between rural and urban areas and standard of living.[27] The economic disparity was profound and distressing when compared with West Pakistan. A deep-rooted feeling that East Pakistan was exploited to build the West aroused a strong feeling of alienation and deepened antipathy. The idea of Bengali homeland had already gained currency. The most crucial and turning point having far-reaching implications, which generated a driving force to propel a massive movement in search of autonomy at first and then territorial sovereignty, was the dismissal of the elected government of East Pakistan in 1954. It gave the Bengali Muslims a bitter taste of alien rule in the name of religion. Just as economic disparity, political suppression and the demeaning attitude of the ruling elite towards Bengali culture and language hurt the sentiment of the people living in this part of Pakistan, which provided enough ground for secession, the urge to find an expression of national identity in its fullest form, to ensure economic prosperity and to exercise political sovereignty also inspired them to fight for the attainment of an international personality of the Bengali nation-state, obviously outside the framework of religion.[28]

A series of nerve-wrecking developments took place, leading to the resurgence of Bengali nationalism entrenched deeply in the Bengali language. On January 26, 1952 the Muslim League declared that Urdu would be the only official language of Pakistan. The people of East Pakistan declared February 21 as the State Language Day even though it was anticipated that the Pakistani soldiers would ruthlessly suppress the observance of the day. Thousands participated in the massive demonstration in support of linguistic solidarity of the Bengalis. The brutal police action to disperse the demonstrators led to the death of seven and injury to several hundreds. This was the flash point for the emergence of Bengali nationalism based on linguistic solidarity, which finds expression even today in the form of commemoration of 'Ekushey' (twenty-first).[29] Three important components– language, culture and social processes created a syncretism that encompassed all domains of life in Bengal, including religion.[30]

The language issue steered an emotional appeal for solidarity under the banner of Bengali nationalism. Initially it was a movement to secure autonomy for East Pakistan so that a distinct shape of Bengali nationalism could emerge.[31] It is noteworthy that the Muslim identity of the movement was subtle and less focused to enable all Bengali speaking people irrespective of religious affiliation, to come under a common banner to spearhead a movement towards restoration of Bengali pride. The core issue for the people as a whole in East Pakistan was the attainment of political autonomy, so that they could decide their own fate even within the loose concept of a federal structure in Pakistan in which the protection and promotion of Bengali nationalism could be possible. The articulation of the issue eventually led to the formation of the Awami League, a party formed after the split of the Awami Muslim League. It went on to register an overwhelming victory in the 1970 general elections. In the 313 member Pakistan Nation Assembly, the Awami League captured 167, while the Pakistan People's Party of Z.A. Bhutto got 88 seats. In utter disregard of the parliamentary practices, there was a conspiracy to appoint Bhutto as the Prime Minister. The attempt to hijack the electoral mandate by the ruling elite of West Pakistan, in order to deprive Sheikh Mujibur Rehman from his legitimate claim for Prime Ministerial position, ignited a civil war in East Pakistan leading immediately to the declaration of independence of Bangladesh, and finally to the surrender of the Pakistani army to the Indian army on December 16, 1971 and the birth of a secular and democratic new nation.[32]

Once Bangladesh was born after a colossal loss of millions of life during the war of liberation, Sheikh Mujibur Rehman, the father of the nation, made serious efforts to give a territorial, cultural and linguistic outline of Bengali nationhood, which is undoubtedly a political concept. Sheikh Mujib had made it clear about Bengali nationalism even before the proclamation of Bangladesh. He said in unequivocal terms: "I once again reaffirm that every person living in Bangladesh is a Bengali".[33] The statement was political which was bound to hurt those who were not Bengalis by language, as for example, the Hindi speaking Biharis[34] and the tribal Chakmas living in Chittagong Hill Tracts (CHT).[35] What he intended to mean was that Bangladesh as a nation-state was united under the concept of Bengali nationalism and nationhood. Mujib's declaration of Independence moment before his arrest in the early hours of March 26, 1971 clarifies the position he meant by Bengali nationalism. To quote him:

> This is my last message. From today Bangladesh is Independent. I call upon the people of Bangladesh wherever you might be and with whatever you have to resist the army of occupation to the last. Your fight must go on until the last soldier of the Pakistan occupation army is expelled from the soil of Bangladesh and final victory is achieved.[36]

The name of the country Bangladesh literally means the land of the Bangla speaking people. There is no scope for any ambiguity.[37] The nomenclature, as in the case of Malaysia as will be found in Chapter IV, stands for an affirmative position in favour of the Bengali community. It might be obvious and natural, considering the historical development leading to the birth of the new nation in South Asia. As Tajuddin Ahmed, the first Prime Minister of Independent Bangladesh declared while addressing his people at the critical moment of the onset of liberation war, "You have shown that a new Bengali nation has been born amidst the ruin of the battlefield."[38] It was not at all surprising. What for the people of that land had fought against the Pakistani rulers? It was not for equal treatment in sharing national wealth and economic benefit, and not merely to undo the perpetual injustice. They fought to achieve political independence for the ethnic Bengali community. Naturally, the ethnic Bengali nationalism became an all-pervading and overriding emotion that encompassed all other sentiments.

As the new nation emerged out of death and destruction, a national consensus was developed to shape the concept of Bengali nation-state in an identifiable and consolidated manner. The national psyche, which led the entire nation to freedom, was articulated in unmistakable terms during the constitutional debates in parliament in 1972. To quote two leading personalities who played the lead role in the debates is relevant in this context. Sheikh Mujib said:

> Our ideology is clear. The ideology has inspired us to attain independence, and this ideology shall constitute the basis of this state. Nationalism – Bengali nationalism – shall be the main pillar of this state. Bengali nationalism encompasses Bengal's culture, Bengal's heritage, its land and above all the sacrifices made by the Bengalis.[39]

To quote Kamal Hossain, the architect of the Constitution, is equally relevant. While introducing the Constitutional Bill in the parliament in the defining moment of history of Bangladesh, he said:

> This is a memorable day in the history of Bengalis...History will testify that Bengalis never accepted any external domination. We can say with pride that the quest of Bengali nation is an indomitable one.[40]

In other words, Bengali nationalism was projected as the foundation of the new nation-state of Bangladesh. Article 9 of the pre-amended Constitution defines Bengali nationalism in an unequivocal manner:

> The unity and solidarity of the Bengali nation, which deriving its identity from its language and culture, attained sovereign and independent Bangladesh through a united and determined struggle in the war of independence, shall be the basis of Bengali nationalism.

Two other features also deserve attention. The pre-amended Constitution of Bangladesh of 1972 stood for secularism and democracy as enshrined in the Preamble, meaning thereby that Bengali nationalism was inseparably linked with secularism and democracy. The Bengali language was accepted as the national language. Article 6 stipulated that the citizens of Bangladesh were to be known as Bengalis.

The content and the tone of these statements and constitutional provisions have Bengali hegemonic overtones, which were not acceptable to the Chakma population. Their leader Manobendra N. Larma expressed strong disagreement to the Constitutional definition of Bengali nationhood. This added additional worries to the already problematic issue of the Chakma integration into Bangladesh.[41] To the Chakma leaders, the imposition of Bengali language as the foundation for language-based ethnic nation-state meant imposition of Bengali hegemony on other nationalities. That was unacceptable even in view of the existence of Article 28(4) of the Constitution, which talks of preferential treatment to the disadvantaged people. Manobendra Larma made a strong case in the parliament that Chakmas were different people and could not surrender their identity to become Bengalis. He stated:

> You cannot impose your identity on others. I am a Chakma and not a Bengali. I am a citizen of Bangladesh, Bangladeshi. You are also Bangladeshi but your national identity is Bengali...they (the Chakmas) can never become Bengalis.[42]

The Bengali leadership tried to pacify the Chakmas and invited them to subsume themselves under the ambit of Bengali nationality. While addressing a gathering in Rangamati, Sheikh Mujib pronounced: "From this day onwards, the tribals are being promoted into Bengalis".[43] The pronouncement sounded ominous signals to the minority tribal communities of losing their language, culture and tradition in the wake of aggressive Bengali nationalism.

Mujib's emotional appeals and utterances did not change the Chakma national identity as a different social and ethnic group. Rather the Chakmas started asserting their distinct identity in view of the aggressive overtone of the Bengali nationalism and frequent attack on them by army, police and paramilitary forces (Rakkhi Bahini). They became organized under the banner of Shanti Bahini (Peace Force).[44] The Kaptai hydro-electric and irrigation project and the aggressive Bengali nationalism forced thousands of the Chakma to leave their homeland and take refuge in India. After Sheikh Hasina Wajed took over as the Prime Minister of Bangladesh, the process of reconciliation started leading eventually to the return of 60,000 Chakma refugees to Bangladesh and their subsequent rehabilitation.[45]

The spirit of Bengali nationalism got ignited on February 21, 1952 when seven persons lost their lives at the hands of the Pakistani forces and several hundred others were injured during the solidarity demonstration in favour of Bengali language marking the turning point in the history of the young nation. It continued to inspire the nation through all the turbulent period under Pakistani rule to those days of constitutional debates when Bengali nationalism overwhelmed other considerations. Thus, the foundation of the nation-state appeared to have rested on linguistic ethnicity.

As days passed a phase appeared, utterly paradoxical indeed, when the linguistic spirit was sidelined and the religious identity received attention once again. It is important to note that essentials of Bengali nationalism embody the secular and democratic credentials of the people as a whole, who are otherwise religious. The shift in the paradigm of nationhood from ethnicity to religion was a handiwork of the generals, who sought legitimacy by exploiting religion to their advantage.

Islamic identity once again

The history of the birth of Bangladesh appears to have decided once for all the ethnic basis of the newborn country. Bangladesh was founded on a secular nationalist ideology based on Bengali language and ethnicity. This identity is fundamentally different from that of Pakistan, which was created on the basis of the 'Two-Nation' theory. The name of the country itself speaks of its Bengali national and republican character. The creation of Bangladesh dismantled the religious foundation of East Pakistan, if not that of West Pakistan. The establishment of a Bengali nation-state was the culmination of historical process that had started centuries back, aspiration of cultural heritage and construction of a national identity – the Bengali identity, which is both linguistic and cultural, two sides of the same coin. The historic event of December 16, 1971 ending a wanton phase of massacre and brutal suppression and emergence of a new international personality laid the ethno-religious foundation of Bangladesh. The slogan "We are Bengalis" inspired millions to face death and destruction at the hands of a brutal military regime located 1700 km away and enabled the people to sort out a number of political issues, such as democracy, secularism and preeminence of linguistic ethnicity. The overwhelming appeal for Bengali identity during the liberation united all sections, minus the agents of Pakistan, such as, the Jamaat-i-Islami, the al-Badars and the Razakars, to fight for independence. They all suffered, and achieved the goal through suffering. The solidarity they mustered laid the foundation of the one and only Bengali nation-state. Its finest expression is found in the defining principle of secularism so clearly laid down in the Constitution of Bangladesh. The Constitution (Article 9), as already stated, is clear and unequivocal in making a statement on nationalism. The images of national monuments such as Shaheed Minar, the commemoration of February 21 as Ekushey (twenty-first), the language, the tradition and culture, the national song, the national flag, and so on, are transcendental symbols of Bengali nationalism, which have virtually no religious overtones whatsoever.[46]

The concept of Bengali nationalism is diametrically opposite to that of 'one state, one nation and one religion' as the foundation of Pakistan. When it is considered together with the principle of secularism, as was enshrined in Articles 12 and 38 till 1978, when military took over power, it is quite evident that secularism provided a space for all religions. The constitutional arrangement to eliminate communalism in all its forms and doing away with any form of discrimination in the name of religion, reinforced popular faith in the spirit of Bengali nationhood, where religion, not put on the backseat of socio-political arrangements, did not lose its significance.[47] At the same time, the new government of Bangladesh tried to ensure that religion could neither be used to discriminate among citizens nor as a weapon to inflict suffering on the minorities. A secular republic was the best option, which could accommodate religious rights of all citizens. That is why Article 12 adorns the spirit of secularism as one of the cornerstones on which national foundation rests and Article 38 shuns communalism and its practices of all forms. The secular foundation of the country had been the prime concern of Sheikh Mujibur Rehman, the founder of the new nation. While participating in the debates in the Constituent Assembly, which prepared the draft of the constitution of Bangladesh, on November 4, 1972, he made a passionate appeal for secularism in the country. Being aware of the fact that Bangladesh is a Muslim majority country, he tried to disabuse the negative perspective of secularism. He understood the reality from proper perspectives:

> Secularism does not mean absence of religion. The 75 million people of Bangladesh will have the right to religion by law. We do not want to ban religion by law. We have no intention of that kind. Secularism does not mean absence of religion. Muslims will observe their religion and nobody in the state has the power to prevent that. Hindus will observe their religion and nobody has the power to prevent that. Buddhists and Christians will observe their respective religions and nobody can prevent that. Our only objective is that nobody will be allowed to use religion as a political weapon.[48]

Mujib was totally committed to secularism and defended his position in the Constituent Assembly. He argued:

> ...secularism does not mean absence of religion. You are a Mussalman, you perform your religious rites. There is no religiousness on the soil of Bangladesh but there is secularism. This sentence has a meaning and that meaning is that none would be allowed to exploit the people in the name of religion, or create such fascist organizations as al-Badar, razakars etc. No communal party will be allowed in the country.[49]

Article 12 enshrining the secular credentials of Bangladesh reinforced the ethnic foundation of the predominantly Muslim inhabited state. Consequently, it gave equal space to all the minorities in the country with the constitutional guarantee that the traumatic days under Pakistan, when there had been wanton religious persecution, will never return. Bengali ethnicity, rather than religious affiliation, provided a canopied structure for the nation-state. It had the accommodative and inclusive character, a better arrangement for national reconstruction. Just as it created an emotional, psychological and political platform during the war of liberation, it was expected to be the driving force in the ethnicity based nationalism, despite the fact that Islam has a universal appeal. It was difficult for the people to ignore or forget the fact that they were exploited, suppressed and pushed to destruction in the name of religion. The gory images of massacre, leading to the death of more than three million people and the atrocities committed by the religious fanatics, during the war of liberation were fresh in the memory of the people. It was the essence of ethnic and linguistic identity that brought all the people together, and sidelined the religious appeal.

Secularism as enshrined in the Constitution was not merely an ideal. It was the unifying and driving force of Bengali nationalism that led to the emergence of the only Bengali nation-state in the world. At the same time, it also discarded religious nationalism. However, in an overwhelmingly Muslim majority country, religion could not altogether be discarded. As stated in Chapter I, Islam is a religion, which encompasses several aspects of the life of an individual and the community; none, not even Sheikh Mujib could deny it, as we shall see in this Chapter. Mujib's statement in the Constituent Assembly clearly suggested that in his country all citizens would enjoy freedom of religion. But his vision of a secular country and inclusion of secularism in the Constitution could not be articulated and communicated to the masses in the proper spirit. That created a confusion, which the Islamists exploited to whip up anti-Mujib stir even during his lifetime and simultaneously pursue their agenda of bringing religion to the forefront of national politics.

Bangladesh at that historic point of time was not ready for understanding and appreciating secularism in its proper perspective. In 1972, Bangladesh was a war ravaged country; economically and educationally too backward to comprehend properly the texture and spirit of secularism. In popular parlance, 'secularism' was 'Mujibism', a cornerstone of political modernization of the country, a philosophy that would keep all sections of the people united and inspire them in the task of building and consolidating the Bengali nation-state. But the message did not reach the masses. The literal translation of 'secularism', (Mujib often used the Bengali term 'dharma nirapekshota'), was understood to be either 'religious neutralism' or 'anti-religion', which appeared to have borne a negative connotation. Therefore, the term was misunderstood to be anti-thesis to Islam. The common masses, who were highly religious, took secularism as non-religious and thus considered it abnegation of Islam.[50] They felt that secularism had denied the majority religious community a place of primacy by making all religions equal. Further, an impression was widespread that the concept of secularism was incorporated in the Constitution at the instance of India. On the basis of this erroneous perception, the anti-Indian lobby used it in the post-Mujib era to promote Islamic nationalism and religious fundamentalism.[51] One of the leading intellectuals in Bangladesh, Talukdar Maniruzzaman wrote that secularism in Bangladesh did not reflect in societal spirit and history. To him, Sheikh Mujib was "clearly advocating the negative, nondiscriminatory, Indian type secularism".[52] This was what the common masses were unable to understand properly. The Government too failed to convey the message of the inner spirit of secularism to the people which caused a great deal of confusion among the public, a situation that was fully exploited by the religious lobby and the military rulers to their advantage. Taking the religious issue to the public domain, it was somewhat easy for the Islamists to arouse communal passion among the masses, who were mostly illiterate (more than 60 per cent) and deeply religious.

The contesting frontiers of religion and secularism surfaced during Mujib's lifetime. His critics started a campaign that his secularism had been an Indian supplant to weaken the Islamic foundation of the country. They argued that as a preeminently Muslim majority country, Islam has a natural role to play in all walks of life including politics, and Sheikh Mujib had been working against Islam in the name of secularism. Being aware of the adverse political reaction to the concept of secularism which he had not anticipated, Mujib tried to take shelter in Islamic slogans and symbols to prove that he was neither an atheist nor a munafiq (religious deviant) but a devout Muslim. He now used to begin public speeches with "Bismillahir rahmanir rahim (in the name of God, the most benevolent and merciful) and conclude with "Khuda Hafiz" (May God protect you), replacing his usual habit of concluding his speeches with "Joy Bangla" (Glory to Bengal). He started using common Islamic terms such as "insah Allah" (if God wishes), bismillah (in the name of God), "iman" (faith) and so on.[53] He made frequent visit to dargahs (mausoleums of great Islamic Sufi saints), reestablished the already defunct Islamic Academy with a new name, Islamic Foundation, to promote Islamic culture and increased government grants to the madrassas in order to build up his image as a devout Muslim. The change in his political image from a Bengali nationalist to a Muslim leader was undoubtedly a tactical one to pacify the Islamic clerics and organizations and to tame the anti-Mujib lobby's campaign against him as a "munafiq".

These steps could neither impress Mujib's opponents and critics, nor could disabuse the negative impression of the general public about his secularism and also his Islamic credentials. Added to the fast erosion of his popularity owing to misgovernance, intolerance of criticism[54], deterioration of law and order in the country, inability to arrest inflation and handle corruption at all levels, alleviate abject poverty, and manage the 1974 catastrophic flood and famine situation were severe blows to Sheikh Mujib and his government. The most horrific aspect of his authoritarian behaviour was the introduction of a single party government in the name of Bangladesh Krishak Sramik Awami League on February 24, 1975 dissolving all other political parties.[55] It paved the way for religious nationalism to grow as an alternative. The Islamists' anti-Mujib campaign centered around a catchy argument that Mujib's secular approach to politics would allow the minority Hindus to dominate the national politics and ruin the future of the Muslims, who constituted the vast majority of the population.[56] In this way the ascendancy of religion in politics had begun in Bangladesh during the last two years of Sheikh Mujib's rule.

With the assassination of Mujib at the dawn of August 15, 1975, and the emergence of military generals in the political scenario of Bangladesh, first with the appointment of Major General Ziaur Rahman as the Chief Martial Law Administrator on November 28, 1976 and then his occupation of the position of the President of the country on April 21, 1977 paved the way for the Islamic forces to resurface in the country. The military general wanted to legitimize his rule by seeking support from anti-Mujib parties and organizations which had an Islamic agenda. Bangladesh had a long spell of military rule from April 1977 to December 1990 with only a tiny gap of 10-month civilian rule. This was the period when the Islamic groups secured political legitimacy and started to project the Islamic image of the country. Certain important steps were taken in both domestic and external affairs, having far reaching implications, to boost the Islamic image of the country. To cite some of these would be instructive.

The first thing that the successors of the slain leader did was to attack him for promoting secularism at the cost of Islam in a Muslim majority country. They used mass media to convey to the people that Bangladesh was essentially a Muslim country, and therefore, it has to promote the values of Islam. The time allotted to reading Qur'an in the early morning radio broadcast was increased from 5 minutes to 15 minutes, while reading other scriptures remained same. As TV telecast became a part of life, the recitation of the Qur'an received the same attention. It was done to demonstrate that Islam was preponderant over other religions. This was the beginning of trying to forge an Islamic identity for Bangladesh, to be followed by other steps having far-reaching consequences.[57]

President Khandakar Mostaq Ahmed, who assumed office soon after the assassination of Sheikh Mujibur Rehman, released from jail the leaders of Jamaat-i-Islami, who were held and imprisoned for their alleged involvement in war crimes during the war of liberation. This step had three immediate consequences – first, the Jamaat got a new lease of life and started its activities to promote its political agenda with a clear-cut objective of transforming Bangladesh into an Islamic state; second, the release impressed Saudi Arabia and it accorded a till-then withheld recognition to Bangladesh as a sovereign country. The Saudi recognition was an important milestone in the diplomatic history of Bangladesh; it gave this newborn country a space in the community of Islamic brethren. Third, the Saudi recognition gave an opportunity to the suppressed Jamaat to rejoice and accelerate its activities in a big way.

After taking over the seat of power, General Ziaur Rahman initiated three highly controversial but historic steps to present an Islamic face of Bangladesh. The first step was proclamation of an ordinance to incorporate "Bismillahir Rahmanir Rahim" (in the name of Allah the most benevolent and merciful) at the top of the text in the Constitution. Later on, the ordinance received the constitutional sanctity through the 5th Amendment. The insertion of these words changed the very character of the Constitution, which had enshrined secularism as the cornerstone of the country. Through the same proclamation, the principle of secularism was substituted by "the principle of absolute trust and faith in the Almighty, nationalism, democracy and socialism meaning economic and social justice, together with the principles derived from them as set out in this Part, shall constitute the fundamental principles of state policy". Ziaur Rahman faced strong opposition to the ordinance and in the passage of the amendment bill doing away with the principle of secularism. He carved a strategy to deal with the opposition. The passage of the amendment was put as a precondition to lift the Martial Law. The opposition was neutralized and the amendment sailed through, despite stiff opposition from the Awami League. Several Articles were amended to reinforce the Islamic credentials of the country. Article 12, which dealt with secularism and freedom of religion and Article 38, which banned use of religion for political mileage, were dropped. Article 25 was amended to insert Section (2) so as to promote Bangladesh's fraternal relations with Islamic countries.

Several other steps followed to prove that Bangladesh was moving towards an Islamic identity, relegating its ethnic nationalism to a back seat. It was a calculated initiative with three broad objectives – (i) to cultivate a formidable support base among the devout Muslims, who would like to see Bangladesh flourishing as an Islamic country, and thus gain political legitimacy, (ii) to marginalize the Awami League which had been enjoying enormous public support despite the gruesome killing of Sheikh Mujib, his family members and murdering four other top leaders in jail on November 3, 1975 and (iii) to develop fraternal relationship with Muslim countries, more particularly the oil-rich Arab states in the Middle East. A closer relationship with these countries was a priority in the foreign policy agenda of Bangladesh, for, that would ensure much needed inflow of petro-dollars and also enhance its respectability among the Muslim countries in the world. Religion became a privilege point in the agenda of the newly constituted Bangladesh Nationalist Party (BNP) headed by General Ziaur Rahman. The party manifesto released in 1978 soon after its formation defined Bangladeshi nationalism within the framework of Islam. "The fact is well reflected in our stable and liberal national life".[58] To foster the spirit of Islam in the life of Bangladesh became a pronounced objective of the ruling party.

Certain other striking changes followed in quick succession soon after to enhance preponderance of Islam over others. It was a practice that on the opening day of the first session of the Jatiyo Sangsad (National Parliament) there used to be recitation from all the holy books of different religions in Bangladesh. General Ziaur Rahman changed it to begin the session with the recitation of the Qur'an only. The

Bengali slogan of "Jai Bangla", the driving force of Bengali nationalism was replaced by an Urduized "Bangladesh Zindabad". By the time he was assassinated on May 30, 1981, 'Bangladeshi Islamic nationalism' took the place of 'Mujibism' in both domestic and international politics.

On the diplomatic front, India was a natural friend of Bangladesh till the assassination of Sheikh Mujibur Rehman for its historic role in liberating it from Pakistan and for the then much needed immediate diplomatic recognition. The Soviet Union was the other great power with which Bangladesh had a very special relation for the same reason. The Soviet recognition was followed by the recognition of Bangladesh by East European countries, Cuba and Vietnam. Such prompt actions at the diplomatic front gave Bangladesh a formidable place in the community of nations and shaped its international personality. Ziaur Rahman brought about a change in the diplomatic front to move closer to Islamic countries, such as, Pakistan and Saudi Arabia and other Middle East Countries for their standing in the Islamic world with the objective to secure a space in this special world.[59]

General Hossain Mohammad Ershad's military rule (March 24, 1982-December 6, 1990) witnessed a series of initiatives towards Islamization of Bangladesh. In order to project his country's image of Islamic foundation, he steered a constitutional amendment (Eighth Amendment, 1988) to insert Article 2A to read "Islam is the state religion. All other religions can be practiced freely in peace and harmony".[60] He made it clear beforehand while addressing a mammoth gathering of Bangladesh Jamiat-ul-Mudderressin on January 20, 1988 that in view of Islam being deeply rooted in the social and cultural life of the people, it would be imperative on his part to declare Islam as the state religion.[61] There was external compulsion that appeared to have forced him to declare Islam as a state religion through a constitutional amendment. Some of the OIC members put a pressure on him to make this proclamation in order to assert the Islamic identity of Bangladesh. It served another purpose of nullifying Pakistan's frequent and virulent propaganda that Bangladesh was not a Muslim country. The other reason was his effort to seek, like his predecessor General Ziaur Rahman, legitimacy from Islamic clerics and organizations. At any rate, the amendment is a milestone in the political history of Bangladesh. It sanctified Bangladesh's shift from ethnic nationalism to Islamic nationalism. Close on the heels of this, General Ershad introduced a Zakat Fund to raise poor tax in accordance with the fundamentals of Islam and decided to declare Friday as the weekend holiday in stead of Sunday. Although not a devout Muslim, Ershad indulged in much publicized visits to mosques and shrines to convey a message as to how strongly faithful he was.[62] All these exercises clearly implied that Bangladesh was moving towards Islamic nationalism shedding its transitional ethnic nationalism, a guiding spirit that gave birth to this youngest nation-state in South Asia.

The steps to transform Bangladesh into an Islamic state and the constitutional amendment to insert Article 2A inserting "Islam is the state religion" did not go unopposed. The enlightened sections comprising scholars, judges, media persons and the leaders of the Awami League and Left organizations challenged the concept of "Islam as the state religion". To them Islam cannot be the state religion, even though Bangladesh is predominantly a Muslim majority country. To hold Islam as the state religion means to put Islam in operation and control of the state. The Qur'an is silent about the concept of state religion. According to the fundamentals of Islam "Allah is Sovereign". It means that the state, the religion, the machinery of the state and government cannot claim to be sovereign.[63] Secondly, if Islam is the religion of the state, it is imperative to transform Bangladesh into an Islamic country. That automatically means that the national parliament has to enact laws in conformity with Sharia laws; there has to be constitutional amendment to enforce Sharia laws in the country. Whatever General Ershad did was a political piecemeal.

Ershad's politically motivated steps to put the religion of the majority over the most visible ethnic identity, and thereby to ensure consolidation of his dictatorship did not succeed. There was massive movement against his rule in 1990 in which his favourite Jamaat also participated. The unity of action of all the political parties throughout the year, in spearheading a massive movement to restore democracy, once again sidelined the issue of preponderance of the religion over ethnicity, democracy and secularism. Ershad could not withstand the popular assault and had to quit on December 6, 1990. Although the democratic movement was successful in removing military dictatorship, it failed to obviate the influence of the Jamaat in the political process of Bangladesh.

Politics of power sharing

Politics is a domain of all possibilities. The recent political history of Bangladesh testifies to this oft-quoted statement. It is an irony of history that Jamaat-i-Islami, which was almost crushed after the war of liberation and against which public wrath was so strong because of its alleged collaboration with Pakistani forces leading to the massacre of millions of people, and defying all logic, would be rehabilitated in a decade's time and eventually elevated to the political status of a coalition partner of Begum Khaleda Zia as Prime Minister. Most of the top leaders were either summarily executed or put behind bars. Its principal leader Ghulam Azam, who had been in Pakistan since November 1971, was stripped of his citizenship. In other words, the Jamaat was in total disarray and had lost every inch of political ground in Bangladesh.

It is a matter of great astonishment that soon after takeover of power by General Ziaur Rahman, steps were being initiated, first to enable Ghulam Azam to return to

Bangladesh on July 11, 1978 with a Pakistani passport, since he was stripped of Bangladeshi citizenship soon after the liberation[64] and then to allow him to rebuild the party on a solid footing. Although his application for citizenship was rejected by the two military rulers, Ziaur Rahman and Hossain Mohammad Ershad, and he was not allowed to be the President of the Jamaat, because of fear of massive public protest, Prime Minister Begum Khaleda Zia restored his citizenship, and the Supreme Court upheld the restoration on the ground that he was a Bangladeshi by birth. He was allowed to continue his political activities, which eventually led to a phenomenal rise of the Jamaat in no time, less than 8 years, to muster enough political acumen to participate in the election politics of the country.

Jamaat's electoral participation did not so far show a significant shift in voters' choice in its favour. It did not dare to participate in the first election of Bangladesh held in 1973 because of public hostility. It did not participate in 1979 elections, as it had started its political activities only after the return of Ghulam Azam and was too weak to do so. But in the third general elections it launched its political campaign and captured 10 seats in the national parliament securing 4.61 votes (Table 2.2).

Jamaat's political agenda is essentially to transform Bangladesh into an Islamic state to be governed in accordance with the Qur'an and Hadith.[65] Although Jamaat does not claim to be a political party, it has an agenda to advance an alternative paradigm for politics and governance. It believes in election politics and had participated in general elections. It did not receive much support. Yet, even with its miniscule strength of 10 out of 300 in the national parliament after the 2001 elections, it shared power with the BNP, as a coalition partner and enjoying two important berths in the ministry, which is a milestone in its brief political career of 23 years since 1978. However, it is now in an extremely difficult situation after its disastrous performance in the last December 2008 election to the Jatiya Sangshad when it could manage to capture only two seats and polling less than 1 per cent votes.

Table 2.2

Party-wise performance in the general elections in terms of seats and % of votes polled

Parties	*1973*	*1979*	*1986*	*1988*	*1991*	*1996*	*2001*
Awami League	293 (73.20)	39 (24.55)	76 (26.16)	-	100 (33.67)	146 (37.44)	62 (40.18)
BNP	-	207 (41.6)	-	-	140 (30.81)	116 (33..61)	216 (47.06)
Jatiyo Party	-	-	153 (42.34)	251 (68.44)	35 (11.92)	32 (16.40)	14 (7.23)
Jamaat-I-Islami	-	-	10 (4.61)	-	18 (12.13)	3 (8.61)	17 (*)

Source: Aminur Rashid and Mostafa Firoz, *Pramany Sansad* (Dhaka: Tathya Seva, 2002), pp. 19 and 77.

* Percentage of votes polled is not available. It is estimated that Jamaat secured about 8 per cent votes.

Although percentage-wise it could not garner much support, in absolute figures it had around 11 million supporters till December 2008, Jamaat appeared to be quite strong and significant force in a hugely and densely populous country like Bangladesh. Its religious appeal, which intends to sideline ethnic nationalism, had been further sponsored by several militant varieties, which put up a vigorous campaign during the short period from 2001 to 2006, the period when Begum Khaleda Zia was heading the coalition government in which Jamaat was a partner. The militant groups, which have a pronounced agenda to transform Bangladesh into an Islamic country to be governed by Sharia law, reportedly have links with the Jamaat. Among the dreaded such groups, Harkat-ul-Jihad Islami (HuJI), Jamaat-ul-Mujahideen Bangladesh (JMB) and Jagrata Muslim Janata Bangladesh (JMJB) had been indulging in violent campaigns to achieve their political end of capturing power through terror. Now, however, they are maintaining a low profile due to the harsh measures adopted by the caretaker government since October 2006 including quick trial and execution of six militant leaders on March 30, 2007.[66] The return of the Awami League to power with a thumping majority in the December 2008 elections, the public rejection of Jamaat in a significant way testifying to the heavy erosion in its support base and the near collapse of hardcore militancy following the government crackdown on them clearly indicate that political and militant Islamic overtone in Bangladesh is a matter of the past.

Islam appears to figure prominently in Bangladesh when there is a crisis of governance. The country has gone through the most deepening crisis of governance since liberation.[67] In such a vacuum, it is easy to bring in religion to play a dominant role. The Islamic alternative appeared to be attractive, when the democratic and secular one seemingly failed in Bangladesh. The religious card has, though erroneous, a fortuitous image, which carries only a temporizing and palliative impact. It takes no time, as Bangladesh has proved on earlier occasions too, to see the evaporation of the impact. The result of the December 29, 2008 elections has once again proved in unequivocal terms that religion could no longer serve as the panacea of everything that ails Bangladesh. The resounding victory of the 14-party alliance which secured 262 seats in the 300 member Jatiya Sangsad with the Awami League alone capturing 230 seats itself is a clear testimony to the popular rejection of the BNP and the Jamaat, which had to remain content with victory in only 30 and 2 constituencies respectively.[68] *The Daily Star* (January 1, 2009) views that the shocking defeat of the 4-party alliance led by BNP is a result of their hobnobbing with radical Islamists.

The debate as to which way would Bangladesh move is still alive and strong. The civil society, women groups, the

Awami League, the academia, the progressive students having affiliations with the Awami League and the left organizations adhere emotionally and politically to the values of an ethnic-based secular democracy. The BNP claims to be a secular party, but its alliance with the Jamaat, which is essentially a hardcore religious party, tainted by its role during the pre and post 2001 election violence against minority Hindus, cast grave doubt about its secular credentials. Bangladesh has a long history of struggle against oppression and injustice, and for democracy. The attempt to stifle democracy either in the name of religion or in the name of protecting the Constitutional provisions was terrifying. Nonetheless, it did not work. In the struggle for the restoration of democracy in recent years, the Islamic appeal did not surface. The future of the Bangladeshi nation-state appeared to be the rallying point of the 14-party alliance led by the Awami League. The debate as to ethnic and religious foundation of Bangladesh has neither ignored Islam as the religion of the overwhelming majority of the population nor undermined the encompassing and all pervading coverage of Islam in the life of a faithful as well as that of the society, which is essentially composed of the people belonging to this religion. At the same time, the people are aware of the fact that politics centering around the fundamentals of religion had the potentiality of causing havoc in any country, including Bangladesh, as testified to by the evidences left by its history in post-1947 era. The cause and spirit of liberation shared by all sections of the country, with the exception of a negligible section of Bihari community, not only created a canopied structure for all communities of the ethnicity-based nation-state to take shelter under as citizens of Bangladesh but also provided a solid foundation for the country. Yet uncertainty grips the overall political atmosphere of the country, which is being exploited by religious fundamentalists and militant groups. The measures adopted by the caretaker government to check the Islamic militancy were transitional in nature. A lot depends upon how the newly elected

Government of Bangladesh acts upon the rise of Islamists in the country over a considerable period of time. The popular response against religious radicalism by using the power of ballot is expected to guide the ruling political leadership to consolidate decisively and once for all the rationale of the 1971 war of liberation.

The result of the 2008 general elections to the 300 member Jatiya Sangsad is a clear pointer to as to which direction Bangladesh intends to move. There was a massive participation of the electorate (85%) and the poll was conducted in an orderly manner.[69] The results proved to be on expected lines. The Awami League swept the polls, securing 230 out of 300 seats in the Parliament. This was a magnificent victory, considering its poor performance in 2001 securing only 62 seats. The BNP which governed the country from 2001 to 2006 could manage 30 seats only. It is noteworthy that the Awami League and its 14 party alliance kept the hope of the people alive to return the country to democracy and secularism, ever since the *hartal* and *aborodh* commenced in November 2006. Despite the repressive measures designed to corner the 14 party alliance since November 2006, the Awami League could enlist support of the masses. The Jamaat-i-Islami, which was a coalition partner of Khaleda Zia was virtually routed. It could secure only two seats. The media suggested that the BNP's hobnobbing with the militant forces brought about its poll disaster.[70] The trend continues as reflected in the Upzila (sub-district) elections held on January 22, 2009. The Awami League captured more than two-thirds of the 481 Upzilas.[71]

The return of the Awami League to power is a significant development in the political history of Bangladesh. It has revived hopes for reassertion of democracy and secularism. The resounding victory of the 14-party alliance is reminiscent of the first parliamentary elections in 1973; it reaffirmed people's faith in the two basic objectives for which the country was born. There was, however, a qualitative difference in

2008 elections. The first election was held in an atmosphere of victory and euphoria natural for a nascent democracy to nascent independence. In 2008 the political atmosphere was altogether different. A caretaker government appeared to be bent on crushing the top leadership of the party by putting the leader in prison. To spearhead a people's movement to restore democracy, which was shelved for about two years, was an uphill task in view of imposition of emergency in the country clamped down by the caretaker government. Yet there was one advantage. The militant Islamists were in disarray owing to the harsh measures adopted against them. The masses got an opportunity to stand up and say no the hardcore political Islam.

The symptoms of resolution of foundational crisis are surfacing. It has been established that as a country preeminently inhabited by the Muslims, religion occupies an important place in Bangladesh; but that does not mean that the religion of the majority has an overbearing say in the political life of the country. The identity, which created Bangladesh, is an enduring reality. The masses and the institution of governance are to initiate the process of consolidation of the ideals for which the country was born.

The BDR Revolt of February 25, 2009

In the midst of the chilling 30 hour drama that unfolded itself on February 24 when the sepoys of Bangladesh Rifles (BDR)[72] took guns against its top officers and colleagues, one find the unique resoluteness of the government to maintain faith of the country in democracy unshaken. One feels that the message of the last parliamentary election has once again become stronger and louder. The BDR revolt took place reportedly owing to pent up grievances of the ordinary soldiers who had been demanding removal of discrimination in their pay scale compared with those officers coming from army and serving in the organization on deputation, on issues of corruption and allowing the BDR soldiers to serve in the UN peace keeping assignments abroad. The BDR soldiers took guns on February 25, a day after the celebration of the BDR Day, the day when they expected that their chief Major General Shakil Ahmed to place their demands before the Prime Minister during her visit to the headquarters located in Dhaka. The soldiers killed around 76 officers and some of their family members in a brutal manner. The death toll had risen to 142.[73]

There are media reports that the Jamaat, the extremists and foreign militants including the United Liberation Front, Asom (ULFA) had a hand in the sudden revolt.[74] There is some scope to view the latest development as an attempt to dislodge the elected government in order to make Bangladesh to return to either a military regime or to those days of horror and trauma that the country faced during the period of 2001-2006. The firm way the present government handled the situation and demonstrated its ability to take prompt action to force the mutineers to surrender indicate that it means business. The most striking was the display of courage by Home Minister Sahara Khatun and Mehboob Ara Gini, Member of Parliament from Gaibandha, who rushed to the BDR headquarters braving gunfire to ensure surrender. The commitment of the army to restore normalcy and to keep the elected government unaffected by the mutiny, while the media and the public stood behind it testifies to the determination of the country to uphold the values of democracy. Bangladesh might continue to face similar challenges, but the will of the people is a guarantee against any such onslaughts. A newly emergent country has its own difficulties, more so when it has colossal problems of backwardness on social, educational and economic fronts. A secular and democratic ethnicity-based Bengali nation-state will face those challenges with courage and determination as it had done in 1971 and is doing today.

NOTES & REFERENCES

1. F.B. Bradley-Birt, *Dacca: The Romance of an Eastern Capital,*

First published in 1914 (Guwahati: Spectrum Publication, 1992) p. 3.

2. https://www.cia.gov/cia/publications/factbook/geog/bg.html , however, Bangladesh Bureau of Statistics, *2004 Statistical Yearbook of Bangladesh*, puts it to be 128.8 million (Census 2001) while the adjusted population stood 130 million, p. xx.

3. Country Report: *Bangladesh, April 2008* (London: Economic Intelligence Unit, 2008), p.7.

4. Abu Nasar Saied Ahmed, *Fundamentalism in Bangladesh: Its Impact on India* (New Delhi: Akansha Publishing House, 2008), pp. 126-132.

5. Wahid-uz-Zaman, "Editor's Note" in The Quest of Identity, *Proceedings of the First Congress on the History and Culture of Pakistan* held a the University of Islamabad, April 1973 (Islamabad: University of Islamabad Press: 1974) p. iv.

6. Richard M. Eaton, *The Rise of Islam and the Bengal Frontier, 1204-1760* (Berkeley: University of California Press, 1993) and Rafiuddin Ahmed, *The Bengal Muslims 1871-1906: A Quest for Identity* (New Delhi: Oxford University Press, 1981), Chapter 1.

7. Abu Nasar Saied Ahmed, *Fundamentalism in Bangladesh: Its Impact on India,* n. 4, Chapter 3. Also see Richard M. Eaton, *The Rise of Islam and the Bengal Frontier*, 1204-1760, ibid.

8. Andre Wink, *Al-Hind: The making of the Indo-Islamic World,* Vol. I, Early Medieval India and Expansion of Islam, 7th-11th Centuries (Leiden: E.J. Brill, 1990), pp. 65-68.

9. For some details about the early expansion of Islam in the Gangatic plain see Francis Robinson, *Atlas of the Islamic World since 1500* (Oxford: Phaidon Press, 1982) p. 29.

10. For some details on the transformation of Bengal's socio-religious structure taking the 13th century Muslim invasion as the starting point see Rafiuddin Ahmed (ed), *Islam in Bangladesh: Society, Culture and Politics* (Dhaka: Bangladesh Itihas Samiti, 1983), Chapter 1. Also his *The Bengal Muslims 1871-1906: A Quest for Identity*, Chapter 1.

11. For details see Muin-uddin Ahmed Khan, *History of Fariadi Movement in Bengal* (Dhaka: Islamic Foundation, 1984).

12. Abu Nasar Saied Ahmed, "The Concept of Jihad and its Distorted Reality" in *Islam in Contemporary World: Some Indian Perspectives* (New Delhi: Japan Foundation, 2004), pp. 15-36.
13. Muin-uddin Ahmad Khan (ed), *Selections from Bengal Government Records on Wahhabi Trials, 1863-1870* (Dacca: Asiatic Society of Pakistan, 1961), pp. 156-186,
14. Rafiuddin Ahmed (ed), *Understanding the Bengal Muslims: Interpretative Essays* (New Delhi: Oxford University Press, 2001), p. 16.
15. Henry Beverley, *Report on Census of Bengal, 1872* (Calcutta: Secretariat Press, 1872), pp. 12-15.
16. For details on the political basis of Bengali Muslims to join Urdu speaking and culturally different West Pakistan, see Harun-or-Rashid, *The Foreshadowing of Bangladesh: Bengal Muslim League and Muslim Politics 1906-1947* (Dhaka: University Press Limited, 2003), pp. 98-101.
17. *The Times* (London), editorials, June 9 1966 and December 15, 1973.
18. Rupert Emerson, *From Empire to Nation* (Cambridge, Mass: Harvard University Press, 1960), p. 2. Richard V. Weekes is more expressive in terming Pakistan a 'double country'. See his *Pakistan: Birth and Growth of a Muslim Nation* (Princeton: Van Nostrand Company, 1964), p. 3.
19. For details of Jinnah's March 21, 1948 speech entitled "National Consolidation" and another "Farewell Message to East Pakistan" on March 28, 1948 see *Quaid-I-Azam Mohamed Ali Jinnah's Speeches as Governor General 1947-48* (Karachi: Pakistan Publication, n.d).
20. The quotation is cited Rangalal Sen, *Political Elite in Bangladesh* (Dhaka: University Press Limited, 1986), p. 105. For some details on the contentious language issue see Ratan Lal Chakrabarti, *Bhasha Andolaner Dalilpatra* (Documents of Language Movement) (Dhaka: Bangla Academy, 2000).
21. Quoted in Anisuzzaman, *Creativity, Reality and Identity* (Dhaka: International Centre for Bengali Studies, 1993), p. 107.
22. Quoted in Safiqul Islam, "Failure in State-Building: The Case of Pakistan", *Asian Profile,* Vol. 2, No. 6, 1984, p. 585.

23. H.S. Suhrawardy and Sheikh Mujibur Rehman opposed Islamic nomenclature of Pakistan. See *Constituent Assembly Debates*, Vol. 1, No. 51, January 28, 1956, p. 2201.

24. Mohammad Ayub Khan, *Friends, Not Masters: A Political Autobiography* (Karachi: Oxford University Press, 1969), p. 275.

25. Bengali nationalism has specific territorial boundaries and refers consciously to the present geographical map of Bangladesh. It rejects a concept of united Bengal, M.G. Kabir, "Religion, Language and nationalism in Bangladesh" in Rafiuddin Ahmed (ed), *Religion, Nationalism and Politics in Bangladesh* (New Delhi: South Asia Publishers, 1990), p. 45

26. For a perceptive account of the Bengali population see Richard V. Weeks, *Muslim Peoples: A World of Ethnographic Survey* (London: Greenwood Press, 1978), pp. 89-99.

27. For some details see Rehman Sobhan, *Bangladesh: The Problem of Governance* (Dhaka: University Press Limited, 1993) pp. 82-108 and Abu Nasar Saied Ahmed, *Fundamentalism in Bangladesh*, n. 4, pp. 16-17.

28. For a detailed historical perspective on the emergence Bangladesh in the backdrop of regional and economic disparities and political injustice inflicted on the people of East Pakistan by the rulers in the other half, see Emajuddin Ahamed, "East Pakistan to Bangladesh" in Emajuddin Ahamed and Harun-or-Rashid, *State and Culture* (Dhaka: Asiatic Society of Bangladesh, 2007), pp. 81-120.

29. Sufia M. Uddin, *Constructing Bangladesh: Religion, Ethnicity and Language in an Islamic Nation* (New Delhi: Vistaar Publication, 2006), pp. 124-136.

30. For details see Asim Roy, *The Islamic Syncretistic Tradition in Bengal* (Princeton: Princeton University Press, 1983).

31. For a detailed analysis on the rise of Bengali nationalism see Craig Baxter, *Bangladesh: From a Nation to a State* (Boulder: Westview, 1997) and Hasan Zaheer, *The Separation of East Pakistan: The Rise and Realization of Bengali Muslim Nationalism* (New York: Oxford University Press, 1994).

32. For some details see Richard Sisson and Leo E. Rose, *War and Succession: Pakistan, India and the Creation of Bangladesh*

(Berkeley: University of California Press, 1990).

33. *Bangladesh Documents* (New Delhi: Government of India: Ministry of External Affairs, 1971), p. 222.

34. There were more than a million non-Bengali, Urdu speaking Biharis in Bangladesh most of who came from Bihar after partition of India in 1947. After liberation of Bangladesh, they were given the option to remain as the citizens of Bangladesh or to seek repatriation to Pakistan. More than 600,000 opted to remain in Bangladesh while others wanted repatriation. Pakistan accepted 100,000. The rest either still remained in stranded in 81 camps spread out in different parts of Bangladesh or managed to escape to unknown destinations. See *Banglapedia: National Encyclopedia of Bangladesh*, Vol. 2 (Dhaka: Asiatic Society of Bangladesh, 2003), p. 202.

35. The Chakmas are indigenous tribal people living in the Chittagong Hill Tracts. The estimated population is 2,39,417. For authentic details see Sugata Chakma, "Chakma" in *Indigenous Communities*, Vol. 5 (Dhaka: Asiatic Society of Bangladesh, 2007), pp. 36-83.

36. *Bangladesher Swadhinata Juddha Dalil* (Documents of Liberation War of Bangladesh), Vol. 3 (Dhaka: Government of Bangladesh: Ministry of Cultural Affairs, 1982), p. 1.

37. Lawrence Ziring, one of the celebrated foreign scholars writing extensively on Bangladesh writes "The name Bangladesh literally translates itself as the land of Bangla speaking people. See his *Bangladesh: From Mujib to Ershad: An Interpretative Study* (Dhaka: University Press Limited, 1984), p. 4.

38. *Bangladesh Documents* (New Delhi: Government of India: Ministry of External Affairs, 1971), p. 83.

39. *Parliament Debates*, October 12. 1972 (Dhaka: Government of Bangladesh, 1972), p. 20

40. *ibid*, p. 23.

41. The Chakma problem surfaced with the inauguration of the Kaptai hydro-electric dam project in 1967 which led to the displacement and harassment of several thousand people. Later on it took a communal and ethnic dimension leading to escape of Chakmas to Indian states of Arunachal Pradesh, Mizoram, and Tripura. For some details see Syed Nazmul Islam, "The

Chittagong Hill Tracts in Bangladesh: Integrational Crisis between Centre and Periphery," *Asian Survey*, Vol. 21, No. 2, December 1981, pp. 1211-1222; Syed Aziz-al Ahsan and Bhumitra Chakma, "Problems of National Integration in Bangladesh: The Chittagong Hill Tracts", *Asian Survey*, Vol. 29, No. 10, October 1989, pp. 959-979; Suhas Chakma, "Chittagong Hill Tracts: Appalling Violence", *Economic and Political Weekly*, October 17, 1992, pp. 2292-2295; M. Rashiduzzaman, Bangladesh's Chittagong Hill Tracts Peace Accord: Institutional Features and Strategic Concern," *Asian Survey*, Vol. 38, No. 7, July 1998, 653-670.

42. *Parliament Debates*, n. 35, p. 452.

43. Quoted in Sudhin Kumar Chakma, *Prosongo: Parbattya Chattagram* (Context: Chattagong Hill Tracts) (Calcutta: Nath Bros. 1986), p. 49.

44. For some discussion on the Chakma autonomy issue see Amena Mohsin, *The Politics of Nationalism: The Case of the Chittagong Hill Tracts, Bangladesh* (Dhaka: University Press Limited, 2002).

45. For some details on the negotiation between the National Committee on Chittagong Hill Tracts and Parbatya Chattagram Jana Sanghati Samity for normalization of the situation, see *Daily Star*, September 18, 1997. For the full text of the Chittagong Hill Tracts Accord see Avtar Singh Bhasin (ed), *India Bangladesh Relations: Documents-1971-2002*, Vol. V (New Delhi: Geetika Publishers, 2003), pp. 2607-2619.

46. For some discussion on this line see Sufia M. Uddin, *Constructing Bangladesh: Religion, Ethnicity and Language in an Islamic Nation* (New Delhi: Vistaar Publications, 2006), Chapter 4.

47. Talukdar Mariruzzaman, "Bangladesh Politics: Secular and Islamic Trends" in Rafiuddin Ahmed(ed), *Islam in Bangladesh: Society, Culture and Politics* (Dhaka: Bangladesh Itihas Samiti, 1983), pp. 185-219.

48. For the full text of Mujib's speech delivered in Bengali see Khandakar Mohammad Ilias (ed), *Bangladesher Samaj Biplobe Bangabandur Darshan* (Bangabandu's Philosophy for Social Revloution), (Dhaka: Bangladesh Parishad, 1979), p. 118. An English version was published in *Bangladesh Observer*, November 5, 1972.

49. Government of People's Republic of Bangladesh, *Speeches of Sheikh Mujib* (Dhaka: External Publicity Division, Ministry of Foreign Affairs, 1972), pp. 16-17.

50. Muhammad Ghulam Kabir, *Changing Face of Nationalism: The Case of Bangladesh* (New Delhi: South Asian Publishers, 1994), p. 210. It is noteworthy that the campaign against secularism is still strong in Bangladesh. The Jamaat-i-Islami has been doing this for quite sometime and circulating its literature to reach out to the people with the message that secularism is anti-Islam. One of its recent publication in Bengali is *Dharma Niropekshotar Fanchi Sai* (Hang Secularism) (Dhaka: Al-Amin Prakashan, 2006).

51. For some details see Badaruddin Umar, *Juddhotor Bangladesh* (Post-War Bangladesh) (Dhaka: Muktadhara, 1975), Chapter 1.

52. Talukdar Maniruzzaman, "Bangladesh Politics: Secular and Islamic Trends", n. 47, p. 192.

53. Abu Nasar Saied Ahmed, *Fundamentalism in Bangladesh*, no. 4, pp. 96-97.

54. There had been allegation that Sheikh Mujib started behaving like a dictator and did not hesitate to physically eliminate his opponents. One of the most tantalizing killings was that of Sirajul Haq Sikdar popularly known as Siraj Sikdar of Jatiyo Samajtantrik Dal (JSD), for details of some of such killings see Ashraf Kaisar, *Bangladeshe Rajnaitik Hatyakanda* (Political Killings in Bangladesh) (Dhaka: Mawla Brothers, 1998), pp. 34-65.

55. For a detailed discussion on these developments leading to the assassination of Sheikh Mujibur Rehman see U.A.B. Razia Akhtar Banu, "The Fall of the Sheikh Mujib Regime: An Analysis", *Indian Political Science Review*, Vol. XV, No. 1, January 1981, pp. 1-19.

56. For some details see Badaruddin Umar, *Juddhotor Bangladesh*, n. 51, pp. 15-16; Taj J. Hashmi, "Islamic Resurgence in Bangladesh: Genesis, Dynamics and Implications" in Satu P. Limaye *et al., Religious Radicalism and Security in South Asia* (Honolulu, Hawaii: Asia-Pacific Center for Security Studies, 2004), pp. 45-46.

57. Talukdar Maniruzzaman, "Bangladesh Politics: Secular and Islamic Trends", n. 47. pp 197-198.

58. Bangladesh Nationalist Party, *Ghosonapatra* (Manifesto) (Dhaka, 1978), p. 1.

59. Mohammad Abdul Halim and Kamal Uddin Ahmed, "Foreign Affairs: Safeguarding National Interest" in Habib Zafarullah (ed), *The Zia Episode in Bangladesh Politics* (New Delhi: South Asia Publishers, 1996), pp 125-139 and Ali Riaz, *God Willing: The Politics of Islamism in Bangladesh* (New York: Rowman and Littlefield, 2004).

60. The text is almost similar to Article 3(1) of the Federal Constitution of Malaysia which reads "Islam is the religion of the Federation; but other religions may be practiced in peace and harmony in any part of the Federation".

61. Some portion of General Ershad's speech appeared in *Daily Star* and *Prothom Alo* on January 21, 1988.

62. For an interesting analysis on the Generals' taking shelter of Islam to legitimize their dictatorial rule see Emajuddin Ahamed and D.R.J.A. Nazneen, "Islam in Bangladesh: Revivalism or Power Politics?", *Asian Survey*, Vol. XXX, No. 8, August 1990, pp. 795-808 and Peter Custers, "Islamisation and More Aids for the Generals", *Economic and Political Weekly*, June 25, 1988, pp. 1317-1318.

63 For a collection of essays dealing the issue see Muhammad Dilwar Hussain (ed), *Bangladesher Rajnitite Dharma O Dharma Niropekshata* (Religion and Secularism in the Politics of Bangladesh) (Dhaka: Prerona Prokashan, 1993).

64. For details of the return of Ghulam Azam to Bangladesh and widespread protest see leading newspapers such as, *Protom Alo, Daily Star*, and *Ittefaq*, July 12-14, 1978.

65. There are large number of literature on the Jamaat and its agenda published in Bengali language. One such is Ghulam Azam, *Jamaate Islamir Karmaniti* (Policies of Jammaat-I-Islami) (Dhaka: Jamaat-I-Islami Bangladesh, 2005), pp. 32-33.

66. For some details of rise of militant Islam and crackdown of the armed groups see Abu Nasar Saied Ahmed, *Fundamentalism in Bangladesh*, n. 4, Chapter 4.

67. Rehman Sobhan has been writing extensively on the issue of crisis of governance of the new nation, some of which are *Bangladesh: Problems of Governance* (Dhaka: University Press Limited, 1993) and most recent one "Bangladesh's Crisis of Democracy" in John P. Neelsen and Dipak Malik (eds), *Crisis of State and Nation: South Asian States between Nation-Building and Fragmentation* (New Delhi: Monohar, 2007), pp. 119-142.

68. For details of the election results see *The Daily Star*, December 31, 2008.

69. All the leading newspapers reported that there was peaceful and orderly poll. For some details see *The Daily Star* and *Protom Alo*, December 30, 2008.

70. *The Daily Star*, December 31, 2008.

71. *ibid*, January 24, 2009.

72. The BDR is a paramilitary force guarding the 4230 km long international border. It was created in 1795 with the nomenclature of Ramgarh Local Battalion after the battle of Plassey (1757) in which Nawab Sirajuddawla was defeated marking the beginning of the British occupation of Bengal, i.e. present Bangladesh. It was renamed as Eastern Frontier Rifles in 1891 to be named again in 1947 after the Partition as East Pakistan Rifles. It ceased to exit in 1971 when the Bangladesh liberation war took place and most of the officers and ranks deserted it to join the Mukti Bahini. After the liberation, the BDR was established on February 24, 1972.

73. For details see *The Daily Star* and *Prothom Alo*, February 26-28, 2009.

74. The ULFA is a secessionist armed organization born in April, 1979 in Upper Assam, North East India, with the objective of liberating the state from Indian Union. It established its camps in Bangladesh during 2001-2006, reportedly in connivance of the Government of Bangladesh and it has been carrying on its militant activities in Assam. After the victory of the Awami Party, it has been under pressure to dismantle the camps and leave the country for which it reportedly played a role in the BDR revolt to topple the elected government of Bangladesh.

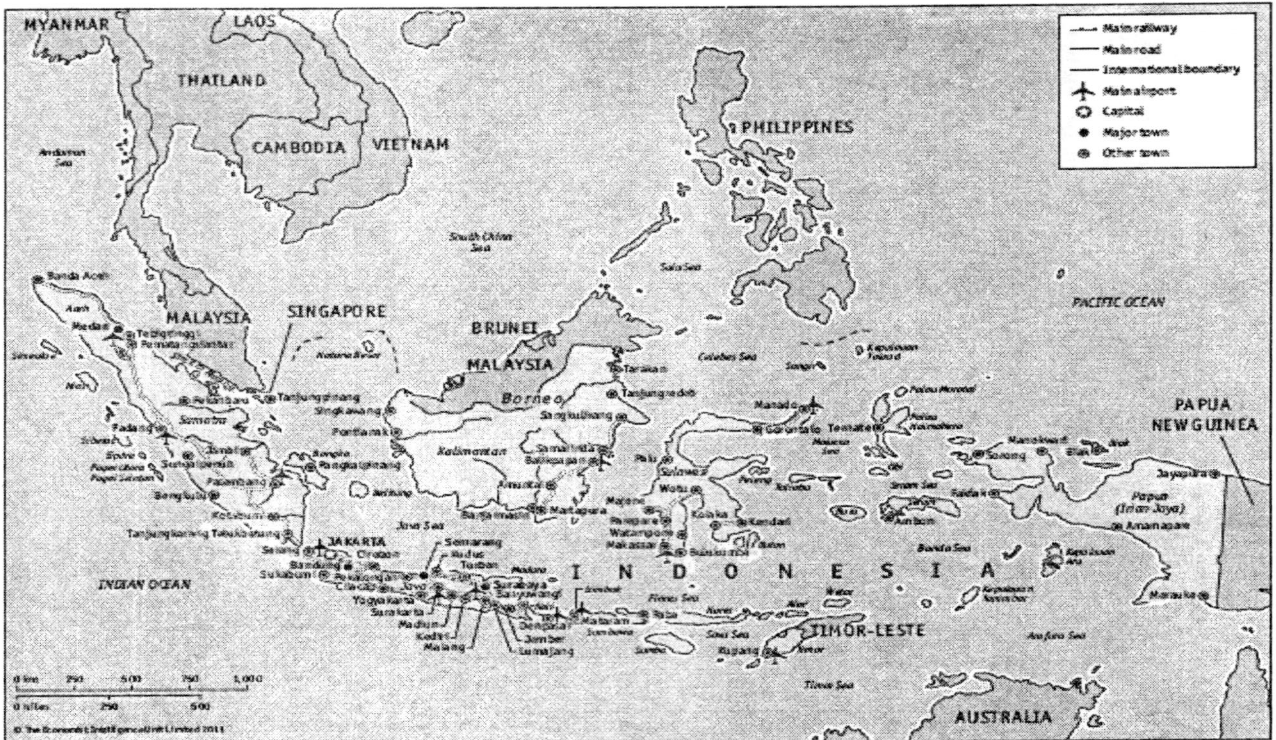
MYANMAR
LAOS
THAILAND
CAMBODIA
VIETNAM
PHILIPPINES
MALAYSIA
SINGAPORE
BRUNEI
MALAYSIA
Borneo
Kalimantan
JAKARTA
INDIAN OCEAN
PACIFIC OCEAN
I N D O N E S I A
TIMOR-LESTE
PAPUA NEW GUINEA
AUSTRALIA
Main railway
Main road
International boundary
Main airport
Capital
Major town
Other town

Indonesia

3

INDONESIA: CAUGHT BETWEEN ISLAM AND ETHNICITY

Indonesia is unique in many ways. It is an archipelagic country of more than 17,000 small and big islands located along the equator in Southeast Asia. Fossilized remains of 'Java Man' indicated that there was human habitation some time during two million to 500,000 years back.[1] Later on the entire stock of people disappeared for reasons beyond scientific explanation. There was rapid and massive migration of people from different parts of the world, mostly from Arabia, Australia, India and China to make it a home of a diversity of cultures, ethnic groups, traditions, social practices, religions and languages. The Europeans, mostly the Dutch, the Portuguese, the Spanish and the British, visited the archipelago in the seventeenth century for the purpose of trade; they struggled among themselves to monopolize the spice trade. The Europeans arrived here in 1512 AD, when Portuguese traders led by Francisco Serrao tried to control the nutmeg trade.[2] The British and the Dutch followed them. The Dutch established the Dutch East India Company (Verenigde Oostindische Compagnie, VOC) in 1602; and their strong footing was followed by tenuous expansion of its territory till the colonization of present Indonesia's current boundaries by the beginning of the 20th century. Indonesia came under the Japanese occupation during World War II.

Two days after the surrender of Japan on August 15, 1945, Indonesia declared Independence. It was followed by a bitter arms struggle against the Dutch, who tried to reestablish their control. Under international pressure, the Government of Netherlands withdrew from Indonesia and recognized it as an independent country on December 29, 1949.[3]

The name Indonesia derives from the Latin word 'Indus' meaning India and Greek word 'nesos' meaning island. The two words form an etymology, which could be 'Indian islands' or Indian archipelago. George Earl, a British ethnologist, suggested a term 'Indunesians' to mean the present Indonesia. At the turn of the last century a German Professor, named Adolf Bastian, popularized the nomenclature 'Indonesia' through his writings. This was acceptable to the people living in the archipelago.[4] All Indies Youth Conference, held in 1928, attended by more than five hundred delegates representing various regional organizations, accepted the nomenclature and made a "pledge of loyalty to one fatherland, Indonesia; one language, Bahasa Indonesia; and asserted themselves to be one people, the Indonesian people".[5] The striking point is that in 1928 itself, the foundation for linguistic nationalism, and not religious or ethnic affiliations, was unequivocally decided upon. The Dutch East Indies, before 1928, had been geographically 'imagined'. The absence of a name of the land propelled the growth of nationalism with the flavour of 'desire to life together'.[6] The commitment remains intact and relevant till date and is likely to withstand any form of deviant assault.

Indonesia is located between 6.08° north and 11.15° south latitude, and from 94.45° to 141.05° east longitude.[7] After the redrawing of administrative divisions in 2005, Indonesia has now 33 provinces, 349 regencies, 91 municipalities, 5,656 sub-districts and 71,563 villages.[8] A hugely populated country with a population of 222.2 millions in 2006 and showing tendency of slowing down the annual growth rate from 1.45 per cent in 1990-2000 to 1.34 during the period of 2000 to 2006. The province of Java has the highest concentration of population around 59 per cent.[9] This factor, as we shall see, has an important role to play in the political process of the country.

Indonesia has the largest Muslim population in the world. The Muslim population is estimated to be 199,959,285, which accounts for 88.20 per cent of the total population. The remaining are Christians (about 6 million) and Hindus (2.5 million) and still smaller groups of Buddhists and various animists. At the same time, the Muslims do not constitute a monolithic structure in Indonesian society. They are divided on ethnic grounds and are not geographically united owing to their dispersed habitation. But the very fact that Indonesia is the largest Muslim country and that Islam as the religion of the Muslim population overwhelms others have a bearing on the socio-economic and political life of the country. As Brian May argues, "no study of Indonesia's problems is of use unless this significant force (Islam) is taken into account".[10]

The advent of Islam in Indonesia

The early history of Indonesia refers to the Dvipantara or Java Dwipa and Sumatra ruled by Hindu kings that flourished since 200 BC. In the sixth and eighth centuries, Hinduism came under the influence of Buddhism.[11] The archeological evidences[12] present a clear idea about the existence of Hindu and Buddhist kingdoms, such as kingdoms of Mataram, Srivijaya. Singhasari and Majapahit in various parts of present Indonesia till the archipelago was virtually overwhelmed by Islam beginning with the thirteenth century.[13] The Arab and Indian and later on Chinese Muslims, who came here since the seventh century in connection with trade[14], brought Islam to this part of the world. But the foreign religion was not immediately accepted by many of the locals, for at least three centuries. The Sufi saints of Shafi order propagated Islam and gradually most of the inhabitants embraced Islam. There is no evidence to suggest that the religious demographic transformation was accomplished through coercion. A well-preserved Arabic epigraph of a young woman laid to rest in Java in 1082 AD is the earliest evidence of the presence of the Muslims.[15] The Muslim tombstones and other historical and archaeological findings in Surabaya and Champa suggest that they had settlement in the region from about the 11th century. The evidences presented by the local historiographies such as *babad* (chronicles) and *hitayat* (historical annals) clearly tells about the Muslim settlements in Aceh, Aru, Samara Perlak and Pasai. There are records that the Pasai ruler sent two Muslim ambassadors to China in 1282.[16] It took hardly three centuries, i.e. thirteenth to sixteenth, to see the region including Malay Peninsula a speedy expansion of Islam. As already stated, the spread of Islam was not accomplished by military might; it was accelerated by the efforts of the Sufi teachers who dovetailed Islamic culture with local traditions and social practices, strongly rooted in Buddhist and Hindu traditions. This is evident from the way Islam was accepted and adopted in a relatively voluntary way without any instance of coercion, sense of conflict and royal patronage.[17] It was basically a handiwork of Sufi saints coming from Arab, India, more particularly from Gujarat, and China, mostly known as *wali* (apostles) with supernatural powers, who converted the local inhabitants to Islam on a massive scale.[18] The Sufis, while undertaking massive conversion, did not disturb the culture, tradition and social practices of the converts, as in the case of present Bangladesh, for which the social fabrics of the region remained intact. Islam in the region became an admixture of the pagan animism and the mysticism of Buddhism and Hinduism. Most of the Indonesian-Malaysian and Western scholars argue that the success of the Sufis in transforming the archipelago could be attributed essentially to presentation of Islam in a way that was found compatible with Hindu-Buddhist mystical background. The interplay of the three religions set the ground for the people to accept Islam. The accommodative and tolerant approach of the Sufis to conversion allowing the local Buddhist and Hindu tradition to remain unaffected shaped Indonesian Islam and its relationship with politics and the state. This led to a peaceful transformation of Indonesia into Islam keeping Hindu and Buddhist tradition intact. The history of Indonesia is one the finest examples of the interface and interaction of three major religions in the world – Buddhism, Hinduism and Islam – that instilled a spirit of mutual tolerance and respect. The arrival of Christianity, once again through trade, did not alter altogether the essentials of the Indonesian social texture.[19]

Although there is scanty documentation of the spread of Islam, it is believed that conversion was the main process of its speedy expansion in the entire archipelago. The common argument is that spice trade brought Islam to the region. In 1292, Marco Polo, the Venetian traveler and author visited the town of Perlak in the northern part of Sumatra and noted the conversion of the people in the area to Islam.[20] The fourteenth century scholar Ibn-Battutah, paid a visit to Java and Sumatra in 1345 and left behind the some notes on the presence of Islam and also conversion of the locals to the religion.[21] As Arnold writes, "long before Ibn Battutah's travel, merchants from Deccan had lived in large numbers in the region and sowed the seed of Islam".[22] Ricklefs writes that two processes probably occurred towards Islamization in Indonesia. To quote him:

> On the one hand, indigenous Indonesians came into contact with Islam and made an act of conversion. On the other, foreign Asians (Arabs, Indians, Chinese, etc) who were Muslims settled permanently in an Indonesian area, intermarried and adopted local lifestyles to such a degree that in effect they became Javanese or Malay or whatever. These two processes may often have occurred in conjunction with each other, and when a piece of evidence survives indicating, for instance, that a Muslim dynasty had been established in some area, it is often impossible to know which of two processes was the more important.[23]

The arrival of the Portuguese in Java in the sixteenth century led to systematic record of the impact of Islam on Indonesian society. The traditional life of the society did not change after conversion. The Muslim traders and saints engaged in the process of conversion followed a mystical form of Islam that had been familiar to Buddhism, Hinduism and local animism. That is why the Muslim mystics could have an astounding impact on the Indonesian-Malaysian peoples. Almost all the highly respected Muslim scholars and religious missionaries were mystics and they alone were responsible for the speedy expansion of Islam.[24] The massive religious transformation of the society in the entire archipelago during the first phase of expansion, from the eleventh to the sixteenth century, was essentially mystic based with a local taste of indigenous tradition, which could not be altered by the series of attempts towards reformation on the line of legal and theological schools of thought of the Middle Eastern puritan variety. This unassailable position in the Indonesian society has a determinant role in its society and polity, which is in its own right different from that of other parts of the world. The early phase of Dutch occupation of present Indonesia is said to have accelerated another phase of conversion apparently to confront the occupation and to assert indigenous identity of the people in that region.[25] Soon after the consolidation of the Dutch rule, the Indonesian Muslims started identifying and associating themselves strongly with Islam and using Islamic symbols, for, the next three centuries, to oppose Europeans and Christians. In this way an alternative way of life quite different from the colonial model started appearing. The anti European hostility was most intense during the Dutch-Acehnese War (1884-1911). The trend continued and became more visible and volatile at the turn of the twentieth century. The Sarekat Islam (Islamic Association), founded in 1912, appeared as the first platform for nationalism to arouse anti-colonial emotions among the people of Indonesia. At the same time, despite its predominant Muslim membership, it had had an inclusive character. That is why it has been regarded as the forerunner of modernist Muslim movements in Indonesia.[26] Later on the Muhammadiyah and the Nahdlatul *Ulama* (Council of the *Ulema*) spearheaded movements for Indonesian as well as Muslim identity to fight the Dutch occupation.[27]

Close on the heels of the movement for nationalism and independence, an Islamic reformist movement also made a mark. Divergent terms, such as Islamic movement, reformist movement, modern reformation movement and modernist movement, are used to name this movement in the entire Indonesian-Malaysian archipelago. The Islamic reformists refer to Islam in the realm of reform in the practices of the Muslims in accordance with the theological principles advanced by Jamal al-Din al-Afghani (1839-1897) and the conceptual foundation prepared by Egyptian reformist Muhammad Abduh (1849-1905) and his disciple Syrian scholar Rashid Rida (1865-1935).[28] Their approach towards purification of the Muslim world through strict adherence to fundamentals of Islam which was sorely needed to strengthen the ailing *ummah* and to rejuvenate it for global leadership, both in secular and sacerdotal fronts reverberated in different countries including Indonesia. A reformist organization named Muhammadiyah was founded in Yogyakarta in 1912 by Kiyai Hadji Ahmad Dahlan, who was inspired by the advocacies of Jamal al-Din al-Afghani and Abduh. It spearheaded a reformist movement to raise the Indonesian Muslims from a state of decline and crisis of faith.[29] It is still a major reformist platform in Indonesia. The Muhammadiyah deeply engaged itself in the task of bringing the community to the straight path of the religion and had the least to do with the political life of the country under the Dutch colonial rule, notwithstanding the fact that in its discourse on Indonesian Muslim identity, there was a heavy dose of anti-Christian and anti-European sentiment that served as a rallying point seeking full independence of the country. Close on the heels of its reformist agenda and awakening call, a new political platform seeking not only reforms but also political independence came up with the name Nahdlatul *Ulama* (NU) in 1926. Both the organizations had deep roots in the Sunni tradition and *Santri* ethnicity. Cutting across the ethnic barriers, the Indonesian Muslims have affiliations to both the Muhammadiyah and the NU. Yet, in the political processes of the country, both do not have a major role to play in terms of formation of government and power sharing.

Indonesian Muslims: a non-monolithic community

As stated in the preceding section, the Indonesian Islam incorporated the older Buddhist-Hindu tradition that served the purpose of building a cohesive society in which Islam played a natural role first in the royal courts during the pre-colonial period in the process of legitimization of kings and at the same time in the integration of many of the pre-Islamic traditions into Islam. The political unity of the kingdom of Java is a classic example of this trend.[30] Java, being the most populous among all the islands and simultaneously Muslim dominated, became the central and rallying point in the struggle against colonial rule. That dynamics of cohesion contributed to the nation-building process in the country in the post-colonial era. Thus, there is no denying the fact that religion and for that matter the Muslims as a community played a role in shaping Indonesia's personality as a nation-state. At the same time, the ethnic base of the Muslim community is Javanese-centric. To be precise, the Javanese constitutes the largest segment of the people of Indonesia (42 per cent of the total population) mostly located in island of Java. They are known in Indonesian terminology as Orang Jawa. Nearly all the Javanese (about 99 per cent) are Muslims.[31]

Yet, divergence of colours and contours could be seen in the religious composition of Indonesia. The Javanese Muslims, who dominate the political processes of today's Indonesia, represent a fascinating texture of the combination of pre-

Islamic tradition of the land with the religion Islam, which is a monolithic one centering around the faith. Indonesian Islam is what Sufism, mysticism and local tradition have determined to be over the years. Their impact is felt in the interior places where the bulk of the population lives. On the other hand, the coastal Muslims, as in the case of Aceh, who were exposed to first contact with the Arab Muslims through trade, emulated the puritan form of the religion. A clear geographic demarcation could be seen in the composition of the puritan and nominal Muslims of Indonesia. That too has a role to play in the political processes of the country, as we go deeper into the problems of ethnicity, religion and politics in Indonesia.

The percentage of the Muslim population in Indonesia (88.20) and the absolute number of the Muslims give an erroneous impression that Islam is preeminently visible in the length and breadth of the country. It is matter of fact that Islam did not spread in the entire Indonesian archipelago. The upland area of Sumatra and the interior part of Kalimantan managed to retain their indigenous religions. The arrival of the Portuguese in the sixteenth century led to the introduction of Catholic Christianity in some of these areas and later on the Protestant variety of Christianity started expanding after the consolidation of Dutch occupation.[32] The island of Bali managed to retain its Hindu identity till today. Other parts of Indonesia, such as Irian province, have continued to practice various forms of animism. The reformist movement under the banner of the Muhammadiyah and the Nahdlatul *Ulama* did not reach these areas, and therefore, the non-Muslims living there were left unaffected. Nonetheless, the two highly populated portions of Indonesia– Java and Sumatra – where the Muslims overwhelm other religious communities, determine the nature of politics of the country.

Yet, like many other countries in the world, where the Muslims have a strong presence in demographic terms, such as India, Muslims are not a monolithic community. The classical division of the Muslim population in Indonesia, as portrayed by Clifford Geertz,[33] still holds good. Indonesian Muslims are divided, though not in watertight compartments, into three segments, namely *abangon* (the nominal and non-practicing Muslims, whose primary identification with Islam is mixed with traditional beliefs and practices of Buddhism-Hinduism and local animism), *santri* (the devout or orthodox Muslims, whose strict adherence to Islam is paramount) and *priyayi* (official or aristocratic Muslims or *abangan* ruling elite). This division makes the Indonesian Muslims far from being homogeneous and monolithic. The *abangan* Muslims are regarded as remnants of animist or Buddhist and Hindu traditions and as syncretistic in their approach to social life. In accepting Islam the people did not abandon their social customs and practices. The non-Islamic practices received religious sanction. Some of the Islamic religious practices such as *fitra* (poor tax) during the month of Ramdan has been made indigenous by branding it as 'rice tax'. Eid-ul-fitr has been celebrated as Hari Raya. Child birth, circumcision of boys, marriage and funerals and similar other socio-religious functions have been performed on the line of customs common to all before the arrival of Islam in the region.[34] The *abangan* population and their culture are overwhelming in the larger islands such as Java, Sumatra and Kalimantan. The *santris* presence along the coastal areas has a limited influence. At the same time, orthodox as they are, the *santris* are not the carbon copies of puritan Muslims of the Middle East. The distribution and distinction between *abangan* and *santri* are not merely matters of individuals who are more or less pious and orthodox or a line of demarcation between more or less secular. At a certain point the distinction becomes too thin to be noticed. For example, any disrespect shown to Prophet Muhammad as done by a Danish cartoonist recently united all the Muslims of Indonesia to organize protest demonstrations throughout the country. To perform Hajj at Mecca is considered a sacred duty by one and all. But the *abangan* Muslims of Java are different in social and religious customs from the *Santri* Muslims of Aceh or of some parts of Sumatra. To put succinctly, the Muslims of Indonesia are not monolithic and homogeneous.

The historical process of Islamization and the divergence of the community did not create a space for the Muslims to play a cohesive role in the political life of Indonesia. The unevenness of demographic structure of the various components of the community in different regions, as indicated in the preceding section, has offered a little scope to community to exercise political collectivism.[35] The Javanese Muslims, who have strong presence in the central and eastern parts of the island, are essentially *abangan* and would not rally behind a demand for Islamization and would oppose the idea of enforcing Sharia laws tooth and nail. On the other hand, the hardliner in Aceh with fragile demographic strength cannot sweep the national politics. This needs further illustration.

Role of Islam in national reconstruction

It is understandable that Islam as a religion has a role to play in the national life of Muslim majority countries, a forbearing point that figures in Chapter I. Indonesia is one of the few Muslim majority countries which kept religion outside the formal domain of politics, in spite of the fact that religion was one of the core components in its struggle against the colonial rule. The war of resistance to Dutch colonialism in the nineteenth century, such as, the revolt spearheaded by Prince Diponogor in Java in the nineteenth century, the Padri, Bentam and Acch wars were essentially Islamic in nature. The fierce fights put up during the colonial period against the Dutch rule were inspired by Islamic slogans. In this way Islam became a rallying point in the political canvas of Indonesia and an important index for identification.[36] Although the freedom movements were crushed, the spirit and determination to oppose colonial rule using Islamic symbols continued to survive. The formation of Sarekat Islam in 1912 as already stated was an expression of the urge of the people to create an independent Indonesian state. With its formation, Islam and the process of Islamization constituted a strong element in the process of building Indonesian nationalism.[37] Although the religious sentiment was one of the cardinal principles behind the foundation of the organization, its leaders subscribed to a modernist approach to life.[38] It had an inclusive character for which people belonging to various shades of political affiliations and ideologies such as communists, modernists, nationalists and Muslim reformists participated in the debates, movements and political rallies organized by it. It is interesting to note that multifarious debates on relationship between the state and religion, socialism and Islam, the demand for and concept of Islamic state, role of women in politics and fundamentals of democracy could be held in a tolerant and accommodative atmosphere.[39]

The Sarekat Islam could not sustain its broad inclusive character due to intense struggle within the organization between the religious nationalists and communists. Various organizations such as the Muhammadiyah, the Nahdlatul *Ulama* and the PKI (Partai Komunis Indonesia or Communist Party of Indonesia) emerged in the scene.[40] The Islamic appeal towards national reconstruction got diluted as the NU's agenda was both political and sacerdotal, while the Muhammadiyah concentrated on issues relating to education, society and religion of the people, and the PKI was obsessed with bringing about a communist movement for liberation of peasants and proletariats. The entire political landscape changed during and after the Japanese occupation of Indonesia. A new political leadership emerged under the leadership of Achmed Soekarno, which believed in shaping Indonesian state on a secular mould. A new emergent Indonesia did not fall under the pressure of demand for a declaration of Islamic state. Indonesian national identity was to grow on a liberal and secular fabric, which transcend till date, despite occasional anti-Chinese riots and jihadi activism.

Prior to the dawn of independence in Indonesia, a fierce debate as to the national identity of the newborn country was initiated. The portents of Japanese defeat and the eventual end of their occupation of Indonesia during World War II was in sight. The nationalist leaders prepared the formulation of a plan of action to handle the affairs of independent Indonesia. On June 1, 1945, Soekarno, the chairman of the preparatory committee for independence, proposed Five Pillars or Pancasila as the foundation for the future of independent Indonesia. The Five Pillars consisted of (1) the belief in One Supreme Divinity, (2) humanism, (3) nationalism seen as the national unity of Indonesia, (4) democracy and (5) social justice. They established a sixty-two member committee to give a definite shape to the ideological foundation of the new state. The debates in the committee clearly showed a line of difference between promoters of secularism and those of an Islamic state. There were other issues too; whether to have a unitary or a federal setup, a republican or monarchical government, whether the head of the state could be designated as Imam or President and what should be the relationship between the state and religion.

The most outspoken advocate for a unitary and secular state of Indonesia, was Muhammad Hatta, devout Muslim from Sumatra, who eventually became the Vice-President of independent Indonesia. He made a passionate appeal for a unitary Indonesia which would keep religion out of the domain of the state affairs. While supporting him Supomo, a Javanese member with impeccable oratory skill argued:

> Creating an Islamic state in Indonesia would mean we are not creating a unitary state. To create an Islamic state in Indonesia would mean setting up a state that would associate itself with the largest religious group in the state, the Islamic. This would create problems with Christians and other minorities, for although an Islamic state would safeguard the interests of such groups, they would not be able to feel involved in the state. The ideals of an Islamic state are not in accordance with the ideals of a unitary state which we all have so passionately longed for.

Three weeks of intense debate between the secular nationalists and those who advocated in favour of Islamic foundation of the state led to the crystallization of a compromise formula to satisfy those who wanted Indonesia to be an Islamic state. It was expressed in what came to be known as the Jakarta Charter of June 22. It served the purpose of a draft to be eventually incorporated as the preamble to the Constitution. To quote:

> ...national independence of the Indonesian people is embodied in the constitution of the state of Indonesia, which takes the form of the Republic of Indonesian state in which the people are sovereign and which is based upon: *Belief in One Almighty God with the obligation to implement the sharia for adherents of Islam* [emphasis added] a just and civilized humanitarianism, the unity of Indonesia, and a Democracy guided by wisdom arising from consultation and representation, which democracy shall ensure social justice for all Indonesian people.[41]

Three weeks after the historic declaration made by Soekarno, on June 22, 1945 a nine member committee proposed a text for the constitution of the country, which came to be known as "seven words" of the Jakarta Charter[42], which were, as translated, "with the obligation to implement the sharia for adherents of Islam".[43] There was huge opposition to the insertion of these words, which hurt the secular Muslims as well as non-Muslim communities. Leading Muslim scholars like Hoesein Djajadiningrat, who later headed Office for Religious Affairs, vehemently opposed these 'seven words' saying that "They may create fanaticism, because it seems that Muslims will be forced to keep the *shariah*".[44] That eventually led to the deletion of these words from the provisional constitution on August 18, 1945 one day after the declaration of independence.[45] Pancasila became a binding force among many communities and races in the country and served the purpose of national reconstruction at the end of the foreign rule. It encompassed all sections of the society, more particularly, the Christian population, numerically smaller, but constituting an important component in army and bureaucracy after *Merdeka* (independence). The entire community, led by Bishop of Jakarta, Albertus Soegijoprajoto, extended support to the cause of national unity under the leadership of Soekarno for his commitment to democracy and secularism.[46] The new leadership could not undermine this fact nor could they wish away the adverse repercussion surfaced as a result of the proposal for adherence to Sharia law.

The omission of the 'seven words' caused severe disillusionment among the pro-Islamic groups, so much so that they fought a civil war against the new state of Indonesia and proclaimed dar-al-salam (domain of Islam) in the three provinces of West Java, South Sulawese and Aceh under the leadership of Kartosuwirjo who assumed the title of Imam. The armed movement to create an Islamic state was crushed and Kartosuwirjo was captured and executed in 1962. The civil war was too localized and limited to dismantle the secular foundation of Indonesian state. The defeat of the radical forces led by Kartosuwirjo virtually marked the end of militant Islamists' quest for an Islamic state of Indonesia.

The first general elections held in September 1955 did not award a clear mandate to any one the three contesting political arrangements. The National Party of Indonesia (NPI) led by Soekarno secured the highest percentage of votes (22.3), the two Muslim factions – Masyumi secured 20.9 per cent and NU 18.3, while the communists garnered 16.4. It is noteworthy that Pancasila ideology as the foundation for Indonesia was not contested in the election campaign. It suggested that the issue was settled. The attempt to upset the already agreed state ideology by the Muslim parties during the period of 1956-1959 could not achieve anything. Soekarno, countered the demand for proclamation of an Islamic state by introducing the Nasakom (Nasional+ agama+ komunist) binding nationalism, *agama* (religion) and communism within the broad framework of Pancasila. Nasakom became a part of national life. It even found a secured place in school curricula. The religiosity of the general people was looked after by the pillar one of the Pancasila, i.e. belief in the One Supreme Divinity.

Soekarno used Pancasila to achieve a broad national consensus on the foundation of Indonesia. His successor General Soeharto used it to crush the communists during the early phase of his 'New Order' regime. At the end of the 'New Order' regime in 1997, the Muslim parties at the interval of half a century of independence piloted an amendment to the Constitution to do away with Pancasila and to proclaim Indonesia as an Islamic state; the attempt finally ended up with a huge flop. When the proposal for an amendment to the Constitution for inserting a clause towards the enforcement of Sharia law and revival of the so-called Jakarta Charter was taken up for debate in the Assembly, it did not survive even a session in a committee meeting. It was overwhelmed by opposition from within and without the Assembly. The opposition did not come from secular Golkar and PDI-P (Partai Demokrasi Indonesia-Perjuangan) or Indonesian Democratic Party-Struggle alone; two other newly formed Muslim parties of PKB (Partai Kebangkitan Bangsa) or National Awakening Party formed in 1998 as based largely on an NU constituency, and PAN (Partai Amanat Nasional) or National Mandate Party founded in 1998 with Amien Rais[47], firmly rejected the idea of reviving the Islamic state. The national consensus was that the preamble of the Constitution containing Pancasila and Article 29 which stipulates "the state is based on the belief in the one Supreme God" and guaranteeing the freedom of religious belief and practice must remain intact.[48] It is important to note that the two largest Muslim civil organizations supported the national consensus to retain Pancasila and Article 29 of the Constitution. To sum up, Pancasila as a state ideology appears to be holding, as testified to by the experience of over five decades.

Despite an Islamic ambience in demographic sense, the religiosity as expressed in amplified call for prayers in the mosques, five times a day, Islam as a religion remains a low-profile component in the public and political domains unless vital issues in the Islamic world disturb and agitate the public mind. The low key profile of Islam in the political life of the country is well reflected in the composition of the national parliament called Dewan Perwakilan Rakyat (DPR), or Peoples' Representative Council where the Muslim parties never won 30% of seats.[49] The end of the 'New Order', the establishment of a popular government headed by B.J. Habibie after the resignation of President Soeharto on May 21, 1998 and the proclamation of *reformasi* era led to the lifting of ban of Islamic parties imposed during Soeharto's time. Indonesia witnessed a mushroom growth of about 48 Muslim parties. This fact indicates the lack of political unity and collectivism among the Muslims parties for which their attempts to capture the majority of seats in the national representative assembly and to win the presidential elections, in both 1999 and 2004, did not succeed. The electoral performance of the Muslim parties in the post-Soeharto era is an indication of their shaky hold among the common Muslims of Indonesia.

The three elections in the post-Soeharto era were path breaking, and therefore, were landmarks in the electoral politics in Indonesia. In clear deviation from the past, these were free and fair elections. Two issues – democracy and Islam in the relations with the state – constituted the major components in the electioneering planks during the first two elections. The issue of economic development, health-care issues, decentralization and good governance dominated the latest elections of 2009. Islam and religion played only a small role. The Islamic parties performed poorly in the April elections to the DPR. After the end of Soeharto's three decades long authoritarian rule, the electorate was committed to strengthen the forces of democracy so that authoritarian rule does not return. The issue of Islam as the religion of more than 88 per cent of the people and its relationship with the state has been alive since the days of the preparation of the Jakarta Charter of 1945. The two issues constituted the core of electioneering in both the 1999 and the 2004 elections. The popular commitment to strengthen democracy and to sustain the secular credentials of Indonesia, which were integral to the spirit of reformasi, was quite visible during the time of electioneering. The election results were predictable.[50] The popular mood was reflected in a decisive manner. A number of presidential decrees ensuring freedom to form new political parties and associations; freedom of both electronic and print media; freedom of workers and peasants to have unions and associations; freedom for the enhancement of the rights of minorities (Chinese, Christians and indigenous peoples) issued by B.J. Habibie and Abdurranhman Wahid helped generate an atmosphere of confidence and freedom which had been denied for three

Table 3.1

Results of Indonesian People's Representative Council elections, 1999

Party	*Valid votes*	*% of votes*	*Seats*	*% seats*
PDI-P	35,706,618	33.7	153	33.0
Golkar	23,742,112	22.4	120	26.0
PPP*	11,330,387	10.7	58	12.6
PKB	13,336,963	12.6	51	11.0
PAN	7,527,936	7.1	34	7.4
Others (16 total)	14,200,921	13.4	46	10.0
Total	105,845,937	100	462	100

Source: Mitsuo Makamura, *Islam and Democracy in Indonesia*, p. 7

* PPP (Partai Pesatuan Pembangunan—(United Development Party) established under pressure in 1973 by amalgamating four Islamic Parties: NU, Parmus (successor to Masyum), Perti (Persatuan Tarbiyah Islamiya i.e. Islamic Education Association) and Sarekat Islam.

decades. The first free and fair nation-wide election held on June 7, 1999 after 45 years since the 1955 general elections and also the first of its kind in the post-Soeharto era put an end to the overwhelming predominance of the Golkar Party of Soeharto.[51] The results pushed forward the reformasi agenda of the PDI-P headed by Megawati Sukarnoputri in a multi-party national legislature, where no party had an absolute majority (Table 3.1).

Besides PDI-P, pro-reformasi forces included new political parties such as PKB, a party that relies on the support of the estimated 30 million members, the NU, an organization dedicated to the task of promoting and ameliorating educational and economic conditions of the Muslims, and the PAN. The others, which include the Muslim parties, failed to make a mark in the elections. All total 48 Muslim parties contested the elections, but none could make their presence felt. Most of them secured less than 2 per cent votes. Consequently, the highest political offices went to the pro-democracy and secular leaders – Abdurrahman Wahid was elected as the President, Megawati Soekarnoputri as the Vice-President and Amien Rais as the Chairman of the parliament.

The political scenario in Indonesia settled down with a decisive mandate for democracy and secularism, despite contesting Islamic forces trying to derail the process of secularization. The three scheduled elections for the national parliament, regional assemblies and local councils in 32 provinces and 400 regencies (administrative units between provinces and sub-districts) and municipalities took place within a span of only six months involving more than 150 million voters. The elections were found to be free and fair, without any instances of violence and rigging. This was a clear departure from the ones conducted during the regime of Soekarno. As in the case of the general elections in 1999, in the subsequent election held in 2004 no party could secure absolute majority in the national parliament (Table

3.2). The pattern remained same. At the same time the hung parliament did not create any political instability, understandably in a presidential form of polity in Indonesia.

Table 3.2

Results of Indonesian People's Representative Council elections, 2004

Party	*Valid Votes*	*% of votes*	*Seats*	*% seats*
Golkar	24,480, 757	21.58	128	23.27
PDI-P	21,026,629	18.53	109	19.82
PPP	9,248,764	8.05	58	10.55
Partai Demorkat	8,455,225	7.45	57	10.36
PAN	7,303,324	6.44	52	9.45
PKB	11,989,564	10.57	52	9.45
PKS	8,325,020	7.34	45	8.18
PBS	2,764,998	2.44	13	2.36
PDS	2,414,254	2.13	12	2.18
PBB*	2,970,487	2.62	11	2.00
Others (Total 14)	14,483,392	12.76	13	2.36

*Partai Bulan Bintang, Cresent Star Party

Source: Mitsuo Makamura, *Islam and Democracy in Indonesia*, p. 13

The Golkar Party bounced back in 2004 and secured the highest number of seats as also the highest percentage of votes, relegating PDI-P to the second position. The rise of the Muslim-based party, PKS (Partai Keadilan Sejaterah or Prosperous Justice Party), securing 7.34 per cent votes and 45 seats in the parliament, is a significant development. The PKS was a new Islamic party formed on July 20, 1998 as the Justice Party, which had failed to meet electoral requirement of 2 per cent votes in 1999 elections, and eventually it was reconstituted as Prosperous Justice Party in April 2002. It is deeply committed to the mandatory implementation of Sharia law, banning of alcohol, pornography and gambling.[52]

The Presidential election of 2004 showed almost an identical trend. No single candidate could secure absolute majority. Susilo Bambang Yudhoyono, an new entrant to politics, was a military general who served the UN forces in Bosnia and also an incumbent minister of politics and security, secured 33.7 per cent votes in the first round of elections and finally defeated Megawati Soekarnoputri in the second round; Yudhoyono secured 60.62 per cent vote while Soekarnoputri slightly improved her tally by 12.77 percent. Amien Rais, a liberal face of among the Muslim leaders secured only 14.66 per cent in the first round. The presence of the Islamic parties was not felt at all.

With only a couple of months to go for the next general elections of 2009, the wind of change to a certain extent could be felt. In 1999 the government passed a law incapacitating parties polling less than 5 per cent votes from participating in the subsequent elections. This elimination process, i.e. parties had to reach the 'threshold' level of 5 per cent poll in their favour to enable them to contest the next elections, reduced the figures indicative of strength of the Muslim parties substantially. In 2004 the 'threshold' barrier was reduced to 3 per cent to enable six parties to contest the elections of 2004. After the 2004 elections only two Islamic parties, the PPP (Partai Persatuan Pembangunan i.e. United Development Party), the only Islamic party that Soeharto allowed to exist and the PKS reached the 'threshold' to be able to contest the 2009 general elections.[53] Proving the political pundits wrong, the Islamic parties romped through the electoral scenario in Indonesia, staging a surprise in regional elections. The PKS and the PAN forged a coalition to win the West Java Governor and Deputy Governor's election held on April 13, 2008. Close on the heels of this development, three days later PKS teamed up to repeat the same victory by winning the posts of Governor and Deputy Governor in North Sumatra.[54] It was a matter of speculation at that point of time that the Islamic forces might perform well in the elections of 2009. The speculation was erroneous, for, the results of April 2008 elections were determined by local issues and factors and were not reflective of the national mood, and therefore, it was ultimately proved wrong. In both parliamentary and presidential elections of 2009, the Islamic parties were no where to match the electoral performance of the national parties.

Indonesia's two recent elections – one for the 560 member People's Representative Council and 132-member Regional Representative Assembly held on April 9, 2009 and the other Presidential elections of July 2009 - reaffirmed the continuation of the already established trend in favour of

Table 3.3

Results of 560-member Indonesian People's Representative Council, April 2009

Parties	*Valid Votes*	*% of votes*	*Seats*	*% of seats*
Partai Democrat	21,703,137	20.85	150	26.79
Golkar	15,037,757	14.45	107	19.11
PDI-P	14,600,091	14.03	95	16.96
PKS	8,206,955	7.88	57	10.18
PAN	6,254,580	6.01	43	7.68
PPP	5,533,214	5.32	37	6.61
PKB	5,146,122	4.94	27	4.82
PGIR*	4,646,406	4.46	26	4.64
PHNR**	3,922,870	3.77	18	3.21

*Partai Gerakan Indonesia Raya, Great Indonesia Movement Party

** Partai Hati Nurani Rakyat, People's Conscience Party

Source: http://en.wikipedia.org/wiki/Indonesian_ legislative_ election,_2009.

democracy and secularism. Out of 60 registered parties only 38 were permitted to join the contest. It is interesting to see that out of 38 parties only 7 parties declared Islam as their political ideology and the rest Pancasila, the cornerstone of national reconciliation and reconstruction. It was a long and grueling campaign that had begun in August 2008 continued till April 5, 2009 four days before the actual nation-wide poll. As predicted, the Democratic Party of President Yudhoyono won 150 seats pushing Golkar to second and Megawati's PDI-P to the third position [Table 3.3].

Out of 38 contesting parties, only 9 parties, as shown in Table 3.3, could reach the People's Representative Council (Dewan Perwakilan Rakyat, DPR). Yudhoyona's Partai Democratic substantially improved its position by 95 seats. The PKS, as predicted also captured 57 seats, a marked improvement by 12 seats. Other Islamic parties were virtually routed in this election. The improvement made by the PKS is a consequential effect of its decision to change its colour soon after its thrilling victory in West Java and North Sumatra in April 2008. It released a 643-page book entitled *Struggling for a Civil Society* on April 20, 2008, which detailed about its political objectives and programme of action for the future. It endorses Islamic values but rejects, in a clear departure from its past position, the idea of making Indonesia an Islamic state.[55] This is a calculated exercise to draw liberal Muslims as well as non-Muslim to its electoral fold, as also, an early warning to the Democratic Party, the Golkar and the PDI-P about the erosion of their bases in 2009 elections. At the same time, it is also an expression of the PKS's realization that how unrealistic it would be to talk of the concept of an Islamic state in a non-monolithic and essentially secular state like Indonesia, where religion and religiosity matter; but the dominance of Islam as a religion over others is not experimented with in the post-colonial history of the country. It will be an uphill task, if not impossible, to transform Indonesian state and society into an Islamic one, adhering to an Islamic way of life of the Taliban mould. The relations between the state and religion could be slightly closer than before. But that is not likely to integrate Indonesia into a theocratic state system. The results of the parliamentary and the presidential elections of 2009 proved once again that religious parties have no future in Indonesia.

The 2009 Presidential election consolidated the gains of the democratic movement ushered in Indonesia since the onset of the *reformasi* era. Within a short span of ten years the democratic reforms gained a formidable space. Soon after the April 2009 elections to the Dewan Perwakilan Rakyat (DPR), a coalition of major opposition political parties to nominate a common candidate to contest the incumbent President Susilo Bamban Yudhoyono was tried when incumbent Vice-President Yusuf Kalla expressed his desire to challenge Yudhoyono in the Presidential election with the support of the PDI-P. After an initial breakdown of talks in this direction were broken off on April 13, 2009, when the Golkar, to which Yusuf Kalla belonged, expressed its coalition commitment to the continuity of the earlier arrangement with the incumbent President, a ten-party loose understanding was forged among the Golkar and the PDI-P, in the event of having a second round of poll. In view of Yusuf Kalla's decision to contest in the election, Yudhoyono chose Boediono, the Governor of Bank Indonesia, as his running mate and entered into a four party alliance with the PAN, the PKS and PKB. It is noteworthy that under the 2008 Presidential Election Law, the candidate must be nominated by a party or coalition of parties that had won at least 25 per cent of valid popular votes or 112 (i.e 20%) of 560 seats of the DPR. This requirement restricted the number of candidates for the election to three – incumbent President Yudhoyon, incumbent Vice-President Yusuf Kalla and former President Megawati Soekarnoputri.

As predicted by psephologists, Yudhoyono returned to power with a thumping majority votes (73,874,562, i.e. 60.80%), undoubtedly with a clear mandate and without, unlike his first election in 2004, requiring for the second round. Megawati polled 32,548,105 (26.79%) and Yusuf Kalla 15,081,814 (12.41%). Once again the hardcore Islamic parties had no role to play.

The politics of demand for Sharia law

Most of the Muslim majority countries, all over the world, encounter the transitional demand for implementation of Sharia law. What is Sharia law? It is Islamic law, which is often considered as the heart of Islam. Sharia means 'path' to life not only in this temporal world but also in thereafter. It is considered as God's guidance for human beings in all aspects of their lives – in their worship and in their relationship with one another. It derives its source from the Qur'an, which contains about ninety verses directly and specifically addressing the questions of law, and the Sunnah (life and activities of Prophet Muhammad) and for practical purposes, from the jurisprudence (*fiqh*) textbooks compiled in the first few centuries of Islam. The *fiqh* textbooks are human efforts to codify Islamic norms, and therefore, are fallible. That is why modern scholars argue that Sharia is not *fiqh*, which could be amended and revised in the light of modern and changing conditions. Sharia derived from the Qur'an and Sunnah cannot be revised and amended.

The fundamental basis of Sharia is that it is the duty of the Muslims to obey God in every walk of life including the social and the personal. According to the 12th century great jurist al-Ghazali (1058-1111) there are five objectives of Sharia laws: (1) protection of religion, (2) protection of life, (3) protection of intellect, (4) protection of human beings and (5) protection of property. There are different interpretations of Sharia law. What is more important from the political point of view is that political parties and organizations utilize the issue of enforcement of Sharia law to garner support from the masses in order to capture power.[56]

As already stated in the Introduction Chapter, to most

of the adherents, Islam is a total way of life, and therefore, they would like to assert that Islam is an integrated religion that offers a solution to all problems of life. Such expressions constitute the core of Islamic revivalism, Islamic resurgence, Islamic revolution and Islamic fundamentalism. Whether or not the ruler (government) has an obligation to implement Sharia law as a definitive step towards Islamization has been debated for centuries together. The central foci of the debate tends to subsume the socio-political, cultural and linguistic identities and differences in submission to God, which could form a normative understanding of submission of the adherents to His all-pervading authority. It could be an ideal, which cannot be translated into reality.[57] The very presence of *adat* (local custom), which decides many a social and family issue and problem, is a classical testimony to interplay of reason, tradition and religion. This implies the diversity of sources of laws in the Indonesian-Malaysian archipelago, making it difficult to build a case for universal acceptance of the idea of implementation of Sharia laws in Indonesia. This consideration is applicable in Bangladesh and Malaysia too.

It is important to note that soon after the proclamation of independence, one of the first major steps that the country took was the establishment of a Ministry of Religion in 1946, which, by implication, presented a role for Islam in the affairs of this secular state. The establishment of a separate ministry meant that the state has an obligation to look after the affairs of religions; Islam being the religion of the vast majority received special attention. Further, despite Indonesia being a secular state, Islam in Indonesia is not a private religion. It has a strong public presence and most of the political parties tend to assert their Islamic identity. The post-Soeharto era witnessed the emergence of a large number of Muslim-based parties, numbering more than 48. The most prominent parties are PPP, PKB, PAN and PBB. This is an unmistakable indication of the relevance of Islam even in the pronounced secular state of Indonesia.

The socio-political activities of national Islamic organizations, such as the NU and the Muhammadiyah, the presence of a large number of Islamic educational institutions and the state-sanctioned religious bodies like the Majelis Ulema Indonesia (Council of Indonesian Religious Scholars) suggest, in unequivocal terms, that Islam has a role to play in all fields of national life of the country, be it political, social, religious, ideological or educational. The all-pervading presence of religion in the secular state prepared the ground for a public face of Sharia in Indonesia.[58]

As in the case of a number of Muslim majority countries, the question of the role of Islam in the governance of a state in general and the place of Sharia in the body polity of a state have remained important in the public discourse in Indonesia ever since the preparation of the Jakarta Charter of 1945. It is still alive even after the defeat of a proposal to incorporate Sharia as mandatory for Muslims in August 2002 in Indonesia's supreme legislative council called MPR (Majelis Permusyawaratan Rakayat i.e. People's Consultative Assembly). Certain unresolved questions about Sharia torment the Muslim mind. Is it a set of laws that always and at all times governs the personal behaviour of an adherent of Islam? Does it mean a code of conduct for secular governance? Does it constitute the foundation of jurisprudence which covers the non-adherents? Is it *sin qua non* of an Islamic state? There is no universally accepted answer to these difficult questions nor there is a complete definition of the term Sharia. That predicament leads people, whether laymen or jurists, to interpret Sharia according to their own convenience.

As for Indonesia, an idea of madhab nasional sharia (National way of Islamic law) was mooted in 1945 to institutionalize Islamic way of education, justice, social system and governance in conformity with the cultural realities of Indonesia.[59] The original discussion on the relationship between the temporal state and Islamic law can be found in the Medina Document of 622 AD, drafted and promulgated at the initiative of Prophet Muhammad.[60] The Document is a common referral point of discourses on Islamic laws. It could be considered as a community-based agreement or a social contract for distribution of power. Such a social contract or agreement in a highly diverse and fragmented country like Indonesia is out of question, for, no organization, neither the NU nor the Muhammadiyah, nor any other political party could ever claim to be representative of the entire population of Indonesia and to forge a social contract or treaty to institutionalize Sharia law in the country.[61]

The first principle of the Pancasila–"Belief in One Supreme God" – replacing the 'seven words' gave the orthodox *santri* Muslims a scope to argue that it carried an Islamic connotation. To them, the state and the adherents of Islam have an obligation to enforce Sharia law. Official formulation holds that Pancasila encompasses all religions, including Christianity, Hinduism, Buddhism, and even animism to make Indonesia a home for all religious beliefs and puts an obligation on the state to stay away from providing a special status to Islam, which has the largest followers.[62] The demand to have a clear constitutional framework for the enforcement of Sharia law in Indonesia is a favourate political plank for all the Islamic parties, notwithstanding the fact that they do not have a coherent understanding of which variety of Sharia law has to be incorporated. In the midst of the dilemma caused by lack of its clear definition, the debate as to the relationship between the state and religion, and as to enforcement of the Islamic law continued for last 50 years with no sign of early emergence of a consensus.

The presence of religious courts in Indonesia and their dispensation of justice in matters of inheritance, marriage, divorce, hajj, *zakat* (charitable alms), *wakf* (religious charitable trust) is a clear indication of adherence to Sharia law in a moderate form. These courts, which have a long history of existence with *qadi* (judge, Indian counterpart *Kazi*), since the spread of Islam in the archipelago, have remained undisturbed during the colonial period and also during the Japanese occupation. They have earned a good reputation for quick and fair dispensation of justice as against the inefficient and corrupt judicial system in the country.[63] On the eve of Indonesia's independence, there was a proposal advanced by many Muslims to constitute a separate ministry for religious affairs. It was rejected not only by the non-Muslims but also by religiously neutral nationalists. Eventually, the Ministry of Religious Affairs was established on January 3, 1946 under the provisions of Article 29 (2) of the Constitution as a move to establish some working relationship between the state and the religions.[64] The article guarantees religious freedom to all the five recognized religions- Islam, Protestantism, Roman Catholicism, Hinduism and Buddhism. Among them, Islam benefits most from the creation of a separate ministry. That proves a point that although Indonesia is a secular state, it provides a special space to Islam. The Islamic courts were transferred to this Ministry, making the Islamic judiciary a part of a conscious effort to establish a relationship between the state and the dominant religion, Islam. At the same time, these courts did not have an equal status, as they were placed under the jurisdiction of civil courts.

In a dramatic move, at the end of Soeharto's 'New Order', the government proposed a draft legislation on January 28, 1989 to the People's Representative Council, DPR, to place Islamic courts under the Supreme Court (Mahkamah Agung) and thus elevate them to enjoy equal status with three other categories of courts – civil courts, military courts and administrative courts. It was designed to end the subordination of Islamic courts, which appeared to have satisfied the sentiments of the Muslim parties. However, the move raised some doubt and suspicion in the minds not only of the Christian and other religious minorities but also of the *abangans*, who constitute the core of the administrative and the military infrastructure of the country.[65] It faced stiff opposition from legal experts; but the Government's position to delimit the jurisdiction of the Islamic courts to matters of marriage and divorce, inheritance, religious endowment (*wakf*) and alms giving (*zakat*) among the Muslims only subdued the opposition and the bill was passed in DPR unanimously.

The people appear to be content with the current position of the Islamic courts as much as they are with the enforcement of Sharia regulations in some of the provinces such as West Sumatra, northern Sulawesi and Aceh to cover social and personal behaviour and dresses.[66]

The question of Sharia law in Indonesia has several dimensions for which the debate on it has now continued for half a century and is yet to see any prospect of early solution. The issue has been discussed and debated since the 1945 in the context of relationship between the state and Islam. The demand for enactment and enforcement of Sharia law has been linked up with the promotion of Islam through constitutional arrangement.[67] The demand could not be translated into reality for obvious reasons. First, there is no consensus about the definition of Sharia law. Second, there is a wide divide between the proponents of Sharia law as enforced in some of the countries in the Middle East and the one that suits Indonesian culture and tradition. Third, there are groups, which want Sharia law for certain specific purposes, such as to contain the problems of alcoholism, gambling, and prostitution. These complexities are too grave and difficult to find a solution in the near future. Considering this, as already stated, the PKS, one of the largest and emerging Muslim parties, has recently made a pronouncement, abandoning the demand for transforming Indonesia into an Islamic state. It maintained a discreet silence on the issue of Sharia law. By implication, it has sidelined the issue in order to play safe in the game of political arithmetic, considering its stakes in the forthcoming general and the presidential elections in 2009. With this, it would be almost impossible for others to launch a movement in favour of making some constitutional arrangement for enforcement of Islamic laws, and for that matter transforming Indonesia into an Islamic state.

Indonesia's two Muslim organizations

The vast profile of Muslim population in Indonesia finds expression in the organizational and operational activities of two highly respected, more or less parallel organizations of Sunni tradition – the Muhammadiyah and the NU. Both came into being at the turn of the last century, when Muslim consciousness began to grow and manifested itself against the backdrop of a popular urge of the *santris* to purify Islam and rescue it from the "corrupting" local influence of popular customs and owing to a dichotomy between modernity and tradition to characterize religious variety in Indonesian society. According to Clifford Geertz, the Muhammadiyah could be considered as modernists, while the more conservative groups such as NU and Persatuan Trabiyah Islamiyah (Perti) are traditionalists. The modernist Muhammadiyah is associated with a 'scripturalist' religious orientation and with a positive concern for rationality, syncretistic social fabric of the society, economic development and western education in order to uplift the conditions of the common masses; on the other hand, the NU represented traditional Islam. It is described as mystical, more rural and otherworldly oriented. Nonetheless, Geertz's analysis based on empirical observation was a matter of research in the 1950's.[68] There has been significant change in the structure and approach of these two organizations during the last half a century. The other important reason for the emergence of the two organizations was the urge to struggle against western colonialism, which was viewed as Christian domination over Muslims. While rural-based NU became involved politically and deeply entrenched with power sharing arrangements both during and after the 'New Order' regime, the urban Muhammadiyah has remained steadfast in its stance as a non-political organization with a modernist approach to Islam and Indonesian society.[69]

The Muhammadiyah came into existence in 1912 to steer religious awakening in Indonesia in conjunction with the development elsewhere on the line of reformist movement spearheaded by Muhammad Abduh and his disciple Rashid Rida of Egypt. It was founded by Hajji Ahmad Dahlan to encourage piety and a serious attitude towards carrying out religious obligations and to purify Islamic beliefs and practices in order to reject the so called animist or Hindu-Buddhist elements in many parts of Indonesia and in opposition to Christian missionary activities.[70] This organization came into being in the backdrop of Dutch colonial rule. Islam became a rallying point of resistance to foreign rule. The resistance was imbued with emotional, national and religious sentiment of the Muslims to stand against Dutch rule, which represented the ethos of expansion of Christianity. At the same time, the united resistance against the Dutch rule did not indulge in any violent movement. It was a peaceful and tolerant expression of the people's will to oppose the foreign rule. Since Indonesia is basically a Muslim dominated country any movement is bound to have a religious dimension. The organization had a women wing named 'Aisyiyah' founded in 1917 in order to involve women with reformist movement aimed at promoting religious education along with general education through a system of girls' schools and exploring opportunities to engage women in social and community services.[71] The striking point is that Muhammadiyah represented the tolerant face of the Indonesian Muslims because of which opponent Christian organizations considered it as rational and safe.[72] It argues in favour of *ijtihad*, which means rational interpretation of scriptures and traditions as against *taqlid* or uncritical acceptance of established opinion or views advanced by the orthodox schools of jurisprudence. Significantly enough it has not tried to gain a political mileage out of the preeminent presence of the Muslims in Indonesia and has been concentrating on the socio-economic betterment of the community as a whole.[73] Despite the fact that its social base is created by the *santri* Muslims, who are known to be conservative in religious practice, the Muhammadiyah presents a liberal and tolerant face of Islam.

Today Muhammadiyah has the reputation of being one of the most important organizations having more than 28 million members. It represents Islamic modernism that believes in inclusiveness and pluralism. It is believed that it learnt from the experience of Masyumi in the 1950s to be more tolerant, innovative and urban-based with strong support in the urban centers of Java and in the outer Islands of Indonesia. It has earned the reputation as moderate and politically quiescent. Unlike the NU, it stays away from the power centers and political planks of parties. Most of the devout Muslim (*santris*) are affiliated to Muhammadiyah as also to NU.[74] Some have dual affiliation, that makes the statistics of membership quite confusing and inflated.

The NU (Nahdlatul Ulama meaning the 'awakening of the ulema) was founded on January 31, 1926 in Surabaya by a group of eminent ulema (religious scholars) most of whom had pesantren (rural Islamic schools) background to strengthen traditional Islam and to unify Indonesian Muslims against the threats posed by the liberal and modernist Muhammadiyah and the heretical Ahmediyah.[75] With astronomical number of membership of about 35 million, the NU is one of the largest organizations under the leadership of the ulema. It was founded as a *jamiah diniah* (religious organization) and started growing steadily to earn the reputation of being thc largest Muslims organization in Indonesia. It drew the attention of the people from late 1930s when it spearheaded a massive campaign against the Dutch rule, which was focused as inimical to Islam. It maintained its non-political character till 1945, when it entered formal politics by becoming an organizational member of the Islamic party, Masyumi (Majelis Syuro Muslimin Indonesia, meaning Indonesian Muslim Consultative Council).

In 1952 it withdrew from the Masyumi, which was in total disarray. Thereafter, it emerged as an independent party and contested the 1955 elections and secured 18 per cent of popular votes. It was Soeharto who incorporated the NU into his corporatist arrangement to sustain his efforts to de-Islamize politics and to create a wider support base for his government.

A passing reference to Masyumi may be relevant. This organization was born in 1945 on the line of Ikhwanul Muslimin (Muslim Brotherhood) of Egypt. Masyumi's origin is a matter of controversy. While some argue that it was born out of an initiative of the Japanese to wipe out the last remnant of Dutch influence, others hold that it was a result of an articulated desire to have an Islamic organization to serve the interests of Muslims in Indonesia. With that broad objective it could attract the other Muslim organizations such as the NU and the Muhammadiyah to come to its fold.[76] In no time this apolitical organization transformed itself into a political party representing all Islamic political interest groups. It tried to dovetail the views and perceptions of both modernists and traditionalists. The NU was one of its constituent groups, which eventually deserted the Masyumi, as already stated, after feeling sidelined. It contested the general elections of 1955 in which it secured 20.9 per cent votes. It is notable that the combined votes of the NU, the Masyumi and all other smaller Islamic groups was 43.9 per cent, much below the majority of votes shared by secular and democratic parties, indicating that the Indonesian people as a whole were in favour of secular and democratic parties.[77] This trend continues till date; in fact, the secular and democratic forces performed better in the parliamentary and Presidential elections of 2004 and 2009. The theory of 'divided majority' of Greg Fealy holds good, despite the emergence of the PKB as a strong Muslim party. The very existence of as many as 48 Muslim parties prove squarely how divided the Muslim community is in the political scenario of Indonesia.

The NU has a political history since 1953, when it joined every cabinet from 1953 to 1971, played a role in dismantling the parliamentary democracy in favour of Soekarno's 'Guided Democracy', actively collaborated with the army in the bloody elimination of the Indonesian Communist Party, and later on, when it earned Soekarno's wrath under the agenda of de-Islmaization of politics, it amalgamated itself with three other Islamic parties to form United Development Party (PPP).[78] But owing to heavy state intervention to rein in the PPP, the NU decided to withdraw from the party in 1984. Although the NU parted with the PPP, which was essentially a sectarian Islamic party,[79] many of its members joined hands with Soeharto, some became members of the Golkar and others of the PDI. All this did not dramatically affect the support base of the NU. The most important point to be noted in this regard is that the organization remained committed to Pancasila, which enabled its national image as a tolerant and inclusive entity.

The NU has remained politically active all through ever since 1953. Its shift in political position is a matter of expediency and it has not altogether changed its moderate image. With growing thaw of relations between Seoharto and the NU in the early 1990s, when its charismatic leader Abdurranhman Wahid became an ardent advocate of democracy and a strong critic of Soeharto's authoritarian rule and then acted as the facilitator of a discussion group called 'Democracy Forum' in 1991, the NU presented itself as a dependable defender of democracy, pluralism, civil society and human rights. That is why it distanced itself from ICMI (Indonesian Council of Muslim Intellectuals or Ikatan Cendekiawan Muslim Indonesia), which had an Islamic agenda favouring enactment and enforcement of Sharia law, just as it also opposed Soeharto's autocratic rule.[80] It joined the nationwide movement against Soeharto and played a role in bringing about his fall in 1998. Abdurrahman Wahid became the President of Indonesia, after the first free election held in 1999. He became the President at a difficult time, when Islamic parties had been trying hard to push through a religious agenda of making Indonesia an Islamic country, when the forces supporting the ousted leader Soekarno were strong enough to destabilize the country and when his opposition to ICMI was too strong to find a reconciliation.[81] At any rate, the NU, despite its conservatism and Islamic content, has maintained its rational and tolerant face and like Muhammadiyah is known for its strong support for Pancasila. It is an ardent advocate of the middle path, neither Islamist to the extreme nor too westernized to demolish the traditional and cultural base of Indonesia.

The salient point in bringing these two mass-based organizations to discussion is that they have been playing a significant role in putting up Islam as a facilitator of developing a moderate and tolerant civil society in Indonesia, which is religious and at the same time accommodative and modern.[82] Both the organizations have remained steadfast in supporting Pancasila ideals of a secular state and in defending the cultural pluralism of Indonesia, which had been shaped by a long historical process. They have been backing a number of reformist intellectuals and NGOs, which have been rendering service to the people to recover from the adverse impact of the economic crisis of 1997. They have a network of large number of NGOs run by IAIN (Institut Agama Islam Negeri or State Islamic Institute) graduates, who have liberal understanding of Islam and also of traditional Indonesian society. They have set up national schools, orphanages, rest houses and hospitals through which they have been making efforts to create the foundation for the basic structure of Indonesian society.[83]

At the same time, both Muhammadiyah and NU are conservative organizations. They are committed to keep intact the Islamic credentials of Indonesia being the largest Muslim country in the world. The urge to preserve the religious faith and character of the Muslim society of Indonesia has been the core of their conservatism. At the same time, such conservativeness has not affected the otherwise harmonious interfaith relationship in the country, even during the series of communal and ethnic clashes of the worst kind during the period 1997-1999.[84] In such difficult times both the organizations worked hard to maintain cordial interfaith relationship. It is, therefore, widely believed that there may be group clashes and violence, though the incidences of such nature have come down dramatically over the years, but that the chance of Indonesia being Talibanized is remote and almost impossible.

Uneasy relationship between the state and Islam

As already stated that at the dawn of independence, a section of the Muslims in Indonesia wanted the newly liberated country to be an Islamic one. A country of more than 88 per cent Muslim population has to be an Islamic one. Rejecting this core argument on which the draft of the Jakarta Charter was drafted, Pancasila emerged as the foundation of the republic. That did not altogether eliminate the transitional demand for the enactment of Sharia laws nor did it bury the issue of relationship between the state and Islam. The formation of political parties on the basis of Islamic ideology and plan of action was a manifestation of the desire of a considerable section, if not the majority, of the Muslim population that Indonesia, being a Muslim majority country, had to present itself as an Islamic state. The enforcement of Sharia laws was considered a concrete step towards the realization of that goal. This aspiration became the sole enterprise of Islamic parties and organizations, and constituted the driving force of political Islam in Indonesia.[85] An almost diametrically opposite position has been taken by other democratic and secular parties, such as, the Golkar, the PPP and the PDI, that have accepted the ideology of Pancasila. This has led to a polarization of ideology, representing political Islam on one hand and nationalist and secular commitment on the other. The early attempt of the Islamic parties and organizations, such as, Masyumi and Partai Sarekat Islam

Indonesia to transform Indonesia into an Islamic state was overwhelmed by nationalist leaders like Soekarno. The latest attempt to amend the Constitution to institutionalize Sharia laws at the end of the 'New Order', too, did not succeed. Despite the setback in 2001, the issue of enforcement of Sharia laws through constitutional amendment remains alive as most of Muslim-based parties tend to secure a political mileage out of it. That is why it remains an important political issue.[86] The failure to achieve the objective was due partly to lack of support from the two main Islamic organizations, the NU and the Muhammadiyah and mainly because of the fact that not all Muslims cherish the idea of an Islamic state.

The diametrically opposite position taken by two broad sections of the society in Indonesia on the fundamental issue of religion has caused an uneasy relationship between the state and Islam.

The religious groups and the parties, right from the days of Masyumi to PKS, took a political position asserting that the state had a religious role to play, implying thereby, that there should be a close relationship between the state and Islam on the simple ground that Islam is the religion of the vast majority of Indonesia. The basic objective of such a position was to be in the corridor of power or to share power, if unable to not capture power. The secular and democratic parties had clear political standpoint to keep the state away from religion. The Soekarno regime had experimented with de-Islamization of politics. Conflict in such a situation is bound to take place in which the Islamist organizations are destined to lose, considering the stratified composition of the society in Indonesia where the *abangan* has a demographic advantage. The defeat and decline of the Islamist organizations could be seen in a series of developments that took place over the years. The Masyumi was banned in 1960 and there was no resistance to this government measure. Soekarno reduced the number of Islamic parties from four (such as NU, Muslimin Indonesia, Partai Sarekat Islam Indonesia, and Persatuan Tarbiah Islam) to just one single Partai Persatuan Pembangunan, sliced down the representation of Muslim parties in the parliament as also in the cabinet and denied the role of Islam as the basis of social and political organization.[87] The 'New Order' regime tried to limit the influence of religion to that extent in which it would be impossible for any Islamic party or groups to pose a formidable challenge to the Government headed by Soeharto. Nothing happened in the country in opposition to these moves. It would be wrong to argue that Soeharto, an *abangan* Muslim, was against Islam. What he wanted to ensure was that political Islam did not get an upper hand to pose a threat to his rule. He was aware of the strength of Islamic organizations like the NU and the Muhammadiyah. He used both organizations, especially the Ansor, the armed wing of the NU, to slaughter hundred thousand PKI members and supporters in 1965-67.[88] He was aware of the threat perception of both the organizations vis-à-vis the PKI and found it easy to enlist their cooperation in the genocide against the communists. Once his objective of eliminating the communist threat was achieved and he felt confident of his position, he projected himself as an ardent supporter or Pancasila, rejecting the Jakarta Charter outright. The Islamic organizations like the NU and the Muhammadiyah felt betrayed, as they had expected the revival of the Jakarta Charter in return of their cooperation in the anti-communist genocide. While the Muhammadiyah adopted a policy of non-cooperation with the government, and remained opposed to the 'New Order', and most of its leading members concentrated on academic activities together with revitalization of 'dakwah' movement[89] through the newly christened Dewan Dakwah Islamiyah Indonesia (Council of Indonesia for the Propagation of Islam, DDII) in order to keep themselves out of politics, the NU joined the government as a strategy to find a breathing space, in view of the drive of Soeharo to de-Islamize politics in Indonesia. In doing so,

Soeharto made all-out efforts to modernize the country with higher educational and economic growth. At the end of the day, when one attempts to assess him in a dispassionate manner, one finds Indonesia under Soeharto "healthier, more literate and more urbanized."[90]

Soeharto's long three decades of power witnessed a crafty shift in internal policy from neutrality in religious matters to identification of government with Islamic interests. It happened in the backdrop of the growing aspiration of the people for democracy and criticism of Soeharto's dictatorial rule and strong opposition posed by Abdurrahman Wahid of the NU and Amien Rais of the Muhammadiyah.[91] The impact of the Iranian revolution in 1979 was felt in Indonesia, despite the fact that it was a basically Shia clerics' resurgence and Indonesia is essentially a Sunni dominated country. Soeharto allowed the dakwah movement to penetrate deep into the educational institutions, university campuses and Islamic schools. While the secular and democratic forces opposed him, Soeharto turned to Islam in order to legitimize his authoritarian rule and downplay the issues of corruption and misgovernance. He increased his religiosity by using his Haji title after performing Hajj in 1991, speaking Arabic very often in public meetings and supporting the Palestinian cause and condemning the massacre of Bosnian Muslims by the Serbs. He often targeted the moderates and ridiculed the liberal and secular Muslims and established close relations with the conservative and anti-West organization called the Komite Indonesia untuk Solidaitas Dunia Islam (Indonesian Committee for Solidarity with Islamic World, KISDI) headed by Ahmad Sumargono which was established by Mohammad Natsir and other members of DDII.[92]

These strategies did not work as pro-democracy movement gathered momentum in 1998. The media, the NU, the Muhammadiyah, students and intellectuals geared up their assault on Soeharto. His attempt to use the KISDI and conservative elements to garner support for his 'New Order' did not succeed.[93] He could not withstand the huge surge of democracy and had to resign on May 21, 1998. In other words, the politics of using Islam to remain in power did not work in Indonesia, just as it had happened in the case of Bangladesh.

The rise of Islamic forces

Soon after the terrible strike of 9/11, Indonesia has been identified along with Algeria, Afghanistan, Sudan, and some other Muslim majority countries as hotbed of Islamic militants capable of committing wanton destruction of innocent lives in different parts of the world.[94] The putative Islamic threat, posed by the al-Qaeda and similar other outfits, all over the world and their organizational establishments in countries where Muslims have a substantial presence, have attracted the attention not only of the policy makers and politicians but also of the academics. The rise of Islamist terrorist activities in Southeast Asia in general and Indonesia, Thailand and the Philippines in particular, has been a major concern after a series of violent activities in the region including the Bali Bombing of 2002 in which more than 202 people were killed.[95] While scholars like Abuza have been sounding an alarm on the emergence of Islamists, John T. Sidel has argued that the alarmist contention is overdrawn, taking into consideration the steady decline, demobilization and disengagement of Islamist forces. The contention of Sidel leads one to suggest that huge divergence in Indonesian population provides no substantive space for the Islamists to grow.[96]

A brief narrative of the rise of the Islamic forces in this context would be relevant. The expansion of Western colonialism to engulf entire Southeast Asia coupled to subjection of the people of Islamic faith under powers preeminently identified as representative of the Christian world is the essence of the conflict between the two religions. At the turn of the last century, the antagonism between the Muslims of Indonesia and western colonialism surfaced.

The Japanese, who occupied Indonesia during World War II (1942-1945), used Islam to build up anti-West sentiment, established Kantor Urusan Agama (Office of Religious Affairs) to promote religious issues and interests and backed the Masyumi to play an overreaching role on all Muslim organizations. Despite the anti-West psyche bolstered by the Japanese, politics of violence of an extreme form was absent at that point of time presumably because of the influence of reformist and modernist organizations like the Muhammadiyah and the NU. Yet, the colonial policy of segregation to keep the small Chinese immigrants confined to urban ghettos, with no scope for integration and at the same time and the Dutch promotion of the Chinese business class created a social divide. The Chinese were about 2.7 per cent of the population at the time of Indonesian Independence, yet they exerted a disproportionate influence in the economy of the country. This imbalance generated a great deal of debate at that time as to how to deal with the Chinese problem.[97] In the past too, there had been bitter clashes between the Chinese and the Muslims, the most serious one taking in 1910 in Central Java.[98] The compartmentalized social composition, with marked and profoundly visible fabulously rich non-Muslim Chinese business class on one hand and the emerging *pribumi* (indigenous) Muslim middle class on the other, in post-colonial Indonesia, continued to generate tension between the two segments, one powerful demographically and the other economically.[99] The seeds of racial and communal tension had been sown while implementing the policy of segregation. The racial antagonism led to large-scale anti-Chinese riots on a number of occasions. The most devastating ones took place in 1995-98 in Kalimantan, Malaku and Sulwesi "which left more Muslims than ethnic-Chinese casualties in their wake."[100] The casualties provoked some Muslim leaders to form militia groups to defend the interests of the community in the wake of bloodsheds; also witnessed was the return of radical Muslim exiles including Abu Bakar Baasyir to Indonesia ostensibly to push through the enactment of Sharia laws by peaceful means, and thus to transform Indonesia into an Islamic state.[101] These leaders established effective network with international agencies and operators to augment resources for implementation of violent agenda.[102] These elements had a dreaded agenda of violence to take a toll of lives of innocents to prove their presence and to draw attention.

The period of 1945 to 1949 was a very crucial one in the history of Indonesia. During that time the secular and the Islamic forces and organizations worked together to fight to the finish the attempt of the Dutch government to re-colonize the country. Soon after the transfer of power from the Dutch authorities to the new leaders of Republic of Indonesia in December 1949, political Islam under the leadership of the Masyumi emerged as a formidable alternative to the secular and democratic forces led by Soekarno. It emerged as the largest party occupying 49 seats in the newly constituted parliament of 236 members. After the 1952 elections the Islamic groups and parties increased their strength in the parliament. The Masyumi, the NU, the PSII and Perti had captured 114 out 257 seats. Yet they could neither use legislative collectivism nor could create a unified political entity to pursue their agenda to promote and protect the interests of the Muslim majority. Such an articulated opinion led the Darul Islam and similar other organizations to challenge the national leadership by taking recourse to insurgencies in different parts of the country.[103]

The rebellion of the Darul Islam under the leadership of Sekarmadji Maridjan Kartosuwirjo could be regarded as the first and formidable challenge to the nationalist leadership of Indonesia. He proclaimed an Indonesian state in West Java on August 14, 1945 but eventually decided to abandon the idea of an Islamic state. He worked with Masyumi in the wake of the Dutch attempt to reoccupy the country soon after the Japanese surrender. Differences that grew between him and the mainstream leaders on the methodology of the struggle against Dutch reoccupation and on the issue of the relationship between the state and religion after the end of foreign occupation led him to declare jihad (holy war) against the Dutch and to proclaim the Negara Islam Indonesia (Indonesian Islamic State) in the Dutch controlled area of West Java.[104] This proclamation was renewed after the capture of Soekarno and Hatta by Dutch forces. The concept of Islamic state was advanced as an alternative to the already proclaimed Republic of Indonesia. The armed conflict continued even after transfer of power from the Dutch to the Republic of Indonesia in December 1949. This time the armed struggle took place between the forces loyal to Katosuwirjo and the Republic of Indonesia, which continued till 1962. The rebel Islamic leader was finally captured and eventually executed for high treason. The long grueling armed conflict resulting in the death of more than 25,000 civilians and rendering more than 120,000 homeless,[105] was the forerunner to armed Islamic movement in Indonesia.

The abortive coup staged by the PKI on October 1, 1965 paved the way for Soeharto to come to power. The immediate enemy of the state was found. The annihilation of the PKI was the principal agenda of the 'New Order'. As already stated, Soeharto enlisted the cooperation of the Muslim organizations in violent destruction of the PKI. An ardent supporter of secularism, Soeharto believed that a strong Muslim backing would be necessary in building the Indonesian state, that too when the communists and ultra-nationalists had been trying to capture power. He was successful in getting the support of the Muslim community in crushing ruthlessly the "anti-God" communists. The Muslim leadership in return expected that the 'New Order' of Soeharto would revive the Jakarta Charter and introduce constitutional arrangements for a special role for the Muslims in the governance. That did not happen. General Soeharto was totally opposed to any special space to the Muslim interests and remained steadfast in his adherence to the state ideology of Pancasila.[106] During his rule the separation of religion from the state was done clearly. His strong belief was that politics should not be influenced and dictated by religion (Islam). In 1985 he compelled all Islamic political organizations to renounce Islam as their ideological basis (Azas). At the same time, Soeharto allowed Islam to occupy a place in the cultural and personal life of the individuals. He promoted the Muslim interests in non-political matters such as performance of Hajj, establishment of Islamic courts to settle religious disputes, Islamic banking, building mosques, and religious propagation (dakwah).[107] He was not in favour of an idea that religion was a mere private and personal matter. It has a public space, but not in politics. At the same time and paradoxically enough, he skillfully exploited religious consciousness by making the citizens to carry their identity card in which the individual's religious identity was recorded. The 'New Order' proclaimed the recognition of five national religions – Buddhism, Catholicism, Hinduism, Islam and Protestantism. Further, it was obligatory on the part of students studying in government-funded schools and colleges to devote two hours in a week to understand the basic tenets of their religions.

In order to demonstrate his neutrality in matters of religion, Soeharto in course of time sidelined Masyumi totally. It was the first step to de-Islamize politics. He set in place strict control on Islamic political organizations. The challenge to the state by the Islamic forces was contained. It was also a part of his strategy to de-politicize the society and weaken the party system thoroughly. At the same time he promoted non-political religious organizations, which eventually compelled many political organizations to take shelter under Islam as an alternative.[108] In the overall strategy towards de-politicization, the university and college campuses were put under heavy restrictions in the name of 'campus normalization'. His measures successfully prevented resurgence of political Islam. Any Islamic rebellion, such as the one in Jakarta's port district of Tanjung Priok in 1984 and another in Lampung in 1989, were crushed with a heavy hand.[109] But the other variety of tension between the Islamists and the state and the communal tension between the Muslims and the Chinese Christians continued. It is difficult to identify a single group or association, which was responsible for racial and communal violence, as there were many structurally located operators capable of fomenting racial hatred and communal violence.[110] Soeharto fully exploited the situation pitting one religious community against another and it "Left a bitter legacy of state meddling in religious matters, and, by posing religious communities against each other, left relations among communities deeply troubled."[111]

After 25 years of his personalized rule, when he made relentless efforts to de-politicize Indonesian society, Soeharto embarked on a shift in state-Islam relations in the 1990s by co-opting middle class Muslim leaders and critics to various levels in his regime. It was a new strategy to expand his base within the framework of his new concept 'corporatism'.[112] It was formulated as a device to establish institutional linkages between the state, the Islamic community and other political interest groups. The Golkar dominated party system,[113] which included the Muslim dominated PPP and secular democratic PDI, became the cornerstone of the framework of 'corporatism' to which interests of other non-party bodies representing labour, farmers, women, bureaucrats, artists and literary bodies were channelized. This was a part of Soeharto's overall policy of accommodation. The most striking step that Soeharto took was the establishment of the Association of Indonesian Muslim Intellectuals (Ikatan Cendekiawan Muslim Indonesia, ICMI) in 1990, which raised a hope in the minds of the Muslim leaders that their voice would be now heard and that they would be able to secure an access to power. After two decades of his 'de-Islamization', his 'corporatism' paved the way for politicalization of Islam. Along with the ICMI, the Indonesian Council of Ulema (Mejelis Ulema Indonesia, MUI), the Indonesian Mosque Council (DMI) and the Indonesian Dakwah

Council got an opportunity to establish connections in the corridors of power. In other words, the corporatist framework of Soeharto became a spear point for his management of state-Islamic relations with the ultimate motive of keeping him in power.

However, all these arrangements did not keep him in power for a long time. In spite of conscious efforts during the later phase of his rule to focus his Islamic identity, his much publicized Hajj performance in 1991, his support for construction of mosques, Islamic education and banking, and his visible shift in foreign policy to move closer to the Arab world,[114] Soeharto could not prevent the massive people's movement for democracy from toppling him from power.

Close on the heels of racial and communal violence in Indonesia, the developments in the rest of the Islamic world and elsewhere such as,the US-led invasion of Iraq in 1992 and the West's support for Israel at the cost of the Palestinian cause for existence, an atmosphere of radicalization of Islamic forces was built up. A hardcore militant Islamist organization, Jemaah Islamiyah (JI), having links with the al-Qaeda, was born on January 1, 1993.[115] It geared up its activities leading to a series of bombings, the most deadly one being the Bali bombing on October 12, 2002 in which 202 people were killed, including 88 Australian tourists. This feared organization has its origins in the formation of Darul Islam movement of the 1950s. It was loosely affiliated to various domestic puritan Islamic organizations, such as, Dewan Dakwah Islamiyah Indonesia (DDII), Al-Irsyad and Persatuan Islam and some international establishments, such as, Salafi and Wahhabi movements. All these are known for their anti-Christian, anti-Semitic, anti-democratic and anti-secular agenda, activities and propaganda. Despite the government's crackdown on the JI leading to arrest of 340 leaders, the horizontal base remained more or less intact and retained its urban hold capable of unleashing terror in any part of the country.

Indonesia has experienced three more terrorist attacks in the post Bali bombing period – the bombing of J.W. Marriott hotel in Jakarta (August 2003), the bombing of Australian Embassy in Jakarta (September 2004) and the suicide bombings in three Balinese restaurants (October 2005). In all these attacks the JI's hand has been established. After a long lull, there was again another bomb attack on two elite hotels, Ritz-Carlton and JW Marriott, in the heart of Jakarta on July 17, 2009, killing seven and injuring 50 others. No one has claimed responsibility for this attack. It is yet to be proved whether JI was involved in the attacks.

This leads one to wonder how JI in a short span of time since its establishment in 1993 under the leadership of Abdullah Sungkar and Abu Bakar Baasyir, both are of Yemeni descent, made Indonesia an epicenter of terrorism in Southeast Asia.[116] These two clerics considered themselves successors of Sekarmadji Maridjan Kartosuwirjo, the founder of Darul Islam. They were initially associated with Darul Islam but left the organization to join Jamaah Mujahidin Anshorullah, the forerunner of JI. Abu Bakar Baasyir is the key figure in the leadership of JI. He had a close association with a clandestine organization called Indonesian Islamic State (Negara Islam Indonesia, NII) better known as Kamando Jihad, a hardcore outfit fighting for an Islamic state. In 1978 he was arrested along with Abdullah Sungkar under the Anti-Subversion Law. After their release in 1984, they escaped to Malaysia and started activities among the Indonesian community. From there, they established contact with Osama bin Laden and al-Qaeda, and secured their financial support in establishing madrassas in Indonesia, some of which eventually became hotbed of militancy. They inspired a number of Indonesian youths to join Afghan Mujahideen to fight against the Soviet forces. The most notable among the Indonesian fighters in Afghanistan was Riduan Isamuddin, better known as Hambali, who masterminded troubles in Maluku and Central Sulawesi and several other places. He established close contact with

Sungkar and Abu Bakar Baasyir and eventually became a dependable al-Qaeda operator by becoming a member of its Regional Advisory Council (Shura). The JI had easy means of securing funds from Saudi charitable organizations such as al-Haramain, the International Islamic Relief Organization and the Medical Emergency Relief Charity (MERC), whose financial assistance towards social and educational promotion had been diverted to carry out militant and terrorist activities.[117] In this way, in a short period of time JI became a formidable terrorist organization capable of launching deadly attack, including the most ghastly Bali bombing of October 12, 2002.[118] The Bali attack had a devastating impact on the economy of the country. As a great spot of holidaying, Bali used to earn $1.4 billion a year from tourism.[119] Being alarmed at the consequential perilous impact, the Indonesian Government launched a crackdown on JI and arrested over 30 suspects, most of whom had strong links with JI and Abu Bakar Baasyir and Abdullah Sunkar. Baasyir was arrested on October 18. He denied the charge of the Bali Bombing.[120] The most prominent suspects were Ali Ghufron 'Mukhlas', a senior JI leader and his younger brother Amrozi. An auto mechanic having close links with Baasyir, Amrozi made a confessional statement on the act. Amrozi, Imam Samudra and Ali Gufron 'Mukhlas' were convicted and were awarded death sentence. All of them accepted the verdicts with defiance and with no sense of remorse. Another accused named Ali Imron was sentenced to life imprisonment. A number of persons belonging to the victims' families appealed to the Government of Indonesia to commute the death sentences on the two grounds. They did not support the extreme punishment and secondly they did not think that terrorism of any form could be contained and eliminated by award of death sentences to convicts. Despite protests in and outside the country, Amrozi, Samudra and Mukhlas were executed on November 8, 2008.[121] The Government's heavy hand in dealing with the JI operators and members and its systematic plugging of the terrorist funding sources led to a steady decline of the organization. Nonetheless, it is too early to say whether these steps would put the last nail on the coffin of terrorism in Southeast Asia, when similar organizations are reporedly active in Thailand, Myanmar and the Philippines.

The place of Islam in the age of reformasi

The fall of Soeharto in 1998 marked the beginning of a new era, which many would like to brand as an era of reformasi. The historic event opened flood gates of new ideas, new concept and new demands. 'Democracy and decentralization first, good governance later' became the favourite slogan. The new president B.J. Habibie lifted bans on political parties.[122] As many as 48 new 'Islamic' political parties were declared eligible to participate in the historic elections of 1999. It was an indication that there was resurgence of Islamic forces. However, the strong popular support for the secular parties, such as, Megawati's PDI-P and Soekarno's Golkar party indicated in unmistakable terms that the end of Soeharto's regime had not altogether changed the secular character of Indonesian society. There were about 141 formally registered parties. Significant rearrangements took place before the elections of 1999. From the NU, four different parties emerged. These are the PKB, the PKU, the PNU and the SUNI. However, the NU extended its all-out support to the PKB. The support of the NU leader, Abdurrahman Wahid, was itself a matter of moral booster to the PKB. That is why it became the most formidable Islamic party in view of the existence of strong support base of the NU in many of the large provinces, such as East Java, Central Java, South Kalimantan and South Sulawesi. The other Muslim organization, Muhammadiyah, extended support to the PAN, which was formed by Muhammadiyah's former charismatic leader Amien Rais. Many prominent members of the Muhammadiyah became top functionaries of the PAN. The third important party contesting the 1999 elections was PBB, which proclaimed itself to be the successor the Masyumi.

It received the support of the DDII. In this way these three parties – the PKB, the PAN and PBB appeared to be leading Islamic parties which were well ahead of others in the race of popularity.

It is noteworthy that both the PKB and the PAN did not use Islam as *azas* (ideological basis), despite the fact that the two largest Islamic parties had mass bases drawn from the NU and the Muhammadiyah respectively. They were considered to be "informal" Islamic parties because of their loose Islamic agenda. They recognized religion, Islam in particular, as a motive and guiding force in practical politics. They were prepared to work with both the "formal" Islamic parties and also the secular parties like Golkar and PDI-P. In such a confusing scenario, when a large number of Islamic parties suddenly surfaced and the two leading parties took a position that Islam is not the official *azas*, the formal Islamic parties, as stated in an earlier context, could not attract the attention of the voters in the 1999 elections. The result was that only two parties, the PKB and the PAN, secured more than the 'electoral threshold' of 2 per cent votes.

The results of the 1999 elections proved in unmistakable terms that political Islam has no roots in Indonesia. The appearance of numerous Islamic parties created a public debate – whether these parties are genuinely Islamic or their emergence is just an expression of euphoria of reformasi era.[123] The very fact that 48 'Islamic' parties made a sudden appearance is an indication that only a few might be serious about promoting Islamic agenda and thus prove to be genuinely Islamic while others will go down in history unnoticed.

The same trend continued in the 2004 and 2009 elections. The failure of the Islamic parties to win public support in a Muslim majority country, which has already paved the way for resurgence of democracy, could be treated as a failure of political Islam. This has reopened, as in 1999, the debate that had taken place in the early 1990s that Muslim interests were better served in the absence of Islamic political parties.[124] It is argued that Islam has a role in every walk of life. At the same time, the religion has occupied the back seat in power politics. Today's most important issues are related to economic growth and recovery from the slump of 1996-97, agricultural development, decentralization of power and good governance. These issues dominated the elections of 2009. Even the Islamic parties and their coalition partners have little to hover around religious issues.[125] When Abdurrahman Wahid, the leader of the PKB, became the fourth President of Indonesia after the 1999 poll, the scenario pertaining to political Islam did not change. A democrat and an ardent supporter of secularism and pluralism, Wahid had to face criticism of the Islamic groups for not carrying forward the issue of Sharia laws. Wahid was aware of the mood of the people who would go by the slogan of Nurcholish Madjid "Islam yes, *partai* Islam no". His agenda was not Islam and Sharia law; his agenda was different – to take Indonesia beyond the relics of 'New Order' to make it a truly democratic country where people's participation at grassroots level through proper decentralization could be a reality. Challenges to him were enormous. [126] Yet he was successful in putting development and democratization agenda far ahead of the Islamic one, and thus, he could set a trend in the political system of Indonesia.

In search of a middle path

The end of a long era of three decades of authoritarian rule in 1998 was followed by rise of around 48 Muslim political parties, ethnic and communal violence, slowdown of the economy of the country. All this raised a highly debated question – whether Indonesia was heading for political stability or chaos.[127] Indonesia in post-Soeharto era has experienced many upheavals, - the emergence of countless political parties, with many of these dubbing as Islamic, terrorist attempts to destabilize the socio-economic structure, ethnic and communal riots of a grave nature, the conservative ascendancy to occupy a formidable political space, and above all the smooth and bloodless transition of power, together with three free and fair democratic elections in 1999, 2004 and 2009. The issue of democracy and decentralization of power has captured the attention of one and all. In such an atmosphere of political renewal, the foundation of Indonesia on Pancasila has been reinforced with a renewed faith. A stray demand for Sharia law or a few devastating bombing incidents cannot demolish Indonesia's long tradition of tolerance and adjustment.

That is why, despite militants' strikes in the heart of Indonesia and anti-Chinese riots that rocked the country on a number of occasions, Indonesia can never be turned into a country of militant Islam.[128] It cannot and should not be expected to become fully westernized in terms of culture and dress, considering the fact it has a glorious past with a pluralistic setting. How is Indonesia projecting itself? As the most populous Muslim country in the world, no one can deny a space for Islam there. Islam as a political force declined long back during the days of 'New Order', but cultural Islam is active and visible. The adoption of Pancasila as the ideology of the Indonesian state is a *fait accompli* in its politics. Religion has a place in the country, but the religion of the majority has not determined the character of the state. The historic moment of the proclamation of the Indonesia as a Pancasila state on August 18 1945 created the new nation-state and its ideology that there is no majority and nor any minority. All attempts to revert and to implement the Jakarta Charter giving Islam a place of preeminence failed. The JI's terror tactics to advance its agenda for an Islamic identity of Indonesia also failed. The social composition of Indonesia does not leave any scope for the emergence of a hardcore extremist and militant Islamic group capable of capturing the political power. In open confrontation between the radicals and the moderate factions of the Muslims soon after the fall of the 'New Order', the moderates secured massive support as testified to by the three election results in the post-Soeharto era. In view of this, as already indicated, some of the Muslim parties like PKS have changed their Islamic agenda to suit the new liberal atmosphere supported by mass-based Muslim organizations. That suggests the possibility of marginalization of radicals and advancement of liberal Islam marking the end of religious extremism, which, however, was unable to engulf the entire Indonesian society.[129] All this lead one to argue safely that Indonesia cannot be Talibanized nor will there be an Iranian type of revolution to dismantle the existing order to put in place a thoroughly Islamic system based on Sharia law. There lies the future of a liberal Muslim country, a classic example for others to follow.

What is the best option for Indonesia as a Muslim majority country? H. Tarmizi Taher would argue – "a middle path". A former Minister for Religious Affairs, Taher would suggest that Indonesia cannot afford a self destructive and extreme Islamic militant path.[130] History has proved it when armed struggle led by Kartosuwirjo to establish Darul Islam was tried. Indonesia cannot go to the other extreme, rejecting and abandoning its long tradition and harmonious inter-faith relationships. The occasional aberrations in the form of ethnic and communal conflicts and JI's bombing campaigns cannot altogether change the tolerant face of Indonesia. Indonesia in 1998 had been engrossed with a broad national agenda under the slogan "Democracy first; good governance later".[131] In a democracy all have equal space and opportunity and none special privileges to enjoy. Today it wants good governance too.

NOTES & REFERENCES

1. T. Whitten *et al., The Ecology of Java and Bali* (Hong Kong: Periplus Edition, 1996), pp. 309-312.
2 It is believed that nutmeg spice, one of the most valuable commodities, found in abundance in the archipelago, brought Europeans and eventually led to the establishment their colonial rule here.

3 For some details of the history of Indonesia see M.C. Ricklefs, *A History of Modern Indonesia since c.1200 to the Present* (London: Macmillan, 1981) and Jean Gelman Taylor, *Indonesia: Peoples and Histories* (New Haven: Yale University Press, 2003).

4. For some details see Jusuf M. Van der Kroef, "The Term Indonesia; Its Origin and Usage", *Journal of American Oriental Society*, Vol. 70, No. 3, 1951, pp. 166-171.

5. Anthony H. Johns, "Indonesia: Islam and Cultural Pluralism" in John L. Esposito (ed), *Islam in Asia: Religion, Politics, and Society* (New York: Oxford University Press, 1987), pp.202-229.

6. For some discussion on the concept of geographical space for an imagined community see Benedict Anderson, *Imagined Communities: Reflections on the Origins and Spread of Nationalism* (London, New York: Verso, 1991).

7. *Statistical Indonesia*, (Statistical Year Book of Indonesia), 2007, p. 3.

8. For details see *ibid*, Table 1.1, p. 5.

9. See *ibid*, p. xlv. The CIA estimates put it to be 234,693,997 in 2007.

10. Brian May, *The Indonesian Tragedy* (London: Routledge, 1978), p. 20.

11. On the role of Indian Hindu influence in Indonesia which came though trade, see O. W. Wolters, *Early Indonesian Commerce* (Ithaca: Cornell University Press, 1967).

12. Frederik David Kan Bosch, *Selected Studies in Indonesian Archaeology* (The Hague: Marinus Nighoff, 1951).

13. For a detailed study on the fall of Buddhist empire once known to be greatest in the region see Oliver William Walters, *The Fall of Srivijaya in Malay History* (Ithaca: Cornell University Press, 1970).

14. For some details on trade connection in expansion of Islam see D.S. Richards (ed) *Islam and the Trade of Asia* (Oxford: Bruno Cassierer and Philadelphia: University of Pennsylvania Press, 1970).

15. For some details about the early presence of Muslims as testified to by tomb stones, see Alijah Gordon (ed), *The Propagation of Islam in the Indonesian-Malay Archipelago* (Kuala Lumpur:

Malaysian Sociological Research Institute, 2001), pp. 26-27. The tomb stone inscriptions found intact in Terrenganu and Melaka clearly tells about early spread of Islam, see pp. 34-43. For inscriptions on gravestones including one of Malik Ibrahim from Gujarat dated 1419 in Indonesia see M.C. Ricklefs, *A History of Indonesia since c.1200*, n. 3, Chapter 6.

16. K.G. Trengonning, *A History of Modern Malaya* (Singapore: Eastern University Press, 1964).

17. M.C. Ricklefs, "Islamization in Java: Fourteenth to Eighteenth Centuries" in Ahmad Ibrahim *et al., Readings on Islam in Southeast Asia* (Singapore: ISEAS, 1985), p. 37.

18. Kenneth P. Landon, *Southeast Asia: Crossroads of Culture* (Chicago: University of Chicago Press, 1948), pp. 138-139. Also see Ricklefs *A History of Modern Indonesia*, p. 12.

19. For some of such observations see Benedict R. Anderson, *Methodology and Tolerance of the Javanese* (Ithaca: Cornell University Press, 1965). Also see Oliver William Wolters, *Culture and Region in Southeast Asian Perspectives* (Singapore: Institute of Southeast Asian Studies, 1982).

20. K.G. Trengonning, *A History of Modern Malay*, n. 16.

21. For a detailed account of conversion to Islam in different parts of the world see Nehemia Levtzion (ed), *Conversion to Islam* (New York: Holmes and Meier Publishers, 1979), pp. 3-4. Also see Bruce Grant, *Indonesia* (Parkville: Melbourne University Press, 1964).

22. T.W. Arnold, *The Preaching of Islam* (London: Constable and Company, 1913), pp. 364-365.

23. M.C. Ricklefs, *A History of Modern Indonesia*, n.3, p. 3.

24. C.C. Berg, "The Islamization of Java", *Studia Islamika*, Vol. IV, No. 2, 1950, pp. 111-142.

25. Bernhard H.M. Vlekke, *Nusantara: A History of Indonesia* (Bandung: W. Van Hoeve, 1959), pp. 97-98.

26. Deliar Noer, *The Modernist Muslim Movement in Indonesia: 1900-1942* (London: Oxford University Press 1973).

27. Sarekat Islam had its origins as a mouthpiece of the Muslim merchants who sought to organize a boycott against the Chinese goods and firms in 1908. Two years later, when it surfaced in

an institutional form it fostered a spirit of Indonesian nationalism and then voiced for total independence, see Fred R. Von der Mehden, *Religion and Nationalism in Southeast Asia* (Madison: University of Wisconsin, 1963), pp. 74-80.

28. For some details of Afghani, Abduh and Rida see H.A.R. Gibbs, *Modern Trends in Islam* (Chicago: University of Chicago Press, 1949); Malcolm H. Kerr, *Islamic Reform: The Political and Legal Theories of Muhammad 'Abduh and Rashid Rida* (Berkeley: University of California, 1966) and Wilfed C. Smith, *Islam in Modern History* (Princeton: Princeton University Press, 1957), pp. 54-63.

29. For some understanding of Muhammadiyah see Allfian, *Muhammadiyah: The Political Behavior of a Muslim Modernist Organization under Dutch Colonilalism* (Yogyakarta: Gadjah Mada University Press, 1989).

30. Robert W. Hefner, "Religion: Evolving Pluralism" in Donald K. Emmerson (ed), *Indonesia: Beyond Suharto: Polity, Economy, Society, Transition* (New York: M.E. Shape, 1999), p. 208.

31. Richard V. Weekes, *Muslim People: A World of Ethnographic Survey* (London: Greenwood Press, 1978), pp. 184-191.

32. Robert W. Hefner, "Religion: Evolving Pluralism", p. 210.

33. Clifford Geertz, *The Religion of Java* (Chicago: University of Chicago Press, 1976). Geertz's classification, however, did not go unchallenged. Those who do not agree with him argue that the classification is misleading and far from reality. The basic elements on which his classification rests could be found in both abangan and santri. See Deliar Noer, *The Modernist Muslim Movement in Indonesia 1900-1942* (London: Oxford University Press, 1973); Marshall G.S. Hodgson, *The Venture of Islam* (Chicago: University of Chicago Press, 1974) and Mitsuo Nakamura, *The Crescent Arises over the Banyan Tree: A Study of the Muhammadiyah Movement in a Javanese Town* (Yogyakarta: Gadjah Mada University Press, 1983).

34. Harry J.Benda, *Crescent and the Rising Sun* (The Hague: Van Hoeve, 1958), p. 82 and D.G. Stibbe and H. Colijn, *Netherlands Indies* (Amsterdam: N.V. Elsevier, 1935), pp. 210-233.

35. Harold Crouch, "Indonesia" in Mohammed Ayoob (ed), *The Politics of Islamic Reassertion* (London: Croom Helm, 1981), Chapter Ten.

36. Bernhard H.M. Vlekke, *Nusantara: A History of Indonesia*, n. 25, pp. 97-98.

37. For some understanding of the role of religion in the nationalist movement in Indonesia see R.E. Elson, "Islam, Islamization, the Nation and the Early Indonesian Nationalist Movement", *Journal of Indonesian Islam*, Vol. 1, No. 2, December 2007, pp. 231-266.

38 Howard M. Federspiel, *Islam and Ideology in the Emerging Indonesian State* (Leiden: Brill, 2001), pp. 30-31.

39. E.S. De Klerck, *History of the Netherlands East Indies* (Rotterdam: W.L. & C. Bruss, 1938) pp. 545-548 and J.S. Furnivall, *Netherlands-Indie: A Study of Plural Economy* (Cambridge: Cambridge University Press, 1944), pp. 249-250.

40. For a detailed study on PKI see Rex Mortimer, *Indonesian Communism under Sukarno: Ideology and Policies*, 1959-1965 (Ithaca: Cornell University Press, 1974) and Ruth T. McVey, *The Rise of Indonesian Communism* (Ithaca: Cornell University Press, 1968).

41. Quoted in B.J. Boland, *The Struggle of Islam in Modern Indonesia* (Hague: Martinus Nijhoff, 1982), p. 243.

42. In Bahasa Indonesia these 'seven words' are "dengan kewajiban menjalankan Syari'at Islam bagipemeluk-pemeluknya." For details on Muslim organizations pleading for Islamic character of Indonesian Constitution see Saifuddin Anshari, *The Jakarta Charter 1945: Struggle for an Islamic Constitution in Indonesia* (Kuala Lumpur: Muslim Youth Movement of Malaysia. 1979).

43. Arskal Salim and Azyumardi Azra (eds), *Shari'a and Politics in Modern Indonesia* (Singapore, ISEAS, 2003) p. 191.

44. Quoted in Anthony H. Johns, "Indonesia: Islam and Cultural Pluralism" in John L. Esposito (ed), *Islam in Asia: Religion, Politics, and Society*, p. 210.

45. For some details see Karel Steenbrink, *Dutch Colonialism and Indonesian Islam: Contrasts and Conflicts 1596-1950* (Amsterdam: Rodopi, 2006), Chapter 8.

46. *ibid*, p. 141.

47. Amien Rais, was a university teacher, a former leader of Muhammadiyah, known to be a secular person who speaks for

united Indonesia that encompasses all religious and ethnic groups.

48. See Mohamad Atho Mudzhar, *Islam and Islamic Law in Indonesia: A Socio-historical Approach* (Jakarta: Office of Religious Research and Development, and Training, Ministry of Religious Affairs, 2003).

49. *Indonesia Official Handbook 2004*, and for details see Mitsuo Nakamura, *Islam and Democracy in Indonesia: Observations on the 2004 General and Presidential Elections, Occasional Publications 6* (Harvard: Islamic Legal Studies Program, 2005).

50. For some details of such prediction that Megawati Soekarnoputri and Abdurrahman Wahid would form a working coalition at the end of the elections since no party was going to secure absolute majority seats in the national parliament, see John MeBeth, "Political Update" in Geoff Forrester (ed), *Post-Soeharto Indonesia: Renewal or Chaos* (Singapore: ISEAS, 1999), pp. 21-32.

51. For some detailed understanding of election politics in Indonesia see Leo Suryadinata, *Elections and Politics in Indonesia* (Singapore: ISEAS, 2002).

52. An interactive session with leading scholars at LIPI on March 24, 2008 led to an assumption that many of the Muslim based organizations and institutions consider the PKS as rising star in Indonesian politics for its strong opposition to corruption, its steadfast advocacy for transparency and cleanness in politics. The party draws inspiration from Muslim Brotherhood of Egypt.

53. Bernhard Platzdasch, "Indonesia's Political Arena: Outlook bleak for Islamic parties", *The Straits Times*, April 11, 2008.

54. *ibid*, April 17, 2008.

55. Lilian Budianto, "PKS party rejects idea of Islamic state', *The Jakarta Post*, April 21, 2008.

56. For some discussion on Sharia law see Nadirsyah Hosen, *Shari'a and Constitutional Reform in Indonesia* (Singapore: ISEAS, 2007)

57. For an interesting discussion see M.B. Hooker, "Introduction: Islamic Law in South-East Asia" *Studia Islamika*, Vol. 10, No. 1, Special Issue, 2003, pp. 1-22.

58. M.B. Hooker and Tim Lindsey, "Public Faces of Shariah in Contemporary Indonesia: Towards a National Madhhab", *ibid*, pp. 23-64.

59. Michael R. Fenner, "Indonesian Movement for the Creation of National Madhab', *Islamic Law and Society*, Vol. 9, No. 1, 2001 pp.84-113.
60. For the details see Ali Bulac, "The Medina Document" in Charles Kurzman, *Liberal Islam: A Sourcebook* (New York: Oxford University Press, 1998), pp. 169-178.
61. For a bitter and long rivalry and conflict among various Islamic groups and organizations see M.C. Ricklefs, *A History of Modern Indonesia since c1300*, n. 3, pp. 354-382.
62. Michael van Langenburg, "The New Order state: Language, Ideology, Hegemony" in Arief Budiman (ed), *State and Civil Society in Indonesia* (Melbourne: Centre for Southeast Asian Studies, 1990), p. 133.
63. Daniel S. Lev, *Islamic Courts in Indonesia* (Berkeley: University of California, 1972).
64. For some details Muhammad Hisyam, "The Interaction of Religion and State in Indonesia: The Case of the Islamic Courts" in Johan Meuleman (ed), *Islam in the Era of Globalization: Muslim Attitude towards Modernity and Identity* (Jakarta: INIS, 2001), pp. 299-314.
65. *ibid,* pp. 309-310.
66. See Greg Fealy and Virginia Hooker (eds), *Voices of Islam in Southeast Asia; A Contemporary Sourcebook* (Singapore: ISEAS, 2007), pp 184-196.
67. Mohamad Atho Mudzhar, *Islam and Islamic Law in Indonesia: A Socio-Historical Approach* (Jakarta: Ministry of Religious Affairs, 2003).
68. Clifford Geertz, *The Religion of Java*, n. 33, pp. 56-89
69. Abdul Mukti Ali, "The Muhammadiyah Movement: A Bibliographical Introduction" (M.A. dissertation, McGraw-Hill, University, 1958).
70. There are countless publications in Bhasa Indonesia on Muhammadiyah. Some of the works in English language which devote partially and fully are Alfian, *Muhammadiyah: The Political Behavior of a Muslim Modernist Organization under Dutch Colonialism* (Yogyakarta: Gadjah Mada University Press, 1989), Ira Marvin Lapidus, *A History of Islamic Societies* (London:

Cambridge, 2002), Alwi Shihab, "The Muhammadiyah movement and Its Controversy with Christian Mission in Indonesia", unpublished Ph. D. dissertation, August 1995, James L. Peacock, Muslim Puritans, *Reformist Psychology in Southeast Asian Islam* (Berkeley: University of California Press, 1978) also his *Purifying Faith: The. Muhammadiyah Movement in Indonesian Islam* (California: The Benjamin/Cummings Publishing Company, 1978), Noer Deliar, *The Modernist Movement in Indonesia* (London: Oxford University Press, 1973) and Mitsuo Nakamura, *The Crescent Arises over the Banyan Tree: A Study of the Muhammadiyah Movement in a Center Javanese Town* (Ithaca: Cornell University Press, 1976).

71. Sally Jane White, "Reformist Islam, Gender and Marriage in the Late Colonial Dutch East Indies, 1900-1942", unpublished Ph. D thesis (Canberra: Research School of Pacific and Asian Studies, Australian National University, 2004).

72. Alwi Shihah, *ibid,* p. 204.

73. M. Sirajuddin Syamsuddin, "Religion and Politics in Islam: The Case of Muhammadiya in Indonesia's New Order", unpublished Ph. D. dissertation, University of California, Los Angeles, 1991.

74. Greg Barton, "The Prospects for Islam" in Grayson Lloyd and Shannon Smith, *Indonesia Today: Challenges of History* (Singapore: ISEAS, 2001), pp. 244-255.

75. There are large numbers of literature on NU in Bhasa Indonesia. Among a few works in English language the most notable is Greg Fealy and Greg Barton (eds), *Nahdlatul, Traditional Islam and Modernity in Indonesia* (Clayton: Monash Asia Institute, 1996), Greg Barton, "Islam and Politics in the New Indonesia" in Jason F. Isaacson and Colin Rubenstein (eds), *Islam in Asia: Changing Political Realities* (New Brunswick: Transaction Publishers, 2002), pp.1-89, Abdurrahman Wahid, "The Nahdlatul Ulama and Islam in Present Day Indonesia" in Taufik Abdullah and Sharon Siddique (eds), *Islam and Society in Southeast Asia* (Singapore: ISEAS, 1986).

76. For some discussion see Harold Crouch, "Indonesia" in Mohammed Ayoob (ed), *The Politics of Islamic Reassertion* (London: Croom Helm, 1981), pp. 190-207 and George McTurnan Kahin, *Nationalism and Revolution in Indonesia* (Ithaca: Cornell University Press, 1952), p. 156.

77. For some details see B.J. Boland, *The Struggle for Islam in Modern Indonesia* (The Hague: Martinus Nijhoff, 1971) and Greg Fealy, "Divided Majority: The Limits of Indonesian Islam" in Shahram Akbarzadeh and Abdullah Saeed (eds), *Islam and Political Legitimacy* (London: Routledge Curzon, 2003), pp. 150-168.

78. See Introduction Chapter of Greg Fealy and Greg Barton (ed), *Nahdlatul illama Traditional Islam and Modernity in Indonesia,* n. 75, pp. xix-xxvi.

79. For a detailed discussion on the reasons for which NU withdrew from the PPP, see Robert Hefner, *Civil Islam: Muslims and Democratization in Indonesia* (Princeton: Princeton University Press, 2000), pp. 168-169, Douglas E. Ramage, *Politics in Indonesia: Democracy, Islam and the Ideology of Tolerance* (London: Routledge, 1995), pp.47-48, and Greg Barton and Greg Fealy (eds), *Nahdlatul Ulema: Traditional Islam and Modernity in Indonesia,* n. 75, pp. 182-184.

80. For the details of the developments see Darul Aqsha et al. (eds), *Islam in Indonesia: A Survey of Events and Developments from 1988 to March 1993,* (Jakarta: INIS, 1995).

81. For details see Greg Barton, *Abdurrahman Wahid: Muslim Democrat, Indonesian President* (Honolulu, Hawaii: University of Hawaii Press, 2002) and also his *Gus Dur: The Authorized Biography of Abdurrahman Wahid* (Jakarta: Equinox Publishing, 2002).

82. For some discussion on the line, see Greg Barton, "Islam and Politics in the New Indonesia", n. 75, pp 20-23.

83. Based my derivation after having serious discussions with academics at the LIPI and the CSIS, Jakarta during March 2008. I interviewed a number of common citizens, religious leaders and Imams with the help of an interpreter to ascertain their views and impressions about the Muhammadiyah and the NU. All without exception are full praise of these two organizations, which have kept Indonesian society balanced between modernity and tradition.

84. The reasons for communal and ethnic clashes had been different and localized, in which outside forces ignited the violence and participated in killings. For some details see Jason F. Isaacson and Colin Rubenstein (eds), *Islam in Asia: Changing Realities*

(New Brunswick: Transaction Publishers, 2002), pp. 23-27 and Ashutosh Varshney *et.al*, *Pattern of Collective Violence in Indonesia (1990-2003)* (Jakarta: United Nations Support for Indonesian Recovery, July 2004), Working Paper: 04-03.

85. Bahtiar Effendy, *Islam and the State in Indonesia* (Singapore: ISEAS, 2003), p.124.

86. Arskal Salim and Azymardi Azra (eds), *Shari'a and Politics in Modern Indonesia* (Singapore: ISEAS, 2003).

87. *ibid*, p. 150.

88. Benedict Anderson and Theodore Friend, *Indonesian Destinies* (London, Cambridge: The Belknap Press of Harvard University, 2003) pp. 109-116. For a detailed account on the ruthless massacre of communists and their sympathizers see Robert Cribb, *The Indonesian Killings, 1965-1966: Studies for Java and Bali*, Monash Papers on Southeast Asia, No. 21 (Clayton, Australia: Centre for Southeast Asian Studies, Monash Univeristy, 1990) and Robert W. Hefner, *Civil Islam: Muslims and Democratization in Indonesia* (Princeton: Princeton University Press, 2000).

89. Dakwah (call or appeal) was an Islamic movement that spread in the length and breadth of entire Indonesian-Malaysian archipelago for a considerable period of time since early the 1970s to 'purify' Muslim masses. Later on it was increasingly politicized to register the demand for enactment and enforcement of Sharia Laws.

90. Norman G. Owen (ed), *The Emergence of Modern Southeast Asia* (Singapore: Singapore University Press, 2005), p. 431.

91. For a detailed discussion on how Soeharto moved towards Islamic conservatism in the later part of his rule see Robert W. Hefner, *Civil Islam: Muslims and Democratization in Indonesia,* n. 79. Chapters 5-7

92. Zachary Abuza, *Political Islam and Violence in Indonesia* (London: Routledge, 2007), pp. 18-19.

93. For a discussion on Soeharto's overtures to the conservative Muslims see Robert W. Hefner, "Islam, State and Civil Society: ICMI and the Struggle for the Indonesian Middle Class," Indonesia No.56 (1993), pp. 1-35 and R. William Liddle, "The Islamic turn in Indonesia: A Political Explanation", *The Journal of Asian Studies*, Vol. 55, No.3, August 1996, pp. 613-634.

94. John Gershman, "Is Southeast Asia the Second Front?" *Foreign Affairs*, Vo. 81, No. 4, 2002, pp. 20-74.

95. One of the most prominent scholars, who has been writing extensively on the rise of Muslim militancy in Southeast Asia, is Zachary Abuza. Some of his writing are "Tentacles of Terror: Al-Qaeda's Southeast Asian Network", *Contemporary Southeast Asia*, Vol. 24, No. 3, 2002, pp. 427-465, Militant Islam in Southeast Asia: Crucible of Terror (Boulder: Lynne Rienner, 2003), Political Islam and Violence in Indonesia (London; Routledge, 2007).

96. John T. Sidel, *The Islamist Threat in Southeast Asia: A Reassessment, Policy Studies* 37 (Southeast Asia) (Washington: East-West Center, 2007).

97. Robert W. Hefner(ed), *The Politics of Multiculturalism: Pluralism and Citizenship in Malaysia, Singapore and Indonesia* (Honolulu: University of Hawaii Press, 2001), p. 25.

98. For details see Takashi Shiraishi, *An Age in Motion: Popular Racialism in Java*, 1912-1926 (Ithaca: Cornell University Press, 1990), pp. 41-79.

99. Richard R. Robinson and Vedi R. Hadiz, *Reorganising Power in Indonesia: The Politics of Oligarchy in an Age of Market* (London: Routledge Curzon, 2004).

100. John T. Sidel, *The Islamist Threat in Southeast Asia: A Reassessment*, n. 96, p. 7.

101. Zachary Abuza, *Political Islam and Violence in Indonesia*, n. 92, p. 5.

102. Zachary Abuza, *Funding Terrorism in Southeast Asia: The Financial Network of Al-Qaeda and Jamaah Islamiyah, NBR Analysis*, Vol. 14. No. 5 (Seattle: National Bureau of Asian Research, December 2003).

103. For a detailed discussion on the reasons for the emergence of insurgency movements in Indonesia at its formative post-colonial era see Herbert Feith and Daniel S. Lev, "The End of Indonesian Rebellion", *Pacific Affairs*, Vol. 36, No. 1 (Spring 1963); Audrey Kahin (ed), *Regional Dynamics of the Indonesian Revolution: Unity from Diversity* (Honolulu: Hawaii University Press, 1985), Nazaruddin Sjamsuddin, *The Republican Revolt: A Study of the Achense Rebellion* (Singapore ISEAS, 1985),

C.van Dijk, *Rebellion under the Banner of Islam: The Darul Islam in Indonesia* (The Hague: Martinus Nijhoff, 1981).

104. B.J. Boland, *The Struggle of Islam in Modern Indonesia* (The Hague: Martinus Nijhoff, 1971), pp. 9-10

105. Karl D. Jackson, *Traditional Authority, Islam and Rebellion: A Study of Indonesian Political Behavior* (Berkeley: University of California Press, 1980), p. 12.

106. For an analytical discussion see Douglas E. Ramage, *Politics in Indonesia: Democracy, Islam and the Ideology of Tolerance* (London: Routledge, 1995).

107. Rizal Sukma, *Islam in Indonesian Foreign Policy* (London: Routledge, 2003), p. 4.

108. For such an analysis see Ruth T. McVey, "Faith as the Outsider: Islam in Indonesian Politics" in James P. Piscatori (ed), *Islam in the Political Process* (Cambridge: Cambridge University Press, 1983), p. 216.

109. The Tanjung Priok incident was one of the worst in which several hundred Muslim demonstrators demanding freedom of expression and organizations were shot dead by Soeharto's military.

110. A structurally divided society is prone to communal and racial hatred, which in the extreme form and manifestation, causes violence of grave nature. For some theoretical understanding in the context of Southeast Asia see Robert W. Hefner, "On the History and Cross-Cultural Possibility of a Modern Political Ideal" in his edited *Democratic Civility: The History and Cross-Cultural Possibility of a Modern Political Ideal* (New Brunswick: Transaction, 1998), pp. 3-49.

111. Robert W. Hefner, *The Politics of Multiculturalism: Pluralism and Citizenship in Malaysia, Singapore and Indonesia*, n. 97, p. 35.

112. For details on 'corporatism' see Donald J. Porter, *Managing Politics and Islam in Indonesia* (London; RoutledgeCurzon, 2002), Chapter 2.

113. Golkar party of Soeharto became the most dominant party in his framework of corporatism. It has a strong support base among the army and bureaucrats even today after the end of 'New Order'. For some details on Golkar at its zenith of power

see David Reeve, *Golkar of Indonesia: An Alternative to the Party System* (Singapore: Oxford University Press, 1985).

114. Rizal Sukma, *Islam in Indonesian Foreign Policy*, n. 92, Chapter 4.

115. For an in-depth study on JI see Barton Greg, *Jemaah Islamiyah; Radical Islamization in Indonesia* (Singapore: Ridge Books, 2005).

116. A large number of studies have appeared on terrorism in Southeast Asia, and JI has occupied the center stage of attention of all. The most prolific analyst is Zachary Abuza whose two works have already been mentioned. Some of his other studies are, *How the Jemaah Islamiyah Terrorist Network Operates*, Asia Report No. 43, December 11, 2002, *Jemaah Islamiya in Southeast Asia: Damaged But Still Dangerous*, August 26, 2003, *Militant Islam in Southeast Asia* (Boulder: Lynne Rienner, 2003) and "Terrorism in Southeast Asia" in Richard J. Ellings and Aron L. Friedberg (eds), *Strategic Asia 2003-04: Fragility and Crisis* (Seattle: National Bureau of Asian Research, 2003).

117. For details see Zachary Abuza, *Funding Terrorism in Southeast Asia: The Financial Network of Al-Queda and Jemaah Islamiya*, n. 79.

118. For details of Bali Bombing see Bali Province Secretariat, *Bali Bombing* (Bureau of Public Relations and Protocol, 2003), Mike Millard, *Jihad in Paradise: Islam and Politics in Southeast Asia* (London: M.E. Sharpe, 2004), Dewi Anggraeni, *Who Did This To Our Bali* (Victoria: Indra Publishing, 2003) and Bantarto Bandoro, "Bali Bombing and Fight against Terrorism", *The Indonesian Quarterly*, Vol. 33, No. 4, 2005, pp. 324-328.

119. Dewi Anggraeni, *ibid*, p. 72.

120. For details of an interview with Baasyir see Joe Cochrane, "It was Carried Out By America", *Newsweek*, October 22, 2002.

121. *The Jakarta Post*, November 9, 2008.

122. For an analytical presentation of the transition from Soeharto to B.J. Habibie see Leo Suryadinata, "A Year of Upheaval and Uncertainty: The Fall of Soeharto and the Rise of Habibie", *Southeast Asian Affairs 1999* (Singapore: ISEAS, 1999), pp. 111-127.

123. Azyumardi Azra, "The Islamic Factor in Post-Soeharto Indonesia" in Chris Manning and Peter Van Diermen (ed), *Indonesia in Transition: Social Aspects of Reformasi and Crisis* (Singapore: ISEAS, 2000)

124. Munwir Sjadzali, *Muslim Interests are Better Served in the Absence of Muslim Parties: Indonesian Experience* (Jakarta: Ministry of Religious Affairs, 1992).

125. For an interesting insight on this line see Anies Baswedan, "Indonesian Politics in 2007: The Presidency, Local Elections and the Future of Democracy", *BIES* (Bulletin of Indonesian Economic Studies), Vol. 43, No. 3, December 2007, pp. 323-340.

126. For some discussion on this see Yuri Sato, *Indonesia Entering a New Era: Abdurrahman Wahid Government and its Challenges* (Chiba: Institute of Developing Economies, 2000).

127. For a detailed discussion on several issues such as future of democracy, role of armed forces, economic development, Islamic political parties and their future role see Geoff Forrester (ed), *Post-Soeharto Indonesia: Renewal or Chaos* (Singapore: ISEAS, 1999).

128. Jason F. Isaacson and Colin Ruberstein (eds), *Islam in Asia: Changing Political Realities* (New Brunswick: Transaction Publishers, 2002), p. 3.

129. Noorhaidi Hasan, "September 11 and Islamic Militancy in Post-New Order Indonesia" in K.S. Nathan and Mohammad Hashim Kamali (eds), *Islam in Southeast Asia* (Singapore: ISEAS, 2005), pp. 301-324.

130. H. Tarmizi Taher, *Aspiring for the Middle Path: Religious Harmony in Indonesia* (Jakarta; Center for the Study of Islam and Society, 1997).

131. For an interesting discussion on the slogan see Douglas E. Ramage, "Indonesia: Democracy First, Good Governance Later" in Daljit Singh and Lorraine C. Salazar (eds), *Southeast Asia Affairs: 2007* (Singapore: ISEAS, 2007), pp. 135-160.

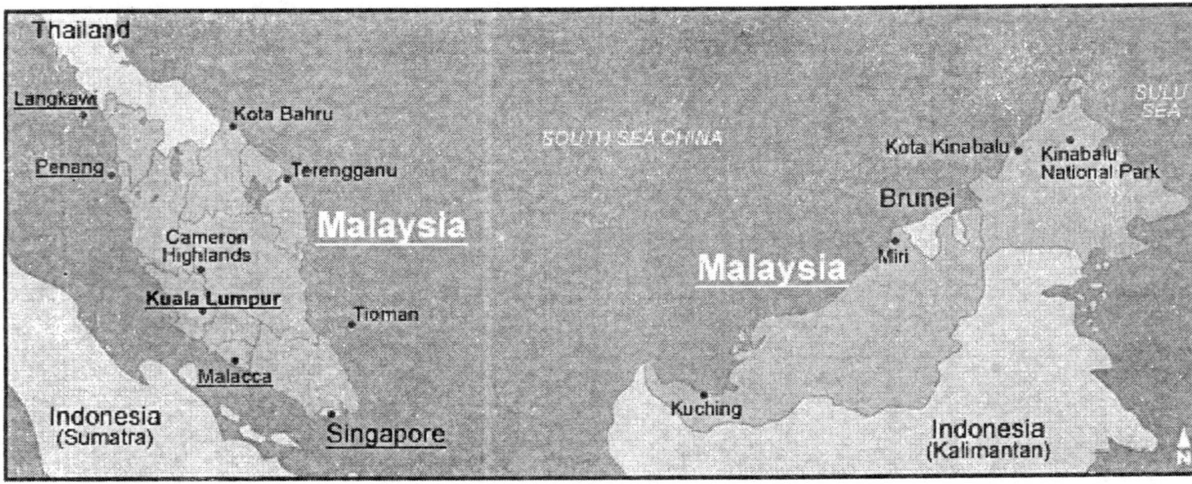
Thailand
Langkawi
Penang
Kota Bahru
Terengganu
Malaysia
Cameron Highlands
Kuala Lumpur
Tioman
Malacca
Indonesia
(Sumatra)
Singapore
SOUTH SEA CHINA
Kota Kinabalu
Kinabalu National Park
SULU SEA
Brunei
Miri
Malaysia
Kuching
Indonesia
(Kalimantan)
N

MALAYSIA

4

MALAYSIA: MALAY FIRST OR MUSLIM FIRST

Malaysia shares many commonalities with Indonesia. It falls in the same archipelago. It has a common historical past, when Buddhist and Hindu kings ruled there. It experienced the same process of Islamization and then colonization of the European powers. It is one of the Muslim majority countries in the region. Being located in the archipelago, Malaysia is closer to Indonesia in terms of religion, language, culture and tradition. At the same time the differences are wide and pronounced. Indonesia is an over-extended country spread from longitude 95 to 140 with more than 17,000 islands, the land area is 1,919,440 sq km, with a huge population of 245,452,739 (estimated in 2006). In comparison, Malaysia is comparatively a smaller country with two peninsular regions – Malaya and Borneo – and separated by the South China Sea; the land area is 329,750 sq km, with a smaller population of about 26.13 million (estimated in 2005).[1] A comparative socio-economic profile has been presented in Chapter V.

Modern Malaysia was born on August 31, 1957 when the British relinquished its sovereignty on the Malaya Peninsula. On September 16, 1963 Singapore, Sabah and Sarawak joined the Malaya Peninsula to form an extended Malaysian Federation. Singapore withdrew from the Federation in 1965. Malaysia till 1980s remained a sleepy agricultural country.

It took less than a decade for it to emerge as a major economic powerhouse, achieving a spectacular success in transforming its agricultural economy to manufacture-industry. The Malaya Peninsula covering 131,573 sq.km. comprises 12 states, and 2 Borneo states of Sabah and Sarawak, which cover around 198,000 sq. km.[2] The Malaya Peninsula and the Borneo territories are separated by the South China Sea. The two territorial regions are characterized by geographic separation, and ethnic and religious differences. Malaysia has a density of 72 persons per sq.km. and a population growth rate of 1.8 per cent. The Malays constitute the majority of the people (50.4%) most of whom live in Malaya peninsula. The Chinese and the Indians constitute 23.3 and 7.0 per cent respectively of the total population. A small indigenous population of about 11 per cent known as *orang asli*, comprising the Iban and Kadazan, could be found in the Borneo region.[3] Malaysia is a multi-ethnic country as evident from the demographic composition of the country detailed above.

Malaysia's development as an economic powerhouse is well known. The UNDP Human Development Report 2010 places it at the 57th position out of 169 countries in the world. With a literacy rate of 93 percent, and with over 97 per cent of seven-year-olds enrolled in schools, a life expectancy of 73 years and the country's high GDP and economic performance[4], Malaysia is now moving faster to posit itself in the list of developed countries by 2020. It has all the potentialities of a developed country with huge natural resources, energy provisions, lower population, least internal troubles and no external threat. The economic policy of the country has been formulated to enable the government to go for higher spending for the realization of objectives of the Ninth Malaysian Plan 2006-2010. At the same time, the perspective planning envisions new taxation, such as, goods and services tax (GST), a comprehensive value-added tax that has been designed to ensure a stable revenue source.[5] Malaysia, with its stable, vibrant and growth-oriented economy, has the capacity to march ahead to engage itself as a leading member of world economy.

Islam and nationalism

Islam landed in present Peninsular Malaysia in the early part of the 12th century AD. But the history of the Malays could be traced to 20,000 years ago when human habitation started in the Niah caves of Sarawak, Kota Tampan in Perak and Tingkayu in Sabah.[6] The Peninsula began its contact with civilizations of other parts of the world during the 2nd century BC. The evidences of existence of Hindu and Buddhist temples in the Bujang valley indicate clearly the international connectivity between the Peninsular Malaysia and the Indian subcontinent. The Hindu-Buddhist rule flourished till the Melaka king accepted Islam in the early part of the 15th century. The 'Srivijaya culture' and rule had strong links with India and China. As already stated in the preceding Chapter, the Srivijay kingdom and its influence transcended the length and the breadth of the entire archipelago, and consequently, the entire historiography of the region covering Java, Sumatra and Malaya peninsula has had similar contour and colour. The entire region during the period of 7th to 12 centuries AD had been the hub of maritime trade, and therefore, experienced prosperity and saw royal power leading the economic, political and strategic domination under illustrious rulers like Sailendra, Kartanegara, Samara, Zebag, Manabharana and Wijiaya. The constellation of the kingdoms of Hindu and Buddhist rulers in many parts of the 'Malay world' paved the way for a multicultural and harmonious zone of peace in Southeast Asia.[7]

With the gradual decline of Srivijaya, a Hindu-Buddhist Malay experienced a major religious transformation with the spread of Islam.[8] The arrival of Islam is traced to the famous 'Terengganu stone', an inscribed pillar in Malay language written in Arabic script, bearing a date equivalent to 1303 AD. It tells that Islam was the local religion. There are divergent opinions about the first arrival of Islam in many of the islands of the archipelago. Islam came from three different places – Arabia, India and China – at different points of time. As in the case of Indonesia, it is widely believed that Muslim traders came to the coastal areas and many of them settled there. That was the first foothold of Islam in the region. It is now an accepted conclusion that there was direct relationship between trade and spread of Islam.[9] There are other reasons such as inflow of Arab Muslims to the region following the fall of Abbasiad Khalifat to the hands of the Mongols in 1258 and growing demand for spice in the non-Malaya world. The spice trade and the route had been controlled and monopolized by the Muslims only till Europeans took over in the 16th century. Then followed the Sufi missionaries' work.[10] It is Sufism that spread Islam in a massive way and also consolidated it in the region. Added to this, in the Malaya peninsula, there was a sudden turn of history around 1404 when being hunted by the Siamese forces, a Hindu king, Parameswara fled from Tumasik (present Singapore) and reached great the entrepot Melaka, which later on came be known as "the Venice of Asia" (as Europeans called it) and established there a new kingdom which could be regarded the cornerstone of the present state of Malaysia.[11] His escape and then establishment of Melaka kingdom has links with the spread of Islam in the peninsula. The conversion of King Parameswara in 1414 to Islam and his adoption of a Muslim name, Megat Iskandar Shah after his marriage with a princess of Pasai, laid the foundation of speedy expansion of Islam. His capital city Melaka became the hub of Islamic missionary activities.[12] Once the Melaka court accepted Islam as the state religion or the religion of the king, the transformation of religious demography became fast and easy. The change was not accomplished through royal coercion or military conquest. The royal patronage reinforced the process of Islamization and its political root. Following this there took place large-scale conversion, leading to fast transformation of the demographic composition of the region.[13] The spread of Islam reached beyond the archipelago; Thailand and the Philippines also experienced the wave. The expansion continued till it was halted by the Portuguese conquest in 1511. Nonetheless, the Muslim resistance to foreign occupation continued. It strengthened the Muslim solidarity and eventually facilitated, in an indirect way, the overthrow of the Portuguese colonization by the Dutch in 1641. The British take over of Melaka from the Dutch in 1795 and the conclusion of the Anglo-Dutch Treaty of 1824 led to the British assurance not to interfere in the religious affairs of the Malaya.[14] That facilitated the religious activities including conversion in the region. By the middle of the 16th century, more than half of the population of the archipelago covering present Indonesia and Malaysia came under the influence of Islam. At the same time, the multi-ethnic composition, with a strong presence of the Arabs, the Chinese and the Indians, shaped Melaka, the base-point of future Malaysia as a multi-cultural pluralist society.

Despite the massive transformation of the religious demography of the Malay world within a short period of time, the cultural unity of the people under the canopied structure of *Melayu* race remained intact. The 15th century Malaya Peninsula earned reputation in commercial and religious interface. At the same time the Malay society was intensely cosmopolitan. The administrative paraphernalia including court language and titles, literature, music and other forms of art, food, dress, social customs and traditions remained staunchly Malay and Malay *adat*. Bangladesh and Indonesia too experienced the same development of ethnic and cultural unity making religion one of the components of socio-political life and not the lone and singular one. It is not clear when and how the word Melayu originated. The Melaka documents of the 15th century and the Chinese and the Portuguese documents of 17th and 18th centuries mention about the Malay language, people and 'Malay world' which had transcended beyond the peninsula to reach Borneo,

Thailand and the Philippines. The Malays call themselves as Orang Melayu who are mostly descendents of the immigrants from Sumatra. They speak the Malay language closer to Bahasa Indonesia.[15] That is why the 'Malay world' has a wider geographical, linguistic, cultural and historical meaning that cuts across the territorial boundaries. The Islamic component of Malay nationhood is a highly complicated and at the same time fascinating. The interface of Islam and Malay ethnicity, which had begun in a massive way in the early part of the 15th century, has had a role in shaping Malay nationalism. With the Malay language as a vehicle for inter-ethnic communication and also for conversion to Islam, Malay secured the status of the "pre-eminent language of scholarship, commerce, diplomacy, and religion."[16] Malay language continues to play a dominant role in the contemporary politics in Malaysia, which rests on the inter-ethnic interface in the country and has presented a canopied structure for the articulation of 'Bangsa Malaysia'.

As already stated, King Parameswara's arrival at Melaka and his conversion to Islam led to a massive expansion of Islam in the Peninsula. The conversion of the King inspired the vast majority of the people. The Sufi saints' missionary zeal added to this emotional, psychological and metamorphic transformation of the people. Along with the unprecedented change in the religious texture of the people in a land of Hindu-Buddhist culture and environment, the role of Islam as a faith had an intense impact on the polity centering round the royal institution.[17] The king came to be known as 'Shadow of God on Earth' (*Khilafah Allah Fil al-Ardhi*), an expression almost similar to the divine origin of the state.

As the Muslim rule in Melaka began to expand, eventually leading to the Islamization of the entire Malaya Peninsula, the region experienced an admixture of religion, ethnicity and polity that continued to prevail through ages. The Portuguese occupation of Malaya in 1511 AD halted, as already stated, the expansion of Islam, but could not alter the religious, political and ethnic texture of the land. On the other hand, migration of Arab and Indian Muslim traders and Sufi missionaries of Shafi tradition continued without affecting the basics of the 'Malay world'. It led to a dovetailing of Malay ethnicity and Islam, a syncretistic tradition was thus born before the European colonial powers landed on present Malaysian soil. The impact of the Islamic Malay tradition was far reaching and enduring. It passed through two colonial periods – the Portuguese and then the British – to reach the modern age of Malaysia without experiencing any dramatic change.

The Islamic character of the Malay world appeared to have faced formidable challenges with the occupation of the land by European colonial powers. The conclusion of the Anglo-Dutch Treaty of 1824 formalized the British occupation of Malaya Peninsula. With that Melaka as a center of Islamic culture and tradition received a major setback. Another Islamic center, Naning, offered stiff resistance to the British under the leadership of Pak Dol Said. Perak followed the example of resistance to foreign occupation and fought against the British under the leadership of Maharaja Lela.[18] However, by 1875 the British control over the entire region was complete. Three striking developments took place. First, as in the case of Dutch Indonesia, where the conversion to Christianity in Muslim dominated areas and among Muslims was not encouraged, the British administration moved cautiously on conversion to Christianity, restricting conversion to the non-Muslims in the Borneo part of Malaya, leaving the predominantly Islamic Peninsula undisturbed by this policy. In 1874, the British officially recognized the preeminent status of Islam in the Malaya states and discouraged conversion of the Malays to Christianity.[19] The institution of monarchy, a symbolic image of Islam, continued in several parts of the peninsula looking after the Islamic religious matters.[20] Second, the British encouraged the migration of educated Chinese people to help in administration and to look after business and commerce. It appeared that the migration proved to be insufficient to cater to the needs of the colonial power. Consequently, the British decided to bring the 'Indian community' to the Peninsula to engage them in rubber plantation. This led to the heavy influx of people mostly of Tamil origin to Malaya Peninsula, and consequently, a visible change in the demographic picture of the region. By 1920 the Chinese overwhelmed the Malays in the Peninsula; they constituted more than 60 percent of the population in federated states of Negeri Sembilan, Pahang, Perak and Selangor.[21] Third, the Malaya Reservation Act, 1913 gave a colonial definition of Malaya, saying that any person belonging to the Malayan race, who habitually spoke Malay or any other Malayan language and who professed Islam was a Malay. This was the forerunner of Article 160 of the Federal Constitution. In short, Islam, which had already become a part of the Malay ethnicity, received statutory confirmation of being integral to Malay macrocosm. Within a short span of time the migrant Muslims from India, China, Java and Sumatra became a part of *orang Melayu* (Malay people), a newly constructed homogenized ethnicity.[22] In the entire process of the construction of the Malay nationalism, the role of Malaya language and Islam is an established fact. That impacted the political process of the country in a formidable way. Diverse ethnicity with roots in the non-Malay world, such as Arabia, China and India led to the emergence of a "plural society", where language and religion Islam had a cementing role to play.

Although British annexation of Malaya, which was complete at the turn of the 20th century, did not adversely affect religious life of the people, as the religious affairs were left to the Sultans located in different parts of the country, the policy of the colonial regime encouraging immigration did affect its demographic composition.[23] The unrestricted immigration of people from India and China to work in rubber plantation and in tin mining changed the demography of Malaya Peninsula. There was least scope for interface of the three communities – Malay, Chinese and

Indian – since they were kept segregated.[24] The ethno-cultural segregation was a part of the colonial policy to divide and rule, a policy universally adopted by all colonial powers, intended to discourage an integration process among the Arabs, the Chinese and the Indian communities into indigenous Malaya society.[25] This led to the Chinese acquiring a special position in the colonial economy. While the immigrants flourished, the Malay remained in the back seat of the national economy. The result was growing tension between and among the communities, with spillover consequences affecting national reconstruction. There was neither cohesion among the ethnic communities nor was there any scope for positive interfacing. The Malaya feared the danger of Chinese supremacy at the end of the colonial era. The segregation and economic backwardness of the natives planted the seeds of conflict in the later period when Malaysia started growing as an independent international personality. Although it is argued that the British colonialism created a pluralistic society in Malaysia,[26] and different ethnic groups lived and worked peacefully in their own ways, without generating strife and social conflict, the century old segregation made the nation-building task more complex and problematic in the post-independence era.[27]

The Japanese occupation of Malaya during World War II, brought some change in the administrative and political set up of the country. The Japanese landed in the Peninsula on December 6, 1941 and swept through it and the Borneo states in less than a month.[28] With its deep-rooted distrust, the Japanese tried to sideline the Chinese in every walk of life and promote the native Malaya instead. At the same time, the Japanese attempt to regulate social customs of Islamic tradition, such as polygamy, caused widespread resentment among both the Malays. Even then, the Japanese occupation helped evolve a pan-Malay sense of community, as the occupation forces promoted the idea of a large and unified Malay nationalism.[29] There was stiff guerrilla resistance to Japanese occupation throughout the period.

The armed movement carried a strong message of Malay nationalism and pledged for national unity among the Malays at the end of the occupation.[30] This was the time when Malay nationalism grew in a formidable way and the emerging elite of the community took full advantage of the support extended by the occupation forces.

The situation once again changed with the surrender of the Japanese at the end of the War and reoccupation of Malaya and Borneo by the British. The simmering racial tension grew as the Chinese, who controlled the economy of the region, tried to settle scores on the Malays for their privileged and patronizing support from the Japanese. There were reprisals against the Malays who extended cooperation to the Japanese. Ethnic tensions rose and clashes occurred in various parts of the country as early as May 1945. In the midst of the tension, the Malays could visualize inevitable steps forward resuscitation of the concept of a Greater Malaya, at the end of the war and the Japanese occupation.

The Malay nationalism was born immediately after the British reoccupation, and was fully expressed in the formation of the United Malays National Organization (UMNO) in 1946. The UMNO spearheaded a massive campaign against the British post-War Malayan Union Plan under which in the new state of Malaya both Malay and non-Malay would have equal rights and citizenship. This would have ended the Malay sovereignty and a new Malayan nation-state would have emerged instead of a Malay nation-state. The UMNO articulated properly the concept of Malay nationhood and fought for the restoration of Malay sovereignty. Eventually, as the process of de-colonization began, the idea of Malay nationalism within the framework of a definite and special role for the Malay put forward by the Malay Reservation Act, 1913 got crystallized. At the end of the long twelve years (1945-1957) of intense articulation by the UMNO and the British officials, independent Malaya was proclaimed on August 31, 1957.[31]

It was during this de-colonization period that three political parties – the UMNO, the Malaysian Chinese Association (MCA) and the Malaysian Indian Congress (MIC) tried to work out a framework for inter-racial cooperation, unity and understanding, to forge a 'Social Contract' among their communities. The three organizations failed to build up a multi-ethnic common platform, as each community could not coalesce around a common cause. While the Malays had been steadfast in their objective of ensuring the protection of their religion, language and culture through constitutional arrangement, the Chinese and the Indians had remained content with the right to citizenship of the new federation. While Malays gained political supremacy, the other two major communities allowed themselves to be pushed to a secondary position. The Malay-Chinese-Indian alliance was formed on unequal terms – Malay preponderance on one hand and back seat to the others. The Malay supremacy has been aptly narrated by Cheah:

> The alliance memorandum to the Reid Commission had, in fact, agreed to all the features of a Malay state: "special position of the Malays", "Malay as the national language", "Islam as the official religion", and the Malay rulers as the "constitutional monarchs". There were also "Malay land reservations" and "reservation for the Malays of a certain proportion of jobs in the civil service". But the controversial questions of citizenship and nationality had been left vague.[32]

The vagueness of the nationality question has raised the foundational issue – in the land of Malaysia, a self-proclaimed showpiece of multiculturalism, where is the space for two of the major communities? That remains unanswered as we proceed to other relevant issue of nation-building.

The alliance of the three communities forged at the time of the constitution making, despite inter-party tensions, remained intact. At a later stage in 1974, they formalized their loose interrelationship to form Barisan Nasional, currently working as a ruling alliance of 14 parties. Even with their mutual distrust and fear the three parties achieved the goal of national reconciliation and reconstruction and were able to form a coalition to contest the first general election in 1955, which they won with a thumping majority capturing 51 out of 52 seats. It was a clear demonstration of the commitment of three major communities for national unity. The disturbances during the period owing to the armed struggle launched by the Malaya Communist Party (MCP) provided a scope for mutual cooperation among the three communities, notwithstanding the fact that the MCP too had followers belonging to Chinese, Malay and Indian communities.[33] The smooth election and its decisive results expedited the process of Independence on August 31, 1957.

The Malaysian Constitution of 1957 has defined Malay in unequivocal terms. The articulation of the Malay nation predates the pre-World War II ethnic Malay nationalism, a nation-state concept that encompassed the Malays only in which the Chinese and other non-Malays had no place.[34] At the time of drafting the Constitution the three major communities – Malays, Chinese and Indians — which had already made arrangements for political segregation, made a distinction between ethnicity and citizenship. While the question of citizenship was addressed with a broad idea of inclusiveness, Malay ethnicity became a matter of exclusiveness from the point of religious consideration. Despite the presence of the idea of exclusiveness, "Malaya for Malays" nation-state, the UMNO-MCA-MIC cooperative leadership worked for a multi-racial and multi-communal state. The pre-1955 cooperation among the three racially and communally different segments of the society, a subtle alliance to confront the surging communist movement, was a social contact through which a multi-ethnic nationalism was achieved.

In the backdrop of the emergence of a post-colonial Malay nationalism, Islam as the religion of the majority remained central to the political process in the country.[35] The Islamic consciousness was oriented, revitalized and expanded at the turn of the 20th century with the enactment of the Muhammadan Law in 1904 empowering the Sultan on matters of public teaching on Islam. It established a linkage between the ruler and the religion, and made the Muslim-Malay national construction rigid and conservative, and to a great extent, Sharia-minded.[36] Consequent upon the enactment of the Muhammadan Law, the ruling elite started to exercise tremendous influence in presenting the Malaya explicitly as being Muslim, and in opposition to Chinese and non-Muslim Indians. They succeeded in conceptualizing Malaya nationalism, not as an anti-colonial nationalism but as a plea for special privilege for the community and against the non-Malay Asian domiciled communities.[37] In the backdrop of the demand for equal citizenship right made by the non-Malay since 1910 through 1946-48, the Malaya elite was successful in mobilizing pressure in favour of ensuring constitutional arrangement for Malay special privileges, together with institutionalization of protection and promotion of Islam through royal patronage.[38] In doing so, the Malay elite buried the idea of inclusiveness of the Malayan nationalism advocated by some sections of their society, in view of the support for their cause extended by the Arab and the Indian Muslims. The stride towards Malay exclusiveness was a case of protection and promotion of Malay Muslims, a sentiment which grew and was nurtured during the entire period of the first half of the last century; this was more ethnic rather than religion based. It was an emotional appeal not to allow non-Malay aliens to take over the Malay land at the end of the colonial rule. All this eventually led to communalization and compartmentalization of politics, ethnic divide, and antagonistic competition in the post-colonial period.[39] Today's Malaysian politics is reflective of the developments that had taken place during the formative period of national reconstruction on the eve of independence.

At any rate, Islam has a striking contribution to the early initiation of the political process in Malaysia beginning in the 15th century. For long Islam has been a precondition of political and social involvement of the masses in the Malay affairs and acted as an upholder of social values and political order. The institution of the Sultan and the influence of the *ulema* have created an elite class, whose loyalty to Islam is pronounced and profound. Islam symbolizes the Malay unity and political legitimacy of the ruling elite and rests on the people's expression of their adherence to Islam.[40]

The Constitutional arrangement for affirmative action

Ever since the Malays realized their vulnerability in demographic composition after the publication of the 1921 census portending the minority status to them, the Malay ethnicity, in combination with Islam as the religion, prevented formation of a multi-communal alliance, despite the efforts made by Onn bin Jaafar.[41] The formation of the UMNO in 1946, which tended to articulate Malay nationalism with special emphasis on Islamic *ummah* (community), could be treated as the beginning of constitutional arrangements for the Malay defined in terms of religion. The cooperation among three ethnic based parties – the UMNO, the MCA and the MIC – continued during the drafting of the Constitution. That itself gave a hope for a stable government in the post-colonial era. The inclusive position taken by Onn bin Jaafar and his associates failed to garner a unanimous plank. There was a split in the UMNO leading to the formation of the first Islamic party named Majlis Agama Tetinggi Malaya (MATA, Malayan Supreme Religious Council) in 1948. Consequently, the British construction of the Malay community as Malay-speaking Muslims, and in difference with the other immigrants, provided the rationale for consolidation of the ethnic definition of the Malay community. In the post-colonial era, however, many indigenous groups, precisely known as *orang asli* (original people) from Sabah and Sarawak were included to construct *bumiputera* (sons of the soil).

The Reid Commission,[42] which drafted the Constitution,

made several provisions for a special status for Islam as the religion of the federation Malaysia, for special position of the Malays and for Malay as the national language. These steps were the result of the UMNO pressure from outside, despite the fact that Tunku Abdul Rahman asked the Reid Commission to ensure that in an Independent Malaya all nationals should be granted equal rights and opportunities, irrespective of race and creed.[43] At the time of drafting the constitution the pressing issue before the five-member Constitution Commission, in which there was not a single representative of the Malays, was not religion and Islamic infrastructures but the post-colonial nation-building task. Therefore, the Commission did not recommend Islam as the religion of the Federation. It was under the pressure from the UMNO that the Constitution incorporated Article 3(1) to ensure the advantage of the Malay-Islam component of the society.[44] It is argued that the inclusion of the provision making Islam the religion of the Federation was driven more by ethnic and national consideration rather than the Islamic.[45] The language of the provisions were carefully drafted, leaving no scope for loose interpretation, clearly implying that the Malay party was successful in dictating terms for the protection of their ethnic and religious advantage. Article 3(1) states precisely the religion of the federation: "Islam is the religion of the Federation; but other religions may be practiced in peace and harmony in any part of the Federation."[46] It is argued that the Article does not state that Islam is the 'official' religion of the Federation, leaving a scope to assert that Malaysia is a secular state as other religions are allowed to be practiced. Article 89 deals with reservation of Malay land for the Malays. This is an enabling article to put the Malays in an advantageous position. Article 152(1) proclaims: "The national language shall be the Malay language", but that "no person shall be prohibited or prevented from using (otherwise than for official purposes), or from teaching or learning, any other language". This Article was inserted to satisfy the Chinese and the Indian Tamils who despite best efforts failed to put their languages at par with Malay. Article 153(2) ensures "reservation for Malays and natives of the states of Sabah and Sarawak" in the public service and in matters of awarding scholarships, educational training, permit or license for operation of trade or business. While federal citizenship was accorded to the Chinese and Indians on the basis of equality, the national identity was denied to them. The most striking is Article 160, which offers the definition of "Malay"; it reads: Malay means "a person who professes the religion of Islam, habitually speaks the Malay language, conforms to Malay customs."[47] This clearly suggests the exclusiveness of the concept of Malay nationality, which was formulated in opposition to the inclusive concept of "Malayan" nationality and nationalism.[48] At any rate all these constitutional provisions have safeguarded and promoted the ethnic Malay, whose religion is Islam, but fragmented the social milieu in which healthy multi-culturalism, consistent with the organic composition of nationalism is not easy. The question of nationalism in the land of Malaysia remains uncertain. If it were an ethnic-driven foundational issue, Malayan nationalism and not Malay nationalism should have been the determinant factor. If it were a religion-driven issue, all the Muslims irrespective of their origins should have come under the coverage of Malay nationalism, for Malay as Muslims belong to the universal concept of *ummah*, and consequently and logically, all Muslim citizens of Malaysia, who speak Malay language and follow Malay tradition, should have been Malays. The exclusive notion of Malay nationalism, and the preeminent position awarded to the religion of the majority, Islam, has caused tremendous stress and strain. The very idea of sidelining the two important segments of the country, the Chinese and the Indians, who are the major players in the economy, was a potentially problematic loophole in the nation-building process. In this way Islam, ethnicity and citizenship remain dialectic and dichotomous in nature.[49] The problem remains unresolved. The inter-ethnic tension continues along with affirmative action in favour of Malays, as Malay supremacy tends to overwhelm others. The agitation for equal treatment spearheaded by the HINDRAF in the latter part of 2007 was a clear testimony to the simmering inter-ethnic tension in Malaysia.

The incorporation of Article 3(1) in the Federal Constitution and a causal comment of Mahathir Mohamad that Malaysia is an Islamic state, which was made to counter the agenda of the Parti Islam SeMalaysia (PAS) to transform Malaysia into an Islamic state led to occasional debate as to whether Malaysia is an Islamic state. A national seminar held in Kuala Lumpur in 2002 tried to address the question "Is Malaysia an Islamic state?". The general consensus of the seminar was that it is not. The proclamation that Islam is the religion of the Federation does not mean transformation of Malaysia into an Islamic state. The Supreme Court in a 1988 case ruled that the effect of Article 3(1) is primarily symbolic. Islamic Sharia law is not the general law of the land. The Sharia courts have limited jurisdiction, only on the followers of Islam and are not superior to civil courts. Allegiance to Islam is not a condition for obtaining citizenship or holding any federal posts and position, other than those of the King and Deputy King.[50] Mahathir Mohamad's comment was understood in terms of demographic consideration of the Muslims who constitute the majority of the population.[51] The comment is an unwitting expression in the context of contesting claims between the UMNO and the PAS over the ownership of Islamic agenda in Malaysia.

UMNO vs. PAS: which one is more Islamic?

As already mentioned, the UMNO was formed at the dawn of Merdeka (independence) in 1946 by Onn Jaafar to register the preeminent role of the Malay Muslims in the affairs of the country and to demonstrate the elite role of the community in the post-colonial political process. It emerged out of a movement against the British plan for a post-colonial unitary Malayan Union that would put all the nine

Malay states under one government and would grant equal political rights to all ethnic groups.[52] A protective role was assigned to the UMNO. It was to replace the sultans as "protector" of the Malays against non-Malays and it was expected that just as the Malays were loyal to the sultans, they were to be now loyal to the UMNO.[53] The UMNO is an exclusive political organization, which has not so far opened its door to non-Muslim Chinese and Indian communities, despite their credentials as people who habitually speak Malay and follow Malay tradition. Despite its exclusiveness, it projected itself as a democratic and liberal organization, refrained from pursuing a hardcore Islamic agenda, such as enforcement of Sharia laws and transforming Malaysia into an Islamic state, and remained steadfast in holding its alliance with the MCA and the MIC without any major hitch. All this infuriated the hardliners within the UMNO who engineered a split in the party in 1948 by forming a new Islamic party MATA. In 1951 the emergence of Parti Islam Se-Malaysia (Pan Malaysian Islamic Party, PAS) led to the replacement of the MATA as a platform to pursue the Islamic agenda. It also posed a major threat to the UMNO, which used to claim the ownership of protecting and promoting the interests of Malay Muslims.[54] The newly formed party challenged the political advantage of the UMNO being the only exclusive Muslim political party in the country. The challenge proved to be real and formidable, as in 1959 elections, it captured power using Islamic card in Kelantan[55] and later on in Terengganu in 1999. Added to this anxiety and threat posed by the PAS, the dakwah movement took shape in Malaysia; as in the case of Indonesia, it is a youth and student movement, which propagated religious radicalism and expressed resoluteness in their agenda and a will to implement Islamic ideals.[56] As the movement campaigned to create a strong Malay-Muslim identity with heightened Islamic consciousness, it could come closer to the PAS. The dakwah movement leaders, as in the case of Indonesia, drew inspiration from the Egyptian Ikhwan-ul-Muslimin

(Muslim Brotherhood) and the Wahhabi cult. The reconstruction of Malay-Muslim identity of the dakwah is characterized by other components of the fundamental doctrine, such as, strict observance of Islamic rituals, clear exhibition of Islamic religiosity in external behaviour and subjection to 'internal conversion' to draw a clear demarcation between 'true' Muslims and 'nominal' Muslims. They were committed to Muslim/non-Muslim dichotomy and wanted to be the real representatives of the resurgent Muslims.[57]

Despite Islam's role of a unifying force in the Malay society, the intra-ethnic conflict surfaced within the community over the issue of political accommodation and space to be made available to other ethnic communities. The UMNO wanted to project itself as a liberal, democratic and tolerant political organization, commanding the confidence of the vast majority of the Malay community, whose interest was a matter of prime concern, a non-negotiable plank. Islam remains as the preeminent symbol of the Malay identity, and therefore, "protection of Islam" is construed as the "protection of the Malays".[58] The Sultan used to play the role of the protector of the Malay society in the pre-independence period. The UMNO took over that role at the dawn of independence. Article 4 of the constitution of the party enshrines that role. The word *"memelihara"* (look after, safeguard, protect) attached to the party vests upon it the responsibility of protecting the Malay community. One of the political objectives of the party is to uphold "the excellence of the religion of Islam and to propagate the same". It did not mean that Islam has a political role to play. This is a core point on which the UMNO tries to project itself as a secular party and continues to sustain its alliance with the MCA and the MIC. The dissentions within the party surfaced when there was a demand that Islam should not be confined to matters of worship and morality, but should play a role in determining the economic and political life of the country – a demand unacceptable to the UMNO's leadership, for, it was feared that a politically dominant role for Islam would transform Malay state into an Islamic one.[59] The very idea of alliance with non-Malay parties was another source of simmering tension between the liberals, such as, Tunku Abdur Rahman and the hardliners. The differences led to a vertical split in the party and the formation of the PAS in 1951.

In the UMNO-PAS rivalry for projection of their respective image as true and real Islamic parties, the UMNO, being the leading coalition partner of the umbrella organization, Barisan Nasional[60], had the advantage of furthering the Islamic agenda at the national level. The PAS, which captured power in Kelantan in 1959, and governed the state till 1996, recaptured power in 1990, and continues to rule till date, and then in Terengganu in 1999 for a brief period, started building its image as an efficient and transparent organization, and in this process, expanded its base in other parts of the Malaysia Peninsula. The core issue for both the parties is Islam on which the differences remain pronounced and profound. In the pursuit of building its image as a Muslim party and to "out-Islam" PAS[61], the UMNO, as the decisive segment in the coalition federal government, took major initiatives, which have far-reaching impact in the political system of Malaysia.

The UMNO's move to out-Islam PAS was influenced by the ideological and political inclination of the middle class Malay Muslims towards the dakwah movement and the PAS in the 1970s. The PAS had already created a base in rural areas of the country. Added to this development, a newly formed youth organization, ABIM[62] (Angkatan Belia Islam Malaysia or Islamic Youth Movement of Malaysia) established in 1971, forged effective links with the PAS. There was an urban-rural divide in these organizations. While the PAS had drawn its support from rural Malays, the dakwah movement and the ABIM remained urban-centric. The UMNO was aware about the cleavage, and therefore, it tried to retain and expand its support base through a series of actions that would overtake PAS in establishing its formidable Islamic credentials. The first step in this direction was the establishment of Islamic Research Centre in 1979, which emerged as a think tank of the party.

The UMNO's geared up its Islamization agenda soon after Datuk Seri Dr. Mahathir Mohamad[63] became the Prime Minister on July 16, 1981. A number of institutions dedicated to the promotion of the Muslims were established, most notably the Islamic Bank (1981), Islamic Insurance (1981) and International Islamic University of Malaysia (1983). There was a visible increase in the Islamic programmes in the government controlled mass media, radio and television. The broadcast of *azan* (call for namaz) five times a day, live coverage of the khutbah (sermon) in the Friday congregational prayer, competition of Qur'an recitation at international level, bringing Anwar Ibrahim, the known and outspoken President of the ABIM to the UMNO were some of the striking steps having far reaching impact that were resorted to in projecting the Islamic face of the party.[64] In this way the process of institutionalization of Islamic values and symbols was accelerated. Together with these steps, the most important one taken by the UMNO was towards steady upward economic mobility of the Malays was the launching of the New Economic Policy in 1971. All these steps proved in a convincing manner that the PAS was busy with rhetoric, while the UMNO had been pursuing Islamic agenda in a vigorous manner. The message was loud and clear – who is more Islamic – the party which talks only and the party which works?

The New Economic Policy (NEP)

The most striking initiative the UMNO leadership took was the adoption of the New Economic Policy (NEP or DEB for Dasar Ekonomi Baru), which made the Malay-non-Malay divide more palpable and pronounced. It was an ambitious and at the same time highly controversial socio economic restructuring affirmative action programme launched by Tun Abdul Rahman in 1971 against the backdrop of the

1969 anti-Chinese riot. It might be relevant to narrate briefly the background events before presenting a narrative of the NEP.

As already stated, Article 153 of the Constitution of Malaysia provided special rights for the Malays. The Reid Commission believed that in due course of time the affirmative action programme stipulated under Article 153 would disappear. The provisions were extended to the Bumiputera in 1963 when Singapore, Sabah and Sarawak were incorporated into the Federation of Malaya, now christened as Federation of Malaysia. The rationale behind Reid Commission's inclusion of the text of Article 153 was to reduce the imbalance between the Chinese and Malays in terms of economic inequality. It was estimated that the Bumiputera share in the economy was about 2.4 per cent while the Chinese enjoyed the lion's share. More than 75 per cent of the people living below the poverty line were Malays.[65] Unemployment among the Malays was the highest among all the communities. They held a mere 1 per cent of investment in registered business. The situation has been aptly revealed by none other than Alex Lee, a member of the MCA:

> The twelve years following Merdeka [Independence] did not, in fact, bring forth the wealth and power which the Malays had expected. They found themselves still to be the rural people with control of the towns very much in the hands of the non-Malays...Their control of the civil service was also being eroded by the influx of non-Malays into the government services and their supremacy in the police force was reduced by the recruitment of non-Malay officers during the Emergency. Their only area of control, therefore, was in the political arena, especially in Parliament where they control two-thirds of the seats. However, the 1969 elections results gave the impression that even this political control was being threatened, and in some States the balance of power seemed to shift to political parties which appealed to Chinese chauvinism.[66]

The striking imbalance in all walks of life relegating the Malays to obscurity was compounded by the pent up tension between the Chinese and the Malays, which eventually led to the infamous anti-Chinese riot of May 13, 1969. The flashpoint of the riot was the elections held on May 10 in which all the opposition parties campaigned against the special position entitled to the Malays and advocated greater use of Chinese, Tamil and English languages as media of instruction in educational institutions.[67] The election results were shocking to the three-party alliance, whose strength was reduced for the first time from two-thirds to a simple majority in the parliament. It failed to secure majority in the states of Kelantan, Selangor and Perak. Tunku Abdul Rahman's strategy to keep both Malay and non-Malay happy did not work.[68] The MCA withdrew from the alliance, which infuriated the UMNO. There was celebration among the Chinese at the political setback of the alliance and better performance of the opposition on the evening of May 13, 1969. This led to a riot in which 196 people were killed and many more were injured.

It was argued that the economic backwardness of the Malays led to the riot of 1969. It was found that the First Five Year Plan of 1966-1970, dedicated to increase rural development and economic prosperity of the poor by uplifting rural economy, did not yield satisfactory results. This realization propelled the Government of Tun Abdul Razak to launch the NEP as a special measure to reduce the economic imbalance among the communities. It was more a political move to salvage the damaged support-base of the UMNO and to satisfy Malay aspirations.[69] Its political dimension could be seen in the projected expectation of greater Malay participation in the affairs of the country, while addressing the problems of poverty and backwardness of the community.[70] The NEP was an interim expression of the Government's desire to secure and uplift the common Malay's economic condition as opposed to the economically well-off non-Malays. The core of the NEP was put in the

Second Malaysian Plan 1971-1975.[71] It was designed within the framework of a broad national unity with a two-pronged approach. To quote the Second Malaysia Plan on the two pronged goals:

> The Plan incorporates a two-pronged New Economic Policy for development. The first prong is to reduce and eventually eradicate poverty by raising income levels and in increasing employment opportunities for all Malaysians, irrespective of race the second prong aims at accelerating the process of restructuring Malaysian society in order to correct economic imbalance, so as to reduce and eventually eliminate the identification of race with economic function. This process involves the modernization of rural life, a rapid and balanced growth of urban activities and the creation of a Malay commercial and industrial community in all categories and at all levels of operations, so that Malays and other indigenous people will become full partners in all aspects of economy to bring the Malay share to 30% was to be achieved by a high rate of growth overall, so that in absolute terms there would be large increases in ownership for non-Malays and foreigners as well as Malays. By 1990, however, the ratios would change to 30% Malay, 40% non-Malay and 30% foreign. Non-Malays were assured that there would be no deprivation of their rights or prospects.[72]

The NEP was formulated to accelerate the process of raising the Malays in all walks of life from 'second class' citizenship to Malay supremacy (*Ketuanan Melayu*). The initial target of the NEP was to move the economic ownership in Malaysia from a 2.4:33:63 ratio of Bumiputera, other Malays, Chinese and other foreigners to a more or less balanced ratio of 30:40:30. This was to be accomplished by way of redistribution of wealth to increase the ownership of enterprise of Bumiputera from the then 2.4 to 30 per cent of the share of national wealth.[73] This was referred to as 'expanding pie theory', which suggested a steady rise in Bumiputera's share of the pie, without reducing the non-Bumiputera's share. Among the specific steps taken to redeem the objectives of the NEP was a requirement that all initial public offerings (IPOs) ought to earmark 30 per cent share for the Bumiputera investors. Most of the Malaysians consider it to be a real national ideology, which propelled economic well-being of the Malay+Bumiputera combination along with spectacular economic growth of the country.[74]

The result of the economic performance under the NEP was impressive. There was a marked improvement in the economic condition of the country. The GNP galloped from RM 1, 142 in 1970 to RM 12,102 in 1979. There was reduction of poverty in a significant manner. The following Table gives an idea of the result of the NEP.

Table 4.1
Distribution of poverty

NEP Benchmarks	*1970*	*1990*	*2004*
Bumiputera equity	2.4%	19.30%	18.7%
Overall poverty	52%	17.10	5.00%
Rural poverty	59.00%	21.8%	11.00%
Household income	RM660	RM1,254	RM2996

Sources: http://en.wikipedia.org/wiki/Malaysian_New_Economic_Policy

The figures in the Table indicate the rate of success in achieving the goals set in the NEP. There was massive use of the government infrastructure to achieve success in the target-oriented policies. Such an endeavour was possible mainly because of the UMNO's special position in the Government. That made the NEP a success, despite the fact that it widened the ethnic division in Malaysia. The NEP had hidden objectives – to dismiss the PAS allegations that the Federal Government of Malaysia did not promote the interests of the Malay Muslims and acted as the tools of the Chinese, as a consequence of which, the Malays continued to remain poor while the Chinese had been prospering. That is why scholars argue that the NEP was a political policy of the UMNO to secure a political mileage.[75] Along with racial tension the cleavage between the rural-urban Malays was sharpened. The Chinese, who were apprehensive of the fallouts of the NEP, did not offer any visible opposition to it mainly due to the fact that the racial riot of May 13, 1969 was still fresh in their memory. They tried to get best out of the policy and eventually they did it. It was an irony that the at the turn of the 1990s, and after twenty years of affirmative action in favour of the Malays, the Chinese had almost doubled their share of ownership. They tried to get the best out of a difficult situation. For example, the Malay would procure necessary license to do business because he has an access to it, and the Chinese would operate it, because he has the expertise and urge to do so. It was an 'Ali-Baba' arrangement, Ali the Malay and Baba the Chinese. The opportunities made available, such as, easy license, training, fund, networking and infrastructure facilities, to the Malays were enormous, but in the absence of a business culture among them they were at a loss as to what to do with these

Table 4.2
Upward mobility of various communities in Malaysia (1970-1990)

Class composition	*% of Bumiputera*		*% of Chinese*		*% of Indian*	
	1970	*1990*	*1970*	*1990*	*1970*	*1990*
Upper & middle class	12.9	27.9	28.6	43.2	23.4	27.3
Working class	18.0	23.2	41.6	33.8	24.7	34.8
Agriculture	62.3	37.4	21.2	13.5	41.0	23.4
Services	6.8	12.4	8.6	8.5	10.9	14.5

Source: Jim Baker, *"Crossroads": A Popular History of Malaysia,* n. 69, p. 356

unfamiliar opportunities and avenues. This offered a unique and an expected opportunity for the Chinese and the Indians to step up their venture of accelerating their business through the good offices of the Malays. In this way, the NEP benefited one and all. The country had made spectacular economic advancement for which it was branded as an 'Asian Tiger'. The Table 4.2 clearly indicated how in 20 years time various ethnic groups had experienced upward mobility.

Notwithstanding the visibility of the benefits being showered on all Malaysian citizens irrespective of race and religion, the Malays enjoyed the largest share of the pie. Consequently, the issue of ethnicity and religion remained deeply involved in the entire agenda of affirmative action in favour of the Malays. The Chinese and the Indians remained dissatisfied all through, and were sidelined in the process of nation-building. There was no visible expression of the dissatisfaction, except for the one in December 2007 when the Indians under the banner of Hindu Rights Action Force (HINDRAF) staged massive demonstrations demanding, among others, equal rights to all citizens irrespective of race and origin of nationality.[76] The movement was crushed. The government took repressive measures to disperse the demonstrators and arrested most of the leaders under Internal Security Act. The heavy action had natural repercussions. The minority Hindus rose against the UMNO and the coalition Barisan Nasional in the general election held on March 8, 2008 leading to a political tsunami in Malaysian politics.[77] The BN suffered heavily. Its two-thirds strength in the national parliament was brought down to a mere simple majority. Being alarmed at the political fallout of the HINDRAF agitation, the Malaysian government banned the organization on October 15, 2008.[78]

The NEP officially came to an end in 1990. But the unofficial stand of the Malaysian government is to continue it indefinitely. In 2005 some of the leading members of the UMNO expressed opinion in favour of official restoration of the policy as a part of the New National Agenda. However, some others in the opposition run states wanted to put an end to it. For example the Chief Minister of Penang, Lim Guan Eng announced on the eve of the March elections that his government would do away with the NEP soon.[79]

Mahathir era and the process of Islamization

Mahathir Mohamad, who ruled for 22 years (1981-2003), the longest serving Prime Minister of Malaysia, is undoubtedly one of the most fascinating personalities in Southeast Asia.[80] His era was marked by a series of historic events and developments such as the spectacular economic resurgence of Malaysia, consolidation of the gains of the NEP, political stability and also his highhanded political decisions, including the sacking of and then putting up for trial his deputy Anwar Ibrahim. He became the Prime Minister in 1981 at the end of the regime of Tun Hussein Onn, which was the briefest of Malaysia's Prime Ministers'. Mahathir's ascendancy to the pivotal position was a welcome development in view of the fact the Onn, though a gentleman, became infamous for his repressive rule, legalistic approach to governance at the cost of human considerations, erosion of fundamental liberties, split in the UMNO and sluggish economic development.[81] A 'young' man of 56 years and with experience in handling various matters of governance under Onn, Mahathir's ascendancy to the highest political office was a welcome development. At the end of his 22-year career as the Prime Minister of the Malaysia, he left behind a huge legacy as an authoritarian, benevolent, visionary and hardworking leader, having thorough and single-minded commitment to the advancement of the Malay people. He tried to make full use of the NEP and the constitutional provisions to further the interests of the Malays. At the same time he was critical of the Malay nature and was aware of the negative impact of the NEP. On August 30, 2000, on the occasion of the 30 anniversary of the NEP, he made the strongest ever criticism of the Malays' 'lazy' character and lamented that he had overstepped his limits in pursuing the affirmative action in favour of the Malays. He said:

> We have, as a result, people who are rather laid-back and not willing to make efforts...I am sad that I will leave without succeeding to change the culture of the Malays. For the Malays, working hard is a good value but in reality

> they do not. It is not because they can't but they don't want to.[82]

He felt that the despite the discrimination, the Chinese minorities proved that hard work did pay. He was disillusioned when a section of the Malays, who enjoyed the benefit of the constitutional arrangement for the affirmative action and the special treatment advanced by the NEP, extended support to the PAS in 1999 elections. He realized that any unqualified support, devoid of meritocracy, to the Malay would not do good to the country, and therefore, advocated in favour of transforming the coalition Barisan Nasional into an all-inclusive political party in which the Chinese, the Indians and the Malays would have equal rights and partnership. This would eventually lead to the transformation of the political scenario into an epitome of Bangsa Malaysia (Malaysian nation) by 2020, when Malaysia would be a "fully developed" country. The outline of the concept of Bangsa Malaysia, which is a part of his "Wawasan 2020" (Vision 2020), ironically synchronizes the ideas of Tunku Abdul Rahman who was in favour of providing an equal opportunity to all ethnic communities which Mahathir himself had opposed so much on the ground that such a position would push the Malays back to sidelines. It could be equated with the earlier broad concept of egalitarian 'Malaysian in Malaysia' in which all the ethnic communities would have an equal share. Naturally, it meant abandoning affirmative action, an idea liked by non-Malay communities and disliked by the Malays.[83] It was a calculated move to resolve the foundational crisis that Malaysia had been facing since its Merdeka in 1957.

Mahathir's moves at the fag end of his 22 year rule were too late to yield any substantive results. He had already overdone to out-Islam the PAS. As he took over as country's Prime Minister, he found the early resurgence of Islamic ideals and groups. The roots of the resurgence could be found in the sentiment to impose Islam in people's private and public lives in order to make Muslims devout and good Malays. What worried Mahathir was the Islamic resurgence that engulfed the youth who believed that the problematic issues of Malay language, Malay poverty and corruption could be resolved within the framework of Islamic ideals and teachings. He was worried to find that the youth in the University Malay started imposing the headscarf on the girl students. They insisted on *halal* food, on not only what could be eaten but also on how the food was prepared. They encouraged the segregation of sexes in the social life of the country. And most alarmingly to Mahathir, the new resurgence groups became involved in the Dakwah movement and moved closer to the PAS. Although there was no single and noticeable impact of the activities of these groups on the social life of the nation, a tendency towards an idea of enforcing Sharia laws emerged.[84] The groups involved in the resurgence were Jaamat Tabligh (known as Tabligh or Tabliq) having international base in New Delhi, Darul Arqam set up by Ustaz Ashaari Mohammad and Islamic Republic Group (IRG), which was an offshoot of the ABIM (Angkatan Belia Islam Malaysia – Malaysian Islamic Youth Movement).

Mahathir, a well-known medical practitioner before he joined active politics, is a liberal, modern and visionary leader, who, as a politician could distinguish between religion and politics. He is a religious person but neither a theologian nor a believer of political Islam. As a successful politician he was aware of what is politically and administratively feasible and workable, and also good for his emergent nation. He was an ambitious person, as all political personalities are, and therefore, to be in power for a considerable period of time was his preferred preoccupation. At the same time, as a visionary he was determined to build up a modern and economically developed Malaysia, which would be able to earn a credibly respectable place in the community of nations. He was aware that a steadfast pursuit on this would also create a solid and enduring legacy for his rule. He needed to prepare strategies to outwit and outsmart the PAS, which posed a formidable threat to his popularity and support base.[85] New institutions focusing the national commitment to Islam and its symbols emerged to prove that he was a better Muslim leader than those in the PAS leadership. In this process, The Islamic Bank and the International Islamic University Malaysia (IIUM) came into being. He co-opted Anwar Ibrahim, a young and charismatic leader of the ABIM into the UMNO to weaken the growing influence of the PAS on the youths of Malaysia. These steps were striking against the backdrop of already initiated steps taken by his predecessors, such as, international Qur'an recitation competition, assistance to Muslims going to the Hajj pilgrimage, establishment of Pusat Islam in 1980 to counter the dakwah movement. The message conveyed to the common Malay through these steps, establishment of the Islamic Bank and the IIUM, and the induction of the Anwar Ibrahim, was that the Federal Government headed by Mahathir Mahamad was making all-out efforts to strengthen the Islamic component of the Malaysian state. The concept of Islamic Bank was to make a paradigm shift of bank interest to bank profit to the customers, mostly the rural ones, who were unhappy with the concept of interest, and therefore, it gained massive popular support.

The IIUM is more or less a replica of the world famous Egyptian Al Azhar University, where many Malaysian nationals studied. The University received added value as the Organization of Islamic Conference became the co-sponsor. The composition of the students and the teachers of the University were international, and religion was not the only criteria for admission of students and appointment of faculty members. The establishment of the IIUM silenced the PAS leadership who had been crying for such a large institution of Islamic nature. The IIUM today is not a theocratic institution, as it is has all branches of knowledge. At any rate, these two steps along with the induction of Anwar Ibrahim into the UMNO and then into the Federal Ministry suited well in Mahathir's strategy to make resurgence of Islam visible.[86] As days passed, Mahathir became an extremely popular leader, a Datuk, a symbol of national aspiration for development of the Malays and the country.

Three new institutions emerged as a part of projecting the Islamic face of Malaysia. The Islamic Economic Foundation emerged as a restructured institution to collect contributions from Islamic sources, such as, the Tabung Hajji, which had been functioning to help needy persons to undertake Hajj pilgrimage. The Institute of Policy Development was founded in 1985 to carry out human development programmes for young student leaders, public servants and junior managers. The third, Institut Kefahaman Islam Malaysia (IKIM, Institute of Islamic Understanding Malaysia) was set up in 1992 with the dual objective of streamlining the challenge of the Islamic resurgence on the line of state-defined boundaries and to provide a plank for a meaningful dialogue with the non-Muslims in and outside Malaysia. The intention was to project to the rest of the world the Malaysian progressive interpretation of Islam and to cultivate friendly relations with the non-Muslim world. And finally, another institution, 'Islamic Hospital' came up in 1999 with the concept of segregation of male and female patients and doctors to project a complete image of Islamic nature of the hospital.

Mahathir's move to out-Islam PAS had economic dimensions also. His 'Vision 2020' (Wawasan 2020) was intended to give the country a giant leap forward in the economic front. Mahathir announced this on February 28, 1991 at the inaugural session of the Malaysian Business Council. It appeared as The Second Outline Perspective Plan (1991-2000), which attempted a review of the achievement of the First Outline Perspective Plan and the NEP. It was an iconography of Mahathir's power and vision to achieve growth, wealth creation, knowledge capital and nation building on an unprecedented scale. It was designed to attain economic maturity and a status of NIC (Newly Industrialized Country).[87] Along with the conceptual framework for a massive economic growth, the Vision contained another concept of attaining

'Bangsa Malaysia' (Malaysian Nation) by 2020, which goes beyond the boundaries of economic development, with the ultimate goal of expediting communal partnership and inclusive Malaysian nationalism. The concept was carved within a catchy phrase of 'Malaysia boleh' (Malaysia can), a precise expression of the ambitious imagination of the Malay people. By 2020 Malaysia would be a "fully developed" country, with an accelerating driving force of industrialization leading to a just and egalitarian nation, in which "a full and fair partnership" towards "a sense of a common and shared destiny" could be possible.[88] In Mahathir's vision, a multi-cultural, multi-religious and fully developed Malaysia in 2020 would make the PAS's concept of an Islamic state irrelevant and redundant. To him what was more important was to promote Islamic values in the society, where the demographic essence was Islam, to make Muslims better citizens and human beings.[89] Once Bangsa Malaysia became a reality, there would be no need to continue the affirmative action in favour of the Malays, and the concept of 'social contract' would also come to an end, making Malaysia a home of all citizens irrespective of race and origin. In Bangsa Malaysia, socio-economic and political life would be based on equal partnership and shared life, the ultimate goal of a liberal and democratic Malaysia. To put in Mahathir's words:

> Bangsa Malaysia means people who are able to identify themselves with the country, speak Bahasa Malaysia and accept the Constitution. To realize the goal of Bangsa Malaysia, the people should start accepting each other as they are, regardless of race and religion.[90]

Elaborating his deep conviction that there could be no state having only one single ethnic group with the exception of Korea and Japan, he eloquently argued that cultural diversity would and should flourish and should be celebrated. He stated:

> Previously, we tried to have a single entity but it caused a lot of tension and suspicions among the people because

> they thought the Government was trying to create a hybrid.
>
> There was fear among the people that they may have to give up their own cultures, values and religions. This could not work, and we believe that the Bangsa Malaysia is the answer.

The non-Malays responded to the concept of Vision 2020 and its political component of creating Bangsa Malaysia enthusiastically. They were enthusiastic about the liberal image of Bangsa Malaysia and started celebrating the National Day in 1995 with enthusiasm and made a wide publicity of the theme Jatidiri Penggerak Wawasan (Our Self-Identity– a Vision). The MCA controlled daily *The Star* published a special supplement on August 31, 1995 containing several articles welcoming the idea of shared nationalism within the framework of Bangsa Malaysia. Nonetheless, a section of the Malays were apprehensive about it for the fear of losing their special status and privileges as guaranteed by the Federal Constitution.[91] Mahathir was clear in mind. He said:

> You cannot say things are going well when everyone is unhappy with his lot. You cannot give everyone everything they ask for. You can only give a portion of what they ask for. If you find that a section of the people is extremely happy with their lot, you can be sure that you have been unfair. It is very important in a multi-racial country not to be seen to be favouring one race over another – you have to compromise.[92]

A section of Malays expressed their displeasure during the time of the 1999 elections when a sizeable section shifted their allegiance either to the PAS or to the Parti Keadilan, the breakaway group of UMNO led by Anwar Ibrahim.[93] However, the Barisan Nasional retained its hold in the parliament by winning 55 per cent of votes and repeated its success on a much bigger scale in 2004 to prove that the Bangsa Malaysia, an inclusive conceptual framework for nation-building, remained valid all through, despite occasional hiccups.

One can see a striking difference between the young, fresh in politics and vibrant Mahathir and the astute and sagacious Mahathir as the Prime Minister, who assumed the uphill task of transforming agricultural Malaysia into a modern manufacturing and export oriented country. He grew as a strong exclusive advocate of Malay rights and privileges over the immigrants. His book *The Malay Dilemma* contains the compelling argument in favour of granting privileges to the Malay community.[94] He confronted Prime Minister Tunku Abdul Rahman on the issue of Malays' special privileges, for which he was eventually expelled from the UMNO in 1969.[95] Spearheading the campaign in favour of the Malays' special rights and privileges in order to uplift the community from economic backwardness and bringing them to the level of non-Malays through legal and constitutional means, earned for him a reputation as a nationalist Malay. Mahathir concentrated on ethnic issues and sidelined the religious dynamics of his community. To him it was a question of ethnicity and poverty. As he wrote:

> The Malay dilemma is whether they should be proud of the poor citizens of a prosperous country or whether they should try to get at some of the riches that this country boasts of, even if it blurs the economic picture of Malaysia a little.[96]

Mahathir did not mix up the issue of the economic development of the Malay people with religion; perhaps, he thought it to be a pointless exercise to bring Islam in his discourse on Malays' rights and privileges. His strategy to bring in religion was a part of his game plan to corner the PAS. It is obvious that Mahathir's development agenda was essentially based on the ethnic foundation of Malaysia and against the backdrop of economic prosperity of the non-Malays, particularly of the Chinese. Mahathir has established a long and enduring legacy to facilitate harmonious existence of ethnicity and religion without leaving scope for a monolithic society. It will be a difficult task for the PAS or any other organization including the UNMO to dismantle the foundation of the multicultural state of Malaysia.[97]

Malaysia and the Islamic world

As in the case of domestic politics, Islamic identity is an important character of Malaysia's external behaviour. The successive Malaysian governments presented its Islamic image to the Muslim world, making Islam as an imperative in the foreign policy of the country.[98]

As the Prime Minister of a Muslim majority country, Mahathir was steadfast in his mission to present the moderate Islamic face of Malaysia before the community of nations. Malaysia is a member of the Commonwealth of Nations and also a supporter of the Non-aligned movement, besides of course, being an active member of the United Nations. It was also a non-permanent member of the UN Security Council for the period 1989-1990. This was the time when the UMNO-PAS conflict was at its height, when the ruling UMNO tried to project its Islamic identity domestically and internationally. The first Gulf War took place at that time, in the wake of Iraq's invasion and occupation of Kuwait in August 1990. Malaysia supported the UN Resolution 678, but at the same time, decided not to send any force to join the multi-national forces engaged to expel Iraq from Kuwait. Malaysia took a carefully drawn stand against aggression committed by a large power on a small neighbour, and at the same time was cautious about the far-reaching consequences of the US and West led invasion of Iraq, an action which might promote the western and the Israeli interests in the region.[99] There was a domestic compulsion in Malaysia to be cautious, as the people had all along been supporting the Palestinian right to exist in their land. The PAS criticized the official position in the Gulf crisis saying that Malaysia surrendered its freedom of action in international affairs by taking a pro-US stand, which would finally benefit Israel.

Palestine remains an overwhelmingly important issue in Malaysia's foreign policy. It supported the peace deal reached between Arafat and Rabin in 1993 but at the same time it would consider sufficiently significant steps to make the peace arrangement permanent. Malaysia has been maintaining a distance from the HAMAS to prove that it does not support any form of extremism; but it is also thoroughly against Zionism. The anti-Zionism sentiment was quite visible when the Government of Malaysia, following an identical move in the Middle East, banned in March 1994 Stephen Spielberg's movie *Schindler's List*, an award winning presentation of horrific experiences of the anti-Semitic Holocaust. The Malaysian Board of Film Censor slapped the ban on the ground that the film depicted "the privileges and virtues of a certain race only" which could be construed as a propaganda material with the objectives of asking sympathy as well as to tarnish the other race".[100] The common Malays, the academia, the political leadership in Malaysia have been always with the Palestinians and their cause for a homeland.[101] No government and no party in a Muslim majority country can think of abandoning the people of Palestine. The print media has given full coverage of the recent Israeli attack on Gaza strip in order to destroy the HAMAS and the widespread condemnation of the massive Israeli attack on civilian population.

It is expected to be quite natural for Malaysia, being a Muslim majority country, to respond and react to any critical issue that adversely affects the community, *ummah*. The issue of Bosnia and the reports of atrocities committed on the Muslim population including the policy of "ethnic cleansing" by Serbian nationalists forced the Government to be vocal in condemning the inaction of the international community in stopping the carnage. It lobbied seriously in different international forums such as, the United Nations, the Organization of African Countries, the Commonwealth of Nations and the Non-aligned Movement to put to an end to the crisis.[102] Besides, the Malaysian force joined the UN Protection Force, along with Bangladesh, Iran, Palestine, Pakistan and Turkey, to protect the Muslims in Bosnia-

Herzegovina. It is important to note that the official interpretation of Malaysian the deployment of Malaysian troops under the banner of the UN Force had a religious colour. The proposal of the Ministry of Defence to seek fatwa from the National Islamic Council on the status of Malaysian soldiers in Bosnia-Herzegovina as participants in jihad testifies to the religious overtones. The proposal did not materialize owing to strong Russian insistence that the Muslim countries participating in the UN peace-keeping efforts must adhere to UN mandate and not to be guided by any notion of religious sentiment in tone and content. The religious sentiment in the country grew as the UMNO organized a massive rally on May 6, 1994 in Kuala Lumpur in which Deputy Prime Minister Anwar Ibrahim announced the commitment of the Government to the cause of the Muslims anywhere in the world.[103] Following this, non-governmental organizations joined together to create the Barisan Bertindak Bosnia (BBB – Bosnia Action Front) to mould international opinion and generate pressure to find a solution to the conflict.

Malaysia's pronounced Islamic character is not the only decisive imperative in the foreign policy process of the country. The Muslim identity is only a part of its foreign policy determinants. The overall foreign policy of Malaysia is to promote friendly relations with all countries in the world. Mahathir's "Look East Policy" was essentially guided by economic considerations; so was also the involvement in the East Asian Economic Grouping and East Asian Economic Caucus, besides of course, the Association of South East Asian Nations. In the pursuit of promoting national interests in the community of nations, the successive governments of Malaysia have not blindly followed an entirely Islam-centric foreign policy. Malaysia's most prominent trading partners are non-Muslim countries. It does not look forward to oil rich Arab countries for its economic development. It has enough resources to be independent of any foreign pressure. It appears that diplomacy, which serves the country's interests in international arena, is different from religious identity, which has a limited objective and limited appeal. Therefore, Malaysia's Islamic identity in the community of nation serves limited purpose only.

The Islamic resurgence

Malaysia experienced Islamic resurgence at institutional level with the emergence of a number of Islamic bodies and organizations and also the dakwah movement spearheaded by young urban students.[104] The scenario was almost parallel to the one Indonesia had witnessed in the 1970s. The PAS was the forerunner of the resurgence. Its formation by the breakaway religious hardliners in the UMNO in 1951, as already discussed, was a manifestation of aggressive Islamic agenda of those who wanted Malaysia to be transformed into an Islamic state, which the UMNO did not approve. Although the vague nebulous concept of Islam as "the best" religion and its encompassing coverage in all aspects of social and cultural life was the motive factor in the formation of the PAS, the urge to put a political challenge and to share power was undoubtedly the most palpable driving force in its formation. In this section a brief note on other Islamic bodies has been presented to make the point that the issue of religion has remained a cornerstone of several organizations in Malaysia.[105] The Dakwah was a middle class Malay movement in the wake of the NEP so as to facilitate the ethnic Malays to be conscious of their majority, constitutional safeguards and affirmative action, and at the same time their religious identity offered a rallying point. After three decades of the dakwah movement, it is viewed as a fervently religious movement, which is now declining, and some consider it to be a social movement of the emergent ethnic Malay middle class, which wanted a preeminent socio-political space in Malaysia.[106] It needs to be noted that Malaysia stands nowhere when compared with Indonesia's two large mass based Muslim organizations – Nahdlatul Ulama and Muhammadiyah – which have not, as discussed in the preceding Chapter, indulged in intolerant and aggressive agenda towards Islamization in that country. In the case of Malaysia, three categories of Islamic resurgence movements could be found, (i) the dakwah movement which included the Jamaat Tabligh and the Darul Arqam, (ii) Islamic youth activist organizations that try to reach out to university and college students, the most prominent and visible one being the ABIM, and (iii) the PAS as a political party with a rural base which is in power in two states of Kelantan and Terengganu.

Jamaat Tabligh

Jamaat Tabligh is a part of the dakwah movement. The literal meaning of the term is council (Jamaat) for communication for a message or revelation. It is a transnational movement for the peaceful propagation of Islam and its ideals among the believers. Set up in Delhi in 1927 by Maulana Muhammad Ilyas, the Tablighi movement has acquired an international character and its presence could be found all over the world. Tabligh movement found a place among the Indian Muslims in Malaysia in the 1950s and eventually spread all over Malaysia. It became popular among the Malay community in rural and urban areas, because of its simple and inoffensive appeal and approach to the youth. Eventually, the highly educated and the professionals became associated with the movement. It is believed that the movement could be popular because of its apolitical character; that is why, the Government of Malaysia has been comfortable with this organization. The principal objective of the Jamaat Tabligh is to encourage the community to behave in a way that was vogue in the seventh century Arabia of the Prophet's time. It was a part of the campaign towards the attainment of Muslim consciousness, and at the same time to affect return to purity and piety on the line of Islamic tradition that included dress codes for both men and women and acceptance of *halal* food.[107] The campaign attracted the attention of various sections of the Malay society, particularly the student community, which believed that strict adherence to the teachings of the Tabligh would remove all social ills so that peace and happiness would prevail.[108] The campaign concentrated more on Islam and the Islamic way of life and had the least to do with ethnic dimensions of the society. Thus, the issue of Malays comes incidentally, as all Malays are Muslims.

Darul Arqam

Darul Arqam (Abode of Arqam) was founded in 1968 by a group of 12 Muslims headed by Ustaz (Teacher) Ashaari Muhammad, a strong critic of the Islamic movements in Malaysia, who argued that the existing Muslim organizations had engaged in useless and wasteful exercises, such as, shouting slogans, organizing seminars and discussions, propagating philosophical concepts of Islam and participating in electoral politic. It believed in armed struggle to establish an Islamic state. The organization was named after Arqam, one of the companions of the Prophet's flight from Mecca to Medina. It started to grow prominently in 1972, and in six years became a formidable militant Islamic organization having a strong anti-establishment bias. This was the period when the PAS was a coalition partner of the Barisan Nasional. It is believed that the decision of the PAS to join the Barisan Nasional disillusioned many protagonists of Islam, who found Darul Arqam as the only alternative to pursue their Islamic agenda, more particularly, in enforcing dress code, five-times daily prayer and acceptance of *halal* food. Moving a step further, the Darul Arqam established their own health clinic and medical centers to enable the female patients to be treated by female doctors and to take *halal* medicines only. It launched severe criticism of the ABIM and the PAS branding them as weak organizations devoid of any tangible capacity of transforming Malaysia into an Islamic state. They were considered un-Islamic organizations for taking up the Malay nationalist causes. To the leaders of the Darul Arqam, there is no place of ethnic cause and consideration in the Islamic world, which is atomized and cannot be fragmented on the basis of ethnicity. The criticism against the Malay Muslim organizations was based on a line of attack as adopted by other Islamic organizations elsewhere, such as, Jamaat-i-Islami of Pakistan and Ikhwanul Muslimin of Egypt, for their failure to emulate the Prophet. It was also critical of the Iranian revolution in 1979, for, it was considered as a Shia movement, which represents a small faction of the Islamic world.[109]

Initially Mahathir Mohamad, after becoming the Prime Minister in 1981, found values in the Darul Arqam for its stand against the ABIM and the PAS. That gave the organization a sense of recognition and legitimacy. Its popularity grew in a substantial manner among the youth who were disillusioned at the rise of superficial materialism that they alleged to have posed a threat to the puritan version of Islam. Eventually, it became a major threat to the political stability in the country, and more to Mahathir, which prompted the Government to ban the organization in 1994. Although banned, it operates underground and has influence among a section of the Malay society, which believes that a puritan Islam is the panacea for all social ills.

In the midst of the anti-government, anti-PAS, and anti-ABIM movement and the campaign for a puritan Islamic way of life propagated by the Darul Arqam, the Memali incident took place on November 1985 in which Ibrahim Mahmood[110], better known as Ibrahim Libya and 13 of his associates were killed in an encounter with the police. Ibrahim Libya worked at a *pondok* (religious school) in Memali, a place situated in the district of Baling, Kedah. The village shot up to prominence in 1970, when ABIM leader Anwar Ibrahim organized a demonstration here against the Government for its failure to handle food crisis in the district. Ibrahim Libya came to be identified as the key figure in the cult-oriented Al Arqam, a radical wing of the PAS which had been campaigning for jihad against the non-Muslims and also the government.[111] The government took strong views on the call for jihad and martyrdom fighting against the UMNO, the Barisan Nasional and the Federal Government. There had been unsuccessful attempts to arrest him along with his followers. On that fateful day of November 19,1985 Ibrahim Libya was surrounded by 576 policemen. Then followed a gun battle for five hours in which four policemen and 14 civilians including Ibrahim Libya were killed.[112] Thus ended the armed struggle of a radical Islamic militant group. Thereafter, Malaysia remained virtually free from any Islamic radical movement. Whatever Islamic movements Malaysia had been experiencing could be treated as a part of peaceful resurgence, despite the fact some Indonesian militant leaders including Jamaah Islamiyah ideologue Abu Bakar Baasyir escaped to Malaysia following a crackdown on them by General Soeharto and remained there till 1998 when the *reformasi* era replaced the New Order regime.

Angkatan Belia Islam Malaysia (ABIM)

ABIM or the Malaysian Islamic Youth Movement, formed in 1971 by several alumni of the National Association of Malaysian Islamic Students with a broad agenda of arousing Islamic conscience among the Malay youth, was a fallout of the 1969 racial riot. The idea of having a strong youth front of the Islamic movement came from a fear of a future violence against the community. It originated on the campus of Universiti Malaya, the only university in Malaysia at that point of time. The main reason behind the establishment of the organization was to build a society based on the principles of Islam.[113] It created a strong support base with the active association of the youth studying in institutions of higher learning. Most of the leaders were studying both in secular and religious educational institutions in and outside the country. The combination served two purposes – one, in exerting and expanding influence among a cross section of the youth, and the other, to build up a broad and intellectual image of the organization. The ABIM drew inspiration from the writings of Indian-born Pakistani ideologue and leader of Jamaat-i-Islami, Sayyid Abul A'la Mawdudi and the activities of the Egyptian Ikhwanul-Muslimin (Muslim Brotherhood). Naturally, one could understand the actual image of an Islamic hardliner organization, which advocated transforming Malaysia into an Islamic state, enactment and enforcement of Sharia Laws, proclaimed that secularism and nationalism were un-Islamic concepts. It established a close relationship with the PAS. Its political agenda included amendment of the Federal Constitution of Malaysia to declare Malaysia an Islamic state, enforcement interest free banking system and replacement existing taxation system by *zakat*. It believed in the preponderance of Islam over Malay race, and therefore, criticized the UMNO for diluting the Islamic identity with Malay nationalism. The ABIM became a prominent organization during the tenure of its leader Anwar Ibrahim (1974-1982) as its president. It started losing its importance after he left it in 1982 to join the UMNO and eventually to rise to the position of Deputy Prime Minister.

The ABIM is definitely more moderate than Darul Arqam. Despite its links with the PAS there has been a degree of tension between them, as ABIM appears to have been critical of the functioning of the PAS governments in Kelantan and Terengganu. While PAS is basically a rural-based political organization, the ABIM is an urban-based students organization, and hence, the inherent contradictions in the relationship between the two.

A thorough analysis on the forces underpinning Islamic resurgence clearly indicates that the centrality of movements around the issue of making Malaysia more Islamic has been ethnicity. The UMNO's Islamic agenda has always been Malay-centric, so is the case with the PAS which has been pursuing an Islamic agenda meant for the Malay.[114] The only organization, that wanted to go beyond ethnicity, is Darul Arqam. It has been crushed. The issue of religion mixed with ethnicity has been always problematic. The contradiction of ethnicity and religion has remained unresolved in Bangladesh, as spelt out in Chapter II. It will remain so in Malaysia for a considerable period of time, without however, leading to any violent disturbances.

The Hudud controversy

As already narrated, the emergence of the PAS in 1951 out of the UMNO was the result of the uncompromising demand of the radical groups to enforce Islamic laws and transform Malaysia into an Islamic state on one hand and the UMNO's refusal to accede to it on the other. To enact and enforce the Sharia laws was one of the core agenda of the PAS. It swept the state elections in Kelantan in 1959 and then in Terengganu in 1999. Kelantan is a Malay dominated (95 per cent) state and comparatively economically backward. Its poverty ratio, 35.1%, is relatively high compared to the national average. Agriculture is the mainstay of the state economy.

In the pursuit of its Islamic agenda PAS tabled and got approved in the Kelantan state assembly the highly controversial laws called *hudud* (legal meaning is punishment) during its session of November 20-25, 1993[115]. The *hudud* laws could be divided into three categories – (i) the first concerns petty crimes and punishments that are specifically mentioned in the Qur'an and the hadith; (ii) the second category deals with crime called *qisas* and proportionate punishments, also mentioned in the Qur'an and the hadith and varies crimes such as murder; and (iii) the third is the category is called *ta'zir*, about which the scriptures are silent. It is up to the Sharia courts to decide on the nature of the crime and the type of punishment to be imposed on the wrong doers. The Kelantan Shariah Criminal Enactment II, known as *hudud*, stipulates harsh and gender bias punishments. For example:

1. Section 8 and 9 state, under the title *Hirabah* (robbery),

that a person, who is found guilty of committing robbery without harming the victim, will have his/her right or left-foot cut. If the victim is harmed the person shall be asked to pay *diyat/irsy* (compensation). If the victim is killed, the criminal will be sentenced to death.

2. Section 12, under the *zina* (adultery), stipulates that a person, who is found guilty of adultery, will be stoned to death if he/she is *mohsan* (married man/woman), or will be whipped 100 time plus one year in jail, if he/she is *ghiru mohsan* (unmarried man/ woman).

The text of the bill aroused strong indignation from all quarters with the exception of the PAS. The "Sisters in Islam" took up the gender-biased and violent nature of the bill at the level of Prime Minister Mahathir Mahamad.[116] The Federal Government took a prompt decision not to approve it, so that the so-called *hudud* laws remained as a bill only and unenforceable in the country. The Government debunked the bill and frustrated the PAS move to implement its Islamic political agenda. Mahathir appeared to be sensitive when he said:

> ...a woman who has been raped, but is unable to produce four witnesses, would not be able to have the rapist punished even if she knows who he is. If she were to have a child as a result [of the assault], she would be guilty of zina (adultery) and could be punished by being stoned to death. By no stretch of the imagination can this be considered.[117]

It is interesting to note that on the eve of a by-election in Terengganu in April 1992, being guided by the dynamics of electoral politics, Mahathir had made an equivocal and diplomatic statement that the Federal Government would not block the implementation of the *hudud* law in Kelantan if it was "really in accordance with the teachings of Islam".[118] The patent argument of the PAS and its supporters' plea are that hudud law was a part of Sharia laws and when a Muslim accepted Islam as his religion, he submitted himself to the laws stipulated in the Qur'an and the hadith. This warranted submission to Sharia laws, which are legal manifestations of the two sacred sources. Reacting to such arguments Mahathir said: "if hudud laws are not implemented, it does not necessarily mean that Muslims are no longer Muslims. If this so, then 90 per cent of Muslims world-wide would no longer be Muslims."[119] To put it precisely, hudud had remained a mere bill and gradually became a dead issue. To make it legally operative, the Federal Constitution would need amendment and for that the PAS needed the support of two-thirds majority, which the PAS is not likely to get in the near or distant future in view of the thorough opposition of the Malays and non-Malays to such a discriminatory, gender hostile and cruel proposition.

Islam Hadhari

After assuming the office of the Prime Minister of Malaysia in 2003, Abdullah Ahmad Badawi threw the concept of *Islam Hadhari* (Civilizational Islam) to the Malays to underline the priorities for steady development and cultivating a progressive forward looking approach to life.[120] In the words of Badawi:

> *Islam Hadhari* is not a new religion. It is not a new teaching nor is it a new mazhab (denomination). It is an effort to bring the *ummah* (the worldwide community comprising all adherents of the Muslim faith) back to the basics of Islam, back to the fundamentals as prescribed in the Quran and the *hadith* which form the foundations for an Islamic civilization.

Based on *ijtihad* (independent reasoning based on reference text) Islam Hadhari has been conceptualized within the framework of a 10 point principles:

1. Faith and piety in Allah;
2. A just and trustworthy government;
3. A free and independent people;
4. A vigorous pursuit and mastery of knowledge;

5. A balanced and comprehensive economic development;
6. A good quality of life;
7. The protection of the rights of minority groups and women;
8. Cultural and moral integrity;
9. The safeguarding of natural resources and the environment; and
10. Strong defence capabilities.[121]

To quote Badawi once more:

> *Islam Hadhari* is complete and comprehensive, with an emphasis on the development of the economy and civilization, capable of building Malay competitiveness. The glorious heritage of the Islamic civilisation in all its aspects must be used as a reference in order to become the source of inspiration for the Malay race to prosper.[122]

Badawi's *Islam Hadhari* denotes the communal perspective of civilization in which non-Malay and non-Muslims in Malaysia have hardly any role to play. It goes against the much-appreciated concept of Bangsa Malaysia, so eloquently enunciated by his predecessor. The exclusiveness in the concept seems to be antithetical to the broader concept of nation-building. While the Chinese have carefully avoided demonstrating a sense of unhappiness, the Tamil dominated Indian community has been apprehensive of such a concept. They are apprehensive of further marginalization of the community, a manifestation of which led to unrest in December 2007.

The recent general elections in Malaysia held on March 8, 2008 appeared to be historic in the sense that for the first time the Barisan Nasional lost its overriding preeminence in the Federal Parliament (Dewan Rakyat). It used to secure two-thirds majority in the parliament all through. In the last election of 2004, it secured 198 out of 222 seats. This

Table 4.3
Party positions in the Dewan Rakyat after the 2008 elections

Parties	*% of votes*	*No. seats*	*% of seats*	*+/-*
Barisan Nasional	50.27	140	63.1	-58
UMNO	29.33	79	35.6	-30
MCA	10.35	15	6.8	-16
MIC	2.21	3	1.4	-6
PGR	2.27	2	0.9	-8
PPB	1.62	14	6.3	+3
SUPP	1.47	6	2.7	-
SPDP	0.65	4	1.8	-
UPKO	0.72	4	1.8	-
PBS	0.55	3	1.4	-1
SAPP	0.38	2	1.4	-2
PBRS	-	1	0.5	-
LDP	0.10	1	0.5	+1
PPP	0.21	0	0	-1
Pakatan Rakyat	46.75	82	36.9	+62
PKR	18.58	31	14.0	+30
PAS	14.05	23	10.4	+16
DAP	13.77	28	12.6	+16
Others (independents	0.81	0	0	-1

Source: Malaysian Election Commission

time in March 2008, it could manage to secure the absolute majority with 140 seats conceding defeat in 58 constituencies. The Opposition three party alliance, Barisan Alternatif (now popularly known as Patakan Rakyat), comprising Anwar Ibrahim led Parti Keadilan Rakyat (People's Justice Party), the Democratic Action Party (DAP) and the PAS made an impressive show of snatching seats from the Barisan Nasional. Table 4.3 presents an idea about the party positions in the national parliament:

Table 4.4
Party-wise position in the Dewan Rakyat

States	*Seats*	*BN*	*PAS*	*DAP*	*PKR*
Perlis	3	3	0	0	0
Kedah	15	4	6	0	5
Kelantan	14	2	9	0	3
Terengganu	8	7	1	0	0
Penang	13	2	0	7	4
Perak	24	13	2	6	3
Pahang	14	12	0	0	2
Selangor	22	5	4	4	9
FT* Kuala Lumpur	11	1	1	5	4
FT Putrajaya	2	2	0	0	0
N. Sembilan	8	5	0	2	1
Melaka	6	5	0	1	0
Johor	26	25	0	1	0
FT Labuan	1	1	0	0	0
Sabah	25	24	0	1	0
Sarawak	31	30	0	1	0
Total	222	140	23	28	31

Source: *The Malay Mail,* March 10, 2008.

*FT stands for Federal Territory

The Barisan Nasional suffered its worst defeat in Kuala Lumpur. It could mange to capture only one out of 11 constituencies – 5 went to the DAP, four to the PKR and one to the PAS. There were several factors, which led to the heavy loss of the Barisan Nasional. The most prominent was that the Chinese voters deserted the MCA and the Indian voters, the MIC, whereas, the Malay favoured the PAS in several areas. The Indian community was heavily influence by the Hindraf movement; the participants of the movement suffered during their agitation for equal rights in December 2007. The UMNO's exclusiveness was another striking reason for losing 30 seats.[123] The erosion of the support base of the ruling alliance, Barisan Nasional and the increase in the gains of the Opposition was reflected in the states too (Table 4.4). In five out of 16 states (Kedah, Kelantan, Penang, Selangor and FT Kuala Lumpur) the Barisan Alternatif outperformed the ruling Barisan Nasional securing majority of the seats.

Table 4.5
Party-wise distribution of seats in state assemblies

States	*Seats*	*BN*	*PAS*	*DAP*	*PKR*	*Ind*
Perlis	15	14	1	0	0	0
Kedah	36	14	16	1	4	1
Kelantan	45	6	38	0	1	0
Terengganu	32	24	8	0	0	0
Penang	40	11	1	19	9	0
Perak	59	28	6	18	7	0
Pahang	42	37	2	2	0	1
Selangor	56	20	8	13	15	0
N. Sembilan	36	21	1	10	4	0
Melaka	28	23	0	5	0	0
Johor	56	50	2	4	0	0
Sabah	60	59	0	1	0	0
Total	505	307	84	73	40	2

Source: The Malay Mail, March 10, 2008

The erosion took place in the five states belonging to the Peninsula Malaysia. However, the two Borneo states of Sabah and Sarawak ensured the emphatic victory of the

Barisan Nasional. It is argued that the Anwar Ibrahim factor coupled with the good governance of the PAS in Kelantan and Terengganu contributed to the rise of the Opposition. The good performance by the PAS did not mean rise of Islamists; rather, the shift in the agenda of the PAS from its pronounced objective of making Malaysia an Islamic state to commitment to developing it to a welfare state attracted both urban and rural voters. Table 4.5 shows that five states went to the Opposition, a marked improvement of its performance compared to that in 2004 when only Kelantan and Terengganu states were captured by the PAS.

The results of the states elections present an identical picture of the party-wise performance in the national parliament. The result was quite shocking for the Barisan Nasional and for that matter for the UMNO. The UMNO made a quick introspection to ascertain where things went wrong. It found that the fault line was inherent in its exclusiveness. Several leaders demanded that time had come when the party needed to be inclusive to face the future challenges offered by the Opposition.[124] The inner party deliberations in the party favouring inclusiveness might eventually lead to concrete measures to embrace all citizens of Malaysia within the canopied structure of Malaysian nationalism in place of Malay nationalism.

The concept of '1 Malaysia'

Soon after Dato Seri Najib Razak took over as the Prime Minister of Malaysia on April 3, 2009, he advanced a new concept called '1 Malaysia' toward national reconstruction in his multi-cultural state. This is the third exercise towards finding a solution of problems of unification of the people of Malaysia under one acceptable category. The concept has been designed to ensure unity of the people irrespective of race, religion, language and place of origin. As already stated, at the time Mardeka in 1957, there was an attempt to articulate, circulate and finally nationally agreed upon "Malaysian Malaysia" ideology mooted by Lee Kuan Yew through the People's Action Party. The concept did not work. Ultimately, Singapore came out of Malaysia in 1965 to become a sovereign republic. The concept remained dear to some of the parties like DAP as their leaders found that such a concept would enable them to find a legitimate space in the national political life and free them from political isolation. Mahathir Mohamad, going a few steps further, propagated the concept of 'Bangsa Malaysia' as a part of his vision 2020 with the same objective of achieving national unity by associating all the communities living and enjoying rights equally in Malaysia as its citizens.

Abdullah Badawi's attempt to draw conservative Malays from the PAS and liberals from the PKR to the UMNO by advancing 'Islam Hadhari' did not work. There is hardly any evidence of inclusiveness in the concept as it addressed mainly the Muslims of Malaysia. The concept did not have a broad framework for national unity and reconstruction. Now, with his departure, it has become a forgotten chapter in Malaysian history.

As already mentioned, the elections of March 8, 2008 ushered a turning point in the political history of Malaysia. The results in the election not only challenged one party domination in the political system of Malaysia but also brought about a paradigm shift in the UMNO. The intense debate in the first post-election general meeting of the UMNO held in April 2008, the idea of inclusiveness was strongly mooted and favoured. The announcement of the new Prime Minister in favour of what is called '1 Malaysia' is the result of such an ongoing discourse on an inclusive framework for national reconstruction.

The critics argue that the new Prime Minister did not have anything new to offer in the concept, as he borrowed the idea of '1 Malaysia' from Anwar Ibrahim, who has made multi-ethnic harmony the cornerstone of his opposition platform. Others say that the Prime Minister's concept is entirely new and is a testimony of his political sagacity.

Still more would like to say that the newness in the concept has been carved to avoid a repetition of what happened with Abdullah's promotion of Islam Hadhari, addressed to the Malay Muslims only, sidelining the other segments of Malaysian society.

What is '1 Malaysia'?

The concept of '1 Malaysia' is a renewed attempt at achieving national unity and reconstruction of the population of a comparatively new nation. Malaysia has a complex ethnic configuration in which three important races manage to have compartmentalized identity formations, and at the same time play a constructive role in the nation-building process. The leading race based parties, such as, the UMNO for the Malays, the MCA for the Chinese and the MIC for the Indians (basically the Tamil speaking population) so far have been working together under an umbrella organization, the Barisan Nasional. There is a growing realization that such a working relationship among race based parties is not enough and such an arrangement has not proved to be helpful towards achieving national solidarity and unity. This is clearly reflected in the advocacy of Anwar Ibrahim who stands for an inclusive political paradigm. Prime Minister Razak's concept of '1 Malaysia' is greatly influenced by the experience of the country for five decades of independence.

The concept of '1 Malaysia' talks centres around 8 values. They are: loyalty, humility, meritocracy, integrity, acceptance, education, perseverance, and culture of excellence.

To put these virtues in a crisp and concise narration using Najib's own words:

(1) **Loyalty** is important but it must not be blind loyalty. It should be tied with loyalty to voters, honesty, corruption-free and trustworthy political environment.

(2) **Humility** is related to showing mutual respect for one another. It is an imperative that requires **understanding**

among the multiracial communities of Malaysia. To understand one another, one needs to learn through continuous interface and open dialogues.

(3) **Meritocracy** is an important principle which needs to be adhered to and can beachieved once racial quotas are removed completely in every sector. Race is not a criterion for merit. The country will have a desired pace of development only when the principle of the best of the best is followed. Those who do not come up to the standard, they have no option but to improve themselves.

(4) **Integrity** is possible when corruption is rooted out. Integrity cannot be achieved in the presence and prevalence of unchecked corruption. Therefore, corruption has to be controlled, if not totally eliminated. Then only one could talk of integrity.

(5) **Acceptance** is a value which can be achieved through understanding and awareness. People should be willing to talk and also be allowed to talk to attain this. At the same time, the government should be able to accept the wishes of its people.

(6) It is possible to impart **education** to the people, but the educator should be of good quality and the contents of the subject should be proper. Education itself should not be politicized. It should an apolitical enterprise.

(7) **Perseverance** is possible if the people are willing to compete to be the best. So long as special treatment [through affirmative arrangement] exists, it is difficult to expect competition from the beneficiaries, and desired performance or genuine accomplishment in any walk of life is remotely possible.

(8) To achieve a **culture of excellence**, the people as a whole must adhere to the above stated 7 values.

The Prime Minister integrated the concept of '1 Malaysia' within a framework comprising three core elements. These are:

- Mutual acceptance amongst the races and peoples of Malaysia
- Nationalism based on principles of the Federal Constitution and the Rukunegara
- Social justice.

One finds some degree of similarity between these principles of '1 Malaysia' and Dr Sun Yat Sen's Three Principles of the People (Mínzú (nationalism), Mínquán (politics and governance) and Mínshing (social welfare or justice)), also known as the San-Min doctrine.

It is argued that '1 Malaysia' is possible when there is a national consensus among the people to build up the country on the basis of equality among all irrespective of races, showing due respect for healthy competition and giving due credence to the principle of meritocracy. But there are certain inherent weaknesses in the concept which are quite problematic. These are as follows:

1. The existence of the constitutionally guaranteed affirmative action will stand on the way of implementation of the concept of '1 Malaysia'.
2. It appears to be an uphill task to arrive at a national consensus to do away with the provisions of the Article 153.
3. The Malay political parties are less likely to accept the matrix of the concept.
4. There is no blueprint to achieve what is conceptualized as '1 Malaysia'.

The efficacy of the concept of '1 Malaysia' has been raised in the public domain. It is a new concept and is yet to revoke thorough and rigorous debate. Whatever have appeared in the print media are passionate arguments for or against the concept. While the supporters concentrate their arguments centering around the much quoted appeal 'Malaysia Boleh', the other view suggests that so long as the constitutional arrangement favouring affirmative action exists and race-based divisive and exclusive politics continue, the concept of '1 Malaysia' will remain in the domain of public debate and discourse only.

The advancement of a new concept towards achieving national reconstruction is a clear indication that Malaysia is still in the process of nation-building and national reconstruction in which the interplay of Malay ethnicity and Islam has not gained consolidation. The exclusiveness of Malay nationalism compounded by constitutional sanctity and affirmative action will remain problematic and generate foundational crises from time to time, even if one ignores the occasional controversies created by the overzealous Islamists to stand for Islam only with utter disregard of Malay ethnicity.

NOTES & REFERENCES

1. For other statistical details see *Buku Tahunan Perangkaan Malaysia* (Yearbook of Statistics Malaysia (Kuala Lumpur: Jabatan Perangkaan Malaysia, November 2005). The recent estimates put the population to be 27.2 million. See *Economist Intelligence Unit,* Country Profile 2007: Malaysia.
2. For some basic information see *Information Malaysia*: 2005 (Kuala Lumpur: Berita Publishing, 2005). For a brief and pointed discussion on the geographic and demographic profile in historical perspective see Barbara Watson Andaya and Leonard Y. Andaya, *A History of Malaysia* (Houndmills, Palgrave, 2001), Chapter 1.
3. For some details about the original people of Malaysia including the orang asli see Robert Knox Dentan *et al. Malaysia and the Original People': A Case Study of Development on Indigenous Peoples* (Boston: Allyn and Bacon, 1997).
4. A comparative profile of economic performance of Bangladesh, Indonesia and Malaysia has been presented in the Chapter V.
5. *The Economist Intelligence Unit,* Country Profile, Malaysia 2010.
6. Virginia Matheson Hooker, *A Short History of Malaysi: Linking*

East and West (Australia: Allen & Unwin, 2003), p. 3.

7. There are major works on early history of Malaysia some of which are David E. Marr and A.C. Milner (eds), *Southeast Asia in the 9th and 14th Centuries* (Singapore: ISEAS, 1985), A.R. Wallace, *The Malay Archipelago*, first published in 1869 (London: Oxford University Press, 1989) and Zainal Abidin A. Wahid (ed), *Glimpses of Malaysian History* (Kuala Lumpur: Dewan Bahasa Dan Pustak, 1970).

8. Several factors including the military expeditions of the Chola kings against the empire led to the fall of Srivijaya. For details see O.W. Wolters, *The Fall of Srivijaya in Malay History* (Kuala Lumpur: Oxford University Press, 1970).

9. Barbara Watson Andaya and Leonard Y. Andaya, *A History of Malaysia*, n. 2, p. 54.

10. For an interesting account on Sufism and its role in spreading Islam in Malaysia see Sayyid Naguib Al-Attas, *Some Aspects of Sufism as Understood and Practiced among the Malays* (Singapore, no press, 1963).

11. Melaka received visitors and traders from Arab, China and India. The visitors were Hindus, Muslims, Christians, tribal animist. Many of them settled down permanently making the city "a pluralistic meeting-point-of the peoples from all over maritime Asia." See Anthony Reid, *Southeast Asian the Age of Commerce, 1450-1680*, Vol. 2, *Expansion and Crisis* (New Haven: Yale University Press, 1993), p. 66 and Luis Filipe Ferreira Reis Thomaz, "The Malay Sultanate of Melaka" in Anthony Reid (ed), *Southeast Asia in the Early Modern Era: Trade, Power, and Belief* (Ithaca: Cornell University Press, 1993), pp. 69-90.

12. For a fascinating account of Melaka in historical perspective see K.S. Sandhu and Paul Weatley (eds), *Melaka: The Transformation of a Malay Capital*, 1400-1980, Vol. I and II (Singapore: ISEAS, 1983).

13. For the details on the process of Islamization in the region see S.Q Fatimi, *Islam Comes to Malaysia* (Singapore: Malay Publishing House, 1963), D.G.E. Hall, *A History of Southeast Asia* (New York: Macmillan, 1966), Chapter 1-4, Hussin Mutalib, *Islam in Southeast Asia* (Singapore: ISEAS, 2008).

14. C. D. Cowan and O.W. Wolters, *Nineteenth Century Malay:*

Origins of British Political Control (London: Oxford University Press, 1961).

15. For some details on Malay see Richard V. Weekes, *Muslim Peoples: A World of Ethnographic Survey* (London: Greenwood Press, 1978), pp. 253-256; N.J. Ryan, *The Cultural Background of the Peoples of Malaysia* (Kuala Lumpur: Longman, 1962); Richard Winstedt, *The Malays: A Cultural History* (London: Routledge and Kegan Paul, 1953) and also Fay-Cooper Cole, *The Peoples of Malaysia* (Princeton, N.J.: Van Nostrand, 1945).

16. James T. Collins, *Malay, World Language: A Short History* (Kuala Lumpur: Dewan Bahasa dan Pustak, 1996), p. 23.

17. For an in-depth analysis see M.B. Hooker, *Islamic Law in Southeast Asia* (Singapore; Oxford University Press, 1984) p. 130.

18. A large number of academic works could be found on anti-British resistance in Malay Peninsula. Some of such work are, Rupert Emerson, *Malaysia: A Study in Direct and Indirect Rule* (New York: Macmillan, 1937), C.N Perkinson, *British Intervention in the Malay States 1867-77* (Kuala Lumpur: Oxford University Press, 1960), D.G.E. Hall, *A History of Southeast Asia* (New York: Macmillan, 1966), Chai Hon Chan, *The Development of British Malaysia* (Kuala Lumpur: Oxford University Press, 1967), Emila Sadka, *The Protected Malay States 1874-1895* (Kuala Lumpur, University Press, 1968).

19. Susan E. Ackerman and Raymond L.M. Lee, *Heaven in Transition: Non-Muslim Religious Innovations and Ethnic Identity in Malaysia* (Honolulu: University of Hawaii Press, 1988), p. 30.

20. *ibid*, p. 175.

21. Anthony Milner, *The Invention of Politics in Colonial Malaya: Contesting Nationalism and the Expansion of the Public Sphere* (Cambridge: Cambridge University Press, 1995).

22. William R. Roff, *The Origins of Malay Nationalism* (Kuala Lumpur: Oxford University Press, 1967) p. 111.

23. For an in-depth analysis on the immigration of the Chinese see Khoo Kay Kim (ed), *The History of Southeast, South and East Asia* (Kuala Lumpur: Oxford University Press, 1977), pp. 78-94 and his "Malaysian Immigration", *JMBRAS*, Vol. LXXI, No. 1, 1998 pp. 1-26. and for Indian immigration see Selvakumaran

Ramachandran, *Indian Plantation Labour in Malaysia* (Kuala Lumpur, S. Abdul Majid & Co, 1994).

24. The Chinese (mostly Buddhist and Christians) were concentrated in the urban areas, the Indians (mostly Hindus) in rubber plantation areas and the Malay (mostly Muslims) in the rural areas. Kamarulnizam Abdullah, *The Politics of Islam in Contemporary Malaysia* (Bangi: Penerbit Universiti Kebangsaan Malaysia, 2003), p. 39.

25. The segregation policy benefited the Chinese, known as 'entrepreneurial minority', most, which eventually germinated the seeds of racial hatred that culminated in the 1969 anti-Chinese riot. For some details of the segregation policy and its impact see Christine Dobbin, *Asian Entrepreneurial Minorities: Conjoint Communities in the Making of World Economy*, 157-1940 (Richmond, England: Curzon, 1996) and Robert W. Hefner, "Society and Morality in the New Asian Capitalisms" in Robert W. Hefner (ed), *Market Cultures; Society and Morality in the New Asian Capitalisms* (Boulder: Westview, 1998),

26. For a discussion on British contribution to the creation of a plural society in a otherwise homogenous pre-colonial Malay land see J.S. Furnivall, *Colonial Policy and Practice* (New York: New York University Press, 1956).

27. Abdul Rahman Embong has been writing extensively on this issue, see some of his writing "The Culture and Practice of Pluralism in Postcolonial Malaysia" in Robert W Hefner (ed) *The Politics of Multiculturalism: Pluralism and Citizenship in Malaysia, Singapore and Indonesia* (Honolulu; University of Hawai'i Press, 2001) pp. 59-85."Islam and Democracy in Malaysia" in Zoya Hasan (ed), *Democracy in Muslim Societies: The Asian Experience* (New Delhi: Sage, 2007), pp.128-176.

28. The fall of Singapore and Japanese occupation of Malay territories is well documented in Paul H. Kratoska, *The Japanese Occupation of Malaya: A Social and Economic History* (London: Hurst and Co., 1998).

29. Barbara Watson Andaya and Leonard Y. Andaya, *A History of Malaysia*, n 1, Chapter 7.

30. For a fascinating narration see F. Spencer Chapman, *The Jungle is Neutral* (London: Chatto and Windu, 1949).

31. For a detailed discussion see Cheah Boon Kheng, *Malaysia: The Making of a Nation* (Singapore: ISEAS, 2002), Chapter 1.

32. *Ibid*, p. 37.

33. The majority of the cadres of the MCP were Chinese, see Richard Clutterbuck, *The Long War: Emergency in Malaysia*, 1948-1960 (London: Oxford University Press, 1966), A Short, *The Communist Insurrection in Malay*, 1948-1960 (London: Oxford University Press, 1975).

34. Chean Boon Kheng, *Malaysia: The Making of a Nation*, n. 31. p. 10.

35. For an in-depth discussion see Safier Ibrahim, "Islamic Elements in Pre-Independent Malay", *Islamic Culture*, Vol. 52, No. 3, 1978, pp. 185-195.

36. Anthony Milner, *The Invention of Politics in Colonial Malaya: Contesting Nationalism and the Expansion of the Public Sphere*, n. 20, p. 150.

37. William R. Roff, *The Origins of Malay Nationalism* (Kuala Lumpur, Oxford University Press, 1967), pp. 235-236.

38. Hussin Mutalib, *Islam and Ethnicity in Malay Politics* (Singapore: Oxford University Press, 1990), p. 28 and Ariffin Omar, *Bangsa Melayu: Malay Concepts of Democracy and Community, 1945-1950* (Kuala Lumpur: Oxford University Press, 1993), pp. 34-61.

39. Hussin Mutalib, *ibid,* p.1 and 21.

40. A.C. Milner, "Islam and the Muslim State" in M.B. Hooker (ed), *Islam in Southeast Asia* (Leiden: E.J. Brill, 1983), pp. 23-49.

41. *ibid,* p. 32.

42. The Reid Commission, appointed by the British Government, started the process of drafting the Constitution for Federation of Malaya from January 18, 1956 under the Chairmanship of Lord William Reid. Other members of the Commission were Sir Ivor Jennings (Britain), Sir Willian McKell (Australia), Justice B. Malik (India) and Justice Abdul Hamid (Pakistan).

43. Cheah Boon Kheng, *Malaysia: The Making of a Nation*, n. 31, Chapter 1.

44. R.S Milne and Daine K Mauze, *Politics and Government in*

Malaysia (Singapore: Times Book International, 1980), pp. 36-38.

45. Hussin Mutalib, *Islam and Ethnicity in Malay Politics*, n. 38, p. 23. He has referred to a statement of Tun Mohamed Suffin Hashmi, the first Chief Justice of Independent Malaysia, who interpreted that the Article was "primarily for ceremonial purposes".

46. The language of the Article is similar to that of Article 2A of the Constitution of Bangladesh.

47. The two other components of the Article are: "(a) was before Merdeka [Independence] Day born in the Federation or in Singapore or born parents one of whom was born in the Federation or in Singapore, or is on that day domiciled in the Federation or in Singapore or (b) is the issue of such a person".

48. For an in-depth analysis on the issue of "Malayan nationalism as against the concept of "Malay" nationality see Cheah Boon Kheng, *Malaysia: The Making of a Nation*, n. 31, pp. 7-15.

49. See Hussin Mutalib, *Islam and Ethnicity in Malay Politics*, n. 38.

50. For a detailed discussion on the issue see the seminar volume Abdul Razak Baginda and Peter Schier (eds), *Is Malaysia an Islamic State? Secularism and Theocracy – A Study of the Malaysian* Constitution (Kuala Lumpur: Malaysian Strategic Research Centre and Konrad Adenauer Foundation, nd).

51. *ibid*, p. 10.

52. For some details of the party see John Funston, *Malay Politics in Malaysia: A Study of the United Malays National Organisation and Party Islam* (Kuala Lumpur: Heinemann, 1981) and also Peter M. Manikas and Laura L. Thornton, *Political Parties in Asia* (Makati, the Philippines: National Democratic Institution for International Affairs, 2002), pp. 150-156,also www.umno.org.my

53. Chandra Muzaffar, *Protector*? (Penang: Aliran, 1979).

54. For a detailed study on the PAS see Farish A. Noor, *Islam Embedded: The Historical Development of the Pan-Malaysian Islamic Party* PAS (1951-2003), Vol. I and II (Kuala Lumpur: Malaysian Sociological Research Institute, 2004).

55. For an extremely analytical work see Clive S. Kessler, *Islam and Politics in a Malay State: Kelantan 1838-1969* (Ithaca: Cornell University Press, 1978).

56. See Oh Myung-Seok and Kim Hyung-Jun, Religion, *Ethnicity and Modernity in Southeast Asia* (Seoul: Seoul National University Press, 1998), pp. 81-101.

57. Muzaffar Chandra, *Islamic Resurgence in Malaysia* (Petaling Jaya: Penerbit Fajar Bakti, 1987), p. 26

58. Chandra Muzaffar, *Protector*, n. 53, pp. 1-32.

59. Malaysia's first Prime Minister Tunku Abdul Rahman while opposing the idea of an Islamic state said that "the attainment of Islamic state would require drowning of every non-Muslim in the country." Quoted in John Funston, "Malaysia" in Mohammed Ayoob, *The Politics of Islamic Reassertion* (London: Croom Helm, 1981), pp. 165-186, quotation p.169.

60. For details see Daine K. Mauzy, *Barisan Nasional: Coalition Government in Malaysia* (Kuala Lumpur: Marican, 1983).

61. Diane K. Mauzy and R.S. Milne, "The Mahathir Administration in Malaya: Discipline through Islam," *Pacific Affairs*, Vol. 56, No. 4 (Winter 1983-84), pp. 617-648.

62. See Chandra Muzaffar, *Islamic Resurgence in Malaysia*, n. 57, pp. 42-48 and Hussin Mutalib, *Islam and Ethnicity in Malay Politics*, n. 38, Chapter 3.

63. A pronounced 'rebel' Mahathir had ups and downs in his political career. He was expelled from the UMNO in 1969 for his opposition to the policies of Tunku Abdul Rahman, readmitted to the party in 1972, then elevated to the position of vice-president and then deputy president, held the portfolio of education (1974-77) and the trade and industries (1977-1981). There are large number of publications on Mahathir in English and Bahasa Malay. Some of the works in English are Khoo Boo Teik, *Paradoxes of Mahathirism: An Intellectual Biography* (Kuala Lumpur: Oxford University Press, 1995), John Hilley, *Malaysia: Mahathirsm, Hegemony and the New Opposition* (London: Zed Books, 2001) and R.S. Milne and Diane K. Mauzy, *Malaysian Politics under Mahathir* (London: Routledge, 2006). J.V. Morais, *Mahathir: A Profile in courage* (Singapore: Eastern University Press, 1982).

64. For a discussion on the similar line see Hussin Mutalib, *Islam, Ethnicity in Malay Politics* and Kamarulnizam Abdullah, *Politics of Islam in Contemporary Malaysia*, n. 24, Chapter 7.

65. There are host of studies telling in details the plight of the Malay people in the early part of post-colonial era. Some of the representative studies are Just Faaland *et.al.*, *Growth and Ethnic Inequality: Malaysia's New Economic Policy* (Kuala Lumpur: Dewan Bahasa dan Pustaka in association with the Michelsen Institute of Norway, 1990), Hussin Mutalib, *Islam, Ethnicity in Malay Politics*, n. 61, Barbara Watson Andeya and Leonard Y. Andeya, *A History of Malaysia*, n. 1, Chapter 8, Jim Baker, *Crossroads: A Popular History of Malaysia* (Singapore: Times Book International, 1999), Chapter 17.

66. Alex Lee, "The Chinese and Malay Dilemmas in Malaysia", *Pacific Community*, Vol. 3, 1971-1972, pp. 561-572, quotation pp. 562-563.

67. James Onkili, *Nation-building Malaysia* (Singapore: Oxford University Press, 1985), p. 201.

68. Karl Von Vorys, *Democracy without Consensus: Communalism and Political Stability in Malaysia* (Princeton: Princeton University Press, 1975) Chapter 13 and 14. The book, known as an excellent presentation of the causes and consequences of the 1969 riot, was proscribed in Malaysia as it contained revealing statements of Tunku Abdul Rahman and a fairly objective assessment of the situation before and after the riot.

69. For a critical analysis of the NEP see R.S. Milne, "The Politics of Malaysia's New Economic Policy", *Pacific Affairs*, Vol. 49, No. 2 (Summer 1976), pp. 235-262.

70. For some understanding on these issues see Jomo Kwame Sundaram, *A Question of Class: Capital, the State and Uneven Development in Malaya* (Singapore: Oxford University Press, 1986), Chapter 10.

71. The full version of the NEP could be found in the *Mid-Term Review of the Second Malaysia Plan 1971-1975* (Kuala Lumpur: Government Press, 1973).

72. The NEP emerged at the initiative of Prime Minister Tun Abdul Razak, who picked up among others two important persons, Ghazali Shafie, a senior civil servant and Just Faaland a

Scandinavian economist, to formulate an economic policy with a political objective – to produce national unity. See *Second Malaysian Plan 1971-1975* (Kuala Lumpur: Government Press, 1971), p. 1.

73. R.S. Milne, "The Politics of Malaysia's New Economic Policy", n. 69, pp. 239-243.

74. James Morgan, "Economic and Social Trends" in *Trends in Southeast Asia: Proceedings and Background Paper of Seminar on Trends in Malaysia*, No. 2 (Singapore: ISEAS, 1971).

75. R.S.Milne, "The Politics of Malaysia's New Economic Policy", n. 69, pp. 256-258.

76. For details of the organization and its 18 point demand in its memorandum submitted to the Government of Malaysia see http://en.wikipedia.org/wiki/File:HINDRAFQueen.jpg

77. For details of the election results see *The Star*, March 9-10, 2008.

78. The announcement of banning the HINDRAF came from Malaysian Home Minister Syed Hamid Alber, see *ibid,* October 16, 2008.

79. "Penang Administration Will Be Free From NEP", *ibid,* March 14, 2008.

80. There are large number of books published in English and Malay language on Mahathir Mohamad. Some more books in English and Malay are in the pipeline, see n. 63.

81. One of Tun Hussein Onn's strongest critics, a leader of the opposition, Tan Chee Khoon wrote severely about the failure of the Prime Minister in all fronts, see Tan Chee Khoon, *Without Fear and Favour* (Singapore: Eastern Universities Press, 1984) and Harold Crouch, "Authoritarian Trends, the UMNO Split and the Limits to the State Power" in Joel S. Kahn and Francis Loh Kok Wah (eds), *Fragmented Vision: Culture and Politics in Contemporary Malaysia* (Sydney: Allen and Unwin, 1992).

82. *New Straits Times*, August 4 and 31, 2001.

83. For a detailed discussion on Bangsa Malaysia' as a part of the Vision 2020 see John Hilley, *Malaysia: Mahathirism, Hegemony and the New Opposition*, n. 63, Chapter 1.

84. Chandra Muzaffar, *Islamic Resurgence in Malaysia*, n. 57, pp.

1-42.

85. R. S. Milne and Daine K. Mauzy, *Malaysian Politics under Mahathir*, n. 80, pp. 85-88.

86. For a perceptive discussion on the strategic initiatives for resurgence of Islam during the early phase of Mahathir's regime see D. Camroux, "State Responses to Islamic Resurgence in Malaysia: Accommodation, Co-option and Confrontation", *Asian Survey*, Vol. xxxvi, No. 9, 1996 pp. 861-866.

87. The details of the document could be found with an Introduction in Ahmad Sarji Abdul Hamid (ed), *Malaysia's Vision 2020: Understanding the Concept, Implications and Challenges* (Petaling Jaya: Pelanduk Publications, 1993).

88. For a critical analysis of the Vision see Khoo Kay Jin, "The Grand Vision: Mahathir and Modernization" in Jeo S. Kahn and Francis Loh Kok Wah (eds), Fragmented Vision: Culture and Politics in Contemporary Malaysia 81 especially pp. 69-79.

89. Koo Boo Teik, *Paradoxes of Mahathirism: An Intellectual Biography of Mahathir* Mahamad, n. 80.

90. *The Star*, September 11, 1995.

91. *New Straits Times*, October 10, 1995, controlled by the UMNO while giving importance to Vision 2020, downplayed the political dimension, reflecting in a shuttle way the reserved support of the Malays for Bangsa Malaysia.

92. Quoted in Robin Adshead, *Mahathir of Malaysia*, n. 80, p. 102.

93. Anwar Ibrahim had a meteoric rise when he was picked by Mahathir in 1983 to become a Minister for Culture, Youth and Sports, then he became the Deputy Prime Minister in 1993 and remained in that position till 1998 when was removed from the position and was arrested for moral corruption. After being disgraced, Anwar engineered a split in the UMNO to form a new party called Parti Keadilan. He served a long jail term and was banned from active politics for six years. In 2008 the ban came to an end and thereafter he contested and won in the parliamentary election held on August 26, 2008. See *The Star*, August 29, 2008.

94. Mahathir Mohamad, *The Malay Dilemma* (Singapore: Asia Pacific, 1970).

95. Mahathir's opposition to the policies of Tunku Abdul Rahman was guided by his Malay nationalism and opposition to awarding larger space to the Chinese in the economic life of the country. He was readmitted to the party in 1972 and then elevated to UMNO's Vice-President before becoming the Prime Minister in 1981. For some details of his conflict with the Prime Minister and his expulsion see Karl von Vorys, *Democracy without Consensus*, n. 68, 371-378.

96. *The Malay Dilemma, ibid*, p. 61.

97. Ismail Noor, *Passing the Baton: From Dr. Mahathir to Abdullah Badawi* (Kuala Lumpur: Thinker's Library, 2004) pp. 122-134.

98. Shanti Nair, *Islam in Malaysian Foreign Policy* (London: Routledge, 1997), Chapter 2.

99. Mahathir Mohamad's statements on the issue could be found in *The Straits Times*, December 1, 1990.

100. *ibid*, March 23 to April 1994 carried out press reports, editorials, and letters to the editor on the issue of banning the film. Among these statement of Junid Megat Ayob, Deputy Home Affairs Minister blasting Spielberg for his passionate propagation of the Jewish cause, *ibid*, (April 7, 1994) is noteworthy.

101. During my visit to Kuala Lumpur and Melaka, I had the opportunity to meet a number of scholars at the University Putra Malaysia, University of Malaya, University Kebangsaan Malaysia and International Islamic University Malaysia, Imams of mosques, students, ordinary citizens, highly articulated car drivers with whom I discussed Malaysia's position in the Islamic world. All of them recognize Israel's right to exist; at the same time, they are for a Palestinian state and their right to exist as a nation-state.

102. Shanti Nair, *Islam in Malaysian Foreign Policy*, n. 98, pp. 253-258

103. *The Star*, May 7, 1994.

104. For details of Islamic resurgence and emergence of Islamic organizations see Chandra Muzaffar, *Islamic Resurgence in Malaysia*, n. 84 and Jomo Kwame Sundaram and Ahmed Shabery Cheek, "The Politics of Malaysia's Islamic Resurgence, *Third World Quarterly*, Vol. 10, No. 2, April 1988, pp. 843-868.

105. K.S. Jomo and Ahmad Shabery Cheek, "Malaysia's Islamic

Movements" in Joel S. Kahn and Francis Loh Kok Wah (eds), *Fragmented Vision: Culture and Politics in Contemporary Malaysia*, 81, pp. 79-106.

106. Oh Myung-Seok, "From Dakwah to New Malays: Islam, Middle Class, and Ethnicity in Contemporary Malaysia" in Oh Myung-Seok and Kim Hyung-Jun, *Religion, Ethnicity and Modernity in Southeast Asia* (Seoul: National University Press, 1998), pp. 81-101.

107. Shamsul A.B., "Identity Construction, Nation Formation, and Islamic Revivalism in Malaysia" in Robert W. Hefner and Petricia Horvatich (eds), *Islam in an Era of Nation-States: Politics and Religious Renewal in Muslim Southeast Asia* (Honolulu: University of Hawaii Press, 1997), pp. 207-227.

108. Zainah Anwar, *Islamic Revivalism in Malaysia: Dakwah among the Students* (Selangor Darul Ehsan: Penaduk Publication, 1987).

109. For a perceptive analysis of Darul Arqam see Greg Barton, "Islam, Society, Politics, and Change in Malaysia" in Jason F. Isaacson and Colin Rubenstein, *Islam in Asia: Changing Political Realities* (New Brunswick and London: Transaction Publishers, 2002), pp.104-110.

110. Ibrahim Mahmood studied in Higher Islamic Studies Center at Nilam Puri, Kelantan. Then he moved to India to study first at Jamaliah College, Chennai and then at Daurl Ulum Madrassa, Uttar Pradesh. Later on he joined Al-Azhar University, Cairo, Egypt to study Sharia. He took a diploma in Islami dakwah in Tripoli, Libya in 1974. On return to Malaysia he worked with the Religious Division, Prime Minister's Department, then known as Pusat Islam, under a project funded by Government of Libya. That is why he came to known as Ibrahim Libya.

111. See White Paper on the Memali Incident 21: 1986. The PAS all along has been asserting that it had no links with the Al-Arqam.

112. For a detailed report on the Memali incident see *Far Eastern Economic Review,* December 5, 1985.

113. Greg Barton, "Islam, Society, Politics, and Change in Malaysia in Jason F. Isaacson and Colin Rubenstein, *Islam in Asia: Changing Political Realities*, n. 109, pp. 110-116.

114. For similar views see J. Nagata, *The Reflowering of Malaysia:*

Modern Religious Radicals and their Roots (Vancouver: University of British Columbia Press, 1984) and Chandra Muzaffar, *Islamic Resurgence in Malaysian,* n. 84.

115. For details see Rose Ismail (ed), *Hudud in Malaysia: The Issues at Stake* (Kuala Lumpur: SIS Forum (Malaysia) Berhad, 1995).

116. For the text of the letter to the Prime Minister see *ibid,* pp. 7-11.

117. *Far Eastern Economic Review,* August 8, 1996,

118. *New Straits Times,* May 1, 1992.

119. *ibid,* May 2, 1992. For the official views of the PAS in support of the hudud see Rose Ismail (ed), Hudud in Malaysia: The Issues at Stake, n. 115, pp. 51-54 and for Mahathir's official position, entitled "Islam Guarantees Justice for all Citizens" see pp. 63-65.

120. Prime Minister Badawi propagated Islam Hadhari for the first time in a prepared speech delivered before the UMNO's 55th General Assembly in Kuala Lumpur on September 23-25, 2004. For details of the concept see Abdullah Ahmad Badawi, *Islam Hadhari: A model Approach for Development* and *Progress* (Petaling Jaya; MPH Publishing, 2006).

121. *ibid,* p. 4.

122. *ibid,* p. 5.

123. For some details of the analysis and comments on the March 2008 elections see *The Star, The Straits Times* and *The Malay Mail,* March 10, 2008.

124. *The Straits Times,* April 10, 2008.

5

GLOBALIZATION, ETHNICTY AND ISLAM

The urge for a change is one of the most fundamental components of human behaviour. Civilizations have grown owing to man's infinite and timeless quest for change and transformation in all walks of life. Wherever the urge was absent, stagnation ensued. The change could be either evolutionary or revolutionary. It could be a resultant of a combination of both, but factors could be manifold and each could be guided by a variety of variables. That is why there had been ups and downs in the course of civilizations. It takes several centuries to get things to settle down. As awareness about ones own identity as a community develops, intermediate variables emerge to raise multi-layers of issues and to promote or hinder the process of developments. An imagined community at one point of time becomes real and vibrant with huge possibilities in the near as also the distant future. This is how many new nations emerged in the post-colonial era with enormous promise. Today, the process of transformation of an imagined community into a real and developed one is unbelievably faster than ever before. So is also the process of the consolidation. One could wonder if globalization had a role in the speedy transformation and consolidation as nation-states of many newly emergent countries. Globalization has also dramatically reduced the possibility of disappearance of small and newly grown communities. It has, as Susan Strange would argue, facilitated interfacing of economic structures and forces, sidelined contentious political issues and has brought to the fore larger issues of market diffusion making communities visible and focused. Consequently, politics has a minimal role to play; whereas economic interests have greater stakes and role in human civilization.[1]

Globalization is one of most latent and absorbing developments in recent times; it has encompassed every aspect of contemporary human civilization. There is no universally acceptable definition of the term, and therefore, has varying degrees of precision, sometimes relating to its theorization and sometimes about the process. Yet, in common parlance, it could be associated with free market, cutting across national and territorial boundaries, with rapid development in all forms of communication, including electronic and information technologies, which have transformed the world into a global village.[2] Along with these, ideas too have spread instantaneously. Massive networking with a plethora of electronic communication means has made interaction of communities and nations a routine affair. A protest in one corner of the world reverberates in other distant corners in no time. A moment of joy in one country becomes a shared trans-national experience. Globalization has not remained confined to the definition of single market economy, nor could it be delimited to integration of national economies into the international economy through trade and direct foreign investment.[3] Today it means shared experience in all frontiers of knowledge, sports, culture, literature, environment and ecology, tourism and travel, and even terror.

In an era of globalization where does a nation-state, which has emerged out of colonial exploitation, stand? This question is obviously irrelevant in the case of Western democracies, which have not suffered under oppressive colonial rule. The countries, that have a long and bitter experience of anti-colonial struggle, where people rallied under the banner of nationalism, against foreign domination, also have the experience of utilizing religion and ethnicity to mobilize mass participation and support to achieve the political objective of independence. Almost all such movements for freedom could not but take recourse to political mobilization through ethnic and religious lines. Primordial affiliations are boundless frontiers of political resources, which no movement could ignore while spearheading a struggle against foreign rule.

Islam is a global religion as outlined in Chapter I. The modern concept of globalization is not foreign to Islamic history and tradition.[4] The concepts of *ummah, jihad, fatwa* and the hajj congregation at Mecca are known manifestations of a global perspective of Islam. The issue of transnational problem of terrorism in the name of Islam and the operational strategy of the al-Qaeda add to the latent global face of Islam. The magnitude of violence committed on 9/11 followed by Bali bombing the next year, the killing spree that has been the order of the day in Afghanistan, Algeria, Iraq, Palestine, Pakistan and Sudan represent a cult of terror of global dimension. Islam as a faith has an atomized, universal and all-pervading outline demonstrated so clearly in the forms of daily five-time prayer, fasting, alms giving (*zakat*) and Hajj. Viewed from that perspective, from Algeria to Indonesia, Islam, as a faith, looks like an undiluted global entity. Beyond that, as 13th century scholar Ibn Khaldun says, Islamic world is diverse and fragmented.

To take the example of the three countries covered in the present study, their economic, political and social domains are so diverse that it becomes a difficult task to locate a meeting point. Bangladesh is one of the least developed countries in the world, whereas Malaysia is an economically prosperous country, and Indonesia stands as a potentially developed one. Their historical processes towards nation-building are different, so are their demographic compositions. The diversities are striking and phenomenal. A comparative panorama of the economic and demographic life of the three countries might help understand their complexities (Table 5.1).

Table 5.1
Demographic and economic statistics of Bangladesh, Indonesia and Malaysia

Basic data	*Bangladesh*	*Indonesia*	*Malaysia*
Population (2005)	153.3 million	226.1 million	25.7 million
Buddhists	0.6%	1.8%	19.2%
Christians	0.3%	8.7%	9.1%
Hindus	9.2%	3.0%	6.3%
Muslims	89.6%	86.0%	60.4%
Ethnicity	Bengali 98%	Javanese 42.0%	Malay 54%
HDI status	140	107	63
Literacy rate	43%	90.5%	91.4%
Per capita US$	2,100	3,724	13,385
GDP per capita*	2,053	3,843	US10,882
Eco. Growth rate	5.4%	5.4%	5.6%
Population growth	2.0	1.2	1.8
Density per sq.km.	1,146	134	83
Import in US$	12.96 billion	62.02 billion	100 billion
Export	9.36 billion	83.64 billion	130 billion

* Compilation of UNDP Report and other sources.

An economically and educationally under-developed Bangladesh is more susceptible to religious fanaticism. The issue of governance is also deeply embedded in the economic performance of the country. Religion tends to fill the vacuum created by low performance economy and poor governance. Where there is a discrepancy between national expectation on one hand and evidence of low performance on the other, transitional forces, such as religion, step in to present an alternative paradigm. Where the bulk of the populace is poor and illiterate, as in the case of Bangladesh, religion hence plays a political role as an alternative approach to governance.[5] A similar situation in Indonesia and Malaysia is unthinkable, understandably, owing to several factors, such as, educational level of the common citizens, economic prosperity and absence of abject poverty, as performing governance is in place. The two massive Muslim organizations in Indonesia, Muhammadiyah and Nahdlatul Ulama, have at no point of time chosen hard-line Islamic agenda based on hate and violence. Neither the UMNO, which stands for the Malay Muslims, nor even the PAS stands for or represents a hardcore militant religious ideology.

The three countries under study present three different settings. Geographically Bangladesh is located in a strategically important region in South Asia. It shares with India and Myanmar common international border, 95.45 per cent international border with India and rest with Myanmar. It has a considerably long coastal access of 580 km, facilitating easy maritime trade with the rest of the world. Indonesia and Malaysia situated in Southeast Asia have common border. Malaysia has international border with Thailand as well in the North. These three countries are Muslim majority ones and the overwhelming Muslim populace follows Sunni tradition. A small Ahmediyah population could be found in Bangladesh and Indonesia. There are occasional demands in these two countries to declare this community as non-Muslim. While Bangladesh witnessed violent demonstration against the community during the period 2001-2006, there has been peaceful agitation against them in Indonesia.

Political situations in these three countries have been different. Bangladesh had experienced military dictatorship twice in its comparatively brief period of history, when two generals – Ziaur Rahman (1978-1981) and Hossain Mohammad Ershad (1982-1990) – ruled the country in the name of restoring law and order. However, the urge for democracy united the people against military dictatorship in 1990, and consequently, democratically elected governments were installed. There is a positive correlation between the chaotic condition and military dictatorship and the rise of Islamic militancy, which wanted to transform Bangladesh into an Islamic country that would follow the Sharia laws.

In Indonesia, a section of the Muslims have always kept the issue of turning the country into an Islamic one alive since 1945, but unlike Bangladesh such forces never secured upper hand. The democratic wave of its early phase of Independence sidelined such a sentiment, for which Indonesia accepted Pancasila as its national ideology based on equality, democracy and secularism. During the first half of the 32 years long 'New Order' regime of General Soeharto, which earned fame as well as disrepute for economic development and dictatorial functioning respectively, a calculated move was made to de-Islamize politics, and therefore, did not provide Islamic groups and parties a space to grow. The bureaucracy and the military played a role in checking the influence of the Islamic parties. The social background of the these two highly influential components of the Indonesian government, bureaucracy and military, are essentially from the *abangon*, who are known to be liberal and less rigid practitioners of the faith and also the *priyayi*, the aristocratic Muslims, who would not trade with the conservative *santris*. Since these constituents of the Indonesian society sway the Indonesian population, they still continue to prevent the Islamic groups and parties from taking over the secular credentials of the country. The post-Soeharto era and for that matter the reformasi era witnessed the emergence of a large number of Islamic parties, but except for two, all of them virtually have no political and popular base. The very fact that the Islamic parties have failed to capture power in the name of religion in an eminently Muslim majority country is a pointer to the importance of non-religious issues of democracy, decentralization and development, and not Sharia law, in the political process in Indonesia. These are the issues which dominated the political planks during the 2009 elections. It is a fine example of the liberal face of Islam, despite certain aberrations, such as, Bali bombing of October 2002 and the July 2009 bombing in the heart of Jakarta city.

Malaysia has remained steadfast in its faith in democracy ever since its inauguration in 1957 as an independent country, despite its predilection to provide a special status to the Malays, who are invariably Muslims. The affirmative action in favour of the Malay was a social contract agreed upon by the UMNO, the MCA and the MIC during the formative period of Malaysian Federation. The contractual arrangement still stands despite the initiative of Mahathir Mohamad to phase it out gradually by 2020 to make his concept of Bangsa Malaysia work in terms not only of economic transformation to make it a developed country but also of communally equal and harmonious relationship within foreseeable time schedule. The latest efforts made by Razak by advancing the concept of '1 Malaysia' is a demonstration of the desire of the political elite to find a universally acceptable framework for national reconstruction. It is early to comment on the efficacy of the new concept, but it is heartening to see the nation is still engaged in the pursuit of finding an inclusive arrangement for equality, justice and mutual respect among all communities living there.

A single common denominator – Islam – could not put the three different countries in a single category. An underdeveloped Bangladesh is quite different from the fast developing Indonesia and the nearly developed Malaysia. The constraints for these countries are immense and sometime appear to be colossal, evading resolution. Bangladesh's economic backwardness is too deep-rooted and all-pervasive to be resolved soon. It would need many more decades to catch up with other developing countries. To pay attention to the issues that need immediate attention should be the overriding concern of the nation rather than reopening an already settled foundational question – as to which one is more important as a yardstick of Bangladeshi identity – Islam or Bengali nationhood. If Islam is the basis of the national foundation of Bangladesh, does it not demolish the basic premises of its separation from Pakistan and emergence as an independent country? It appears that the foundational question is also a philosophical question. Could an emerging country revert back to the days when it was ruled by distant masters in the name of religion? The results of the 2008 elections to the parliament of Bangladesh provide a clue to understand which way the country is moving. The repetition of the electoral wave of 1973 in favour of the Awami League and the crushing defeat of the last remnants of Islamic militant groups is an eloquent answer to the aforesaid query. Islam as the religion of the overwhelming majority of the people will continue to remain important and as such focused in all walks of life. But to exploit religion to devalue the gains of the hard-earned Independence, to demean the values of democracy and secularism and to cast terror in the heart of ordinary citizens appears to be matter of the past.

Similar analogy could be deduced in the case of the largest Muslim country in the world. Islam as the religion of the overwhelming population of Indonesia is a matter of essence of the state. The essence, however, has its limits. A state stands for one and all. Even a microscopic minority has to have a space to flourish, enjoy equal rights and freedom, security against invasion. Likewise, diversity is a core component of creation, and hence, a philosophy of life. Comprising more than 17,000 islands, big and tiny, with human habitation in 10,000, the country is geographically disperse and also culturally diverse. Islam has provided the vast majority of the people with a rallying point for political mobilization. At the same time they are again divided on the basis of ethnicity, class and conservatism. Where does Indonesia stand? Since Islam does not act as a unifying force, *pribumi* steps in and provides a canopied structure where all Indonesian population takes shelter. After a thorough deliberation in 1945, Indonesia resolved the foundational issue by modifying the Jakarta Charter to articulate and accept *Pancasila* as the ideology of the state. Sixty years of Indonesian history has imbued the nation to be proud of diversity on all counts. At the end of 32 years of Soeharto's iron-fist rule when *reformasi* took over, the people rejected the call for restoration of Jakarta sentiment that intended to put the religion of the majority as the determinant of socio-political life of the country. That too shows that religion has been kept out of politics, if not totally but substantially. At any rate the democratic and secular foundation of Indonesia is a matter of *fait accompli.*

Malaysia's dilemma on ethnicity and religion is an admixture of the twin objectives of the Malay people to promote interests of the comparatively disadvantaged Malay nationality and along with that of the Islamic identity. The constitutional guarantee to that end was ensured through trilateral consensus among the leading political parties– the UMNO, the MCA and the MIC -- with the ultimate objective of raising the Malays to the economic level of the Chinese and the Indians. To proceed a step further to look at Malaysia through the prism of Islam only would be an unacceptable proposition, for, the Malay society has ingredients of liberal outlook. The PAS initiated the debate as to whether Malaysia is meant for Muslims alone. The creation of an umbrella organization called Barisan Nasional and its support base suggest that neither the legitimate space for other communities could be compromised, nor could there be a scope for a hegemonic and monolithic religious character for Malaysian nation-state. Malaysia has successfully presented itself as a multi-cultural state where every citizen has a space, despite constitutionally guaranteed affirmative action in favour of the Malays, who are obviously Muslims too. Malaysia passed through an agonizing experience of racial tension; most shocking and disturbing was the anti-Chinese riot on May 13, 1969. Fortunately, however, there was no repetition of similar violence against that ethnic community. The experience in the experiments with affirmative action was not too happy, as Mahathir himself admitted. To the discomfiture of those who advocated vociferously in favour of it now feel that too much of state support to the Malays has created a complacent generation that itself one day would pose as a liability rather than an asset.

At any rate, Malaysia has remained a democratic and progressive country. It has presented itself as a model of harmonious combination of religion and ethnicity. The state has assumed through constitutional arrangement a preeminent role to promote Islam, which is the religion of the state. The Malay question was tagged with it. Consequently, the twin issue of religion and ethnicity of the majority became mutually complementary. Unlike Indonesia, Malaysia has mixed religion with ethnicity with the objective of putting the twin issues in a position of advantage and making the Malays more than equal in comparison with other ethnic and religious communities. This arrangement was a part of the social contract of 1957, but it was destined to affect adversely the process of nation-building. That is why Mahathir's vision of Bangsa Malaysia and Razak's concept of '1 Malaysia' are postulated to do away with the affirmative action in favour of the Malays eventually, has appeared to be a distant goal. At the same time, the PAS quest for total Islamization of Malaysia appears to be an unacceptable gimmick, designed to capture power in the name of religion. When faced with the reality, it has made a paradigm shift towards welfare and good governance. This testifies to the limits of dynamics of religion in politics.

The attempt of the two generals in Bangladesh to dilute the spirit of nationalism shaped during and immediately after the liberation war, by pouring in the religious sentiment has now appeared to be a transitional mechanism in the wake of reassertion of Bengali nationalism, an overriding and enduring national spirit and ideology. As already stated, the generals had limited political strategy to use Islam to legitimize their rule. The overthrow of General Ershad in 1990 proved once again that application of religious symbols and sentiments is short-lived, in the face of popular urge for democracy. Currently Bangladesh has witnessed the third wave of democracy, which is likely to endure, and politics in the name of religion will fade away in favour of consolidation of the ethnic nation state. The current resurgence of democracy has delimited the political role of Islam in Bangladesh.

An uneasy uncertainty still prevails in all these three Muslim majority countries when religious issues get mixed up with domestic and international politics. As already stated, Islam has a globalized connotation transcending national and international boundaries. The transnational character of Islam leaves enormous space for reflection of national, regional and international issues and problems. There are shifting trends. Issues that affect any Muslim population in any part of the world, be the Israeli invasion and massacre of civilian population in Gaza, Serbian massacre of the Muslims of Bosnia, Soviet invasion of and occupation of Afghanistan (1979-1988), US invasion of Iraq in search of weapons of mass destruction and its war on Taliban in Afghanistan, Danish cartoonist depiction of Prophet Muhammad as a terrorist, find emphatic expression in the Islamic world with concern, condemnation and indignation. Globalization has made it easy to keep people informed about the happening in and around the Islamic world. When such issues invite concern of the Muslims, the *ummah* sentiment prevails over all other considerations. One can see the sentiment in the minds of those Bangladeshi volunteers who fought against the Soviet forces in Afghanistan, the Malay troops engaged as a part of the UN peace keeping forces in Bosnia-Herzegovina or Indonesian public demonstrating in front of the Danish Embassy in Jakarta against the cartoonist who insulted the Prophet. In such a situation the Muslims are united cutting across the cultural, ethnic, geographical barriers. That unity of thought and sentiment becomes a transcendental experience, not easily found in other faiths. These are all short-lived transitional issues for the community, who are not directly affected by the events. The more enduring day to day matters of economy, politics, governance, education, rights, culture, livelihood, local issues of peace and conflict, and similar worldly matters keep the Muslims, like any other communities, busy. These are matters having virtually least connection with religion. Naturally religion becomes a matter of private faith and has limited scope to prevail upon all affairs of the statecraft. Religion comes to the forefront in politics when matters affect the community belonging to the said religion, when problems are articulated as problems of the community and when the support for a cause is focused in the name of religion.

Which one – religion or ethnicity - is all-pervading, and offers a canopied identity of the Muslims? None in absolute sense, if one takes the examples of three countries in South and Southeast Asia. Both behave some times as independent and at other times as mutually dependent variables. There lies the tendency towards the development of a plural society understood within the definition of J.S. Furnivall, a British administrator and political thinker, who writes while presenting his perspectives about the region which is known today as Southeast Asia covering today's Indonesia, Malaysia and Singapore, that a plural society is a society that comprises "two or more elements or social orders which live side by side, without mingling, in one political unit."[6] Despite the absence of common will among the segregated communities in Bangladesh, Indonesia and Malaysia, some kind of common will has been shaped over the years. There were social tensions, violent conflicts and riots, but the communities have learnt to live together under one common national banner. Just as the Bengali Hindus and Muslims have agreed to live as Bangladeshis under the canopied structure of Bengali nationalism, the Chakmas, despite their cultural distinctiveness, have learnt to live as Bangladeshi citizens, without mingling, in Furnivall's definition, in one monolithic racially identified social category. Social order has been established in Bangladesh in recent years, despite attempts made by the Islamic radicals to dismantle it with a fanatical agenda. The results of the 2008 elections could be considered as consolidation of the common will to instill a plural social order in that country. Indonesia for last six decades has experienced ethno-religious riots. That has, however, not defaced the profoundness of the diversities in its plural society. The ethnicity-based segregation of Malaysian society was a product of social contract achieved in 1957, an expression of common social will that has united all Malaysian citizens, without any major crisis since 1969 riot.

Social order is dependent on the existence and efficacy of social demand, as Adam Smith and host of other economists argue. Furnivall views social demand as shared identities, markets, values, and tastes. One could find such an atmosphere in all the three countries, where people have a shared life, despites occasional hitches. The most enduring index of a shared life is market economy, a meeting place of all ethno-religious communities, which offers an all-pervading avenue for understanding and interface of economic interests.

Globalization has brought the issues of shared market interest along with other related ones for debate in public domain. As already stated, globalization is not entirely new to Islam. The concept of universal Islam understood within the framework of *ummah*[7] is more or less uniform, though the intensity of its involvement is divergent on the basis of local variation. For example, the Javanese attachment to *ummah* is not as pronounced and strong as that of Bengali Muslims. Yet, certain symbolic issues such as dress code, *halal* food, Friday prayer, fast during Ramdan month and Hajj tend to impact the life of the Muslims all over the world. So also the political issues, such as, the Wahhabi movement[8], a homeland for Palestinians, the US invasion of Iraq, introduction of Sharia law, have a global perspective. Terrorism in the name of Islam through instruments of terror propagated and spearheaded by al-Qaeda and its international networking is a violent global manifestation. The degree of involvement of the Muslims in all these political and non-political or cultural issues varies in degree and commitment and also depends on local conditions and ethos. There is always a distinction between globalization and localization. When engrossed with a local issue of importance and significance, people have least time and energy to devote to extra-national problems and concerns affecting their Muslim brethrens living in a distant land. As John Obert Voll argues: "In the Islamic world, local conditions vary, and each movement is in some way unique. It is therefore important to keep in mind the specific circumstances of each area and movement."[9] Massacre of Palestinians in Gaza by the invading Israeli forces might be a concern of Muslims all over, but the massacre of Bengali Muslim in 1971 did not shock all. Massacre of Kurds by Saddam Hussein might invite concern of many in the Muslim world, but when Turkish soldiers commit the same crime the reaction might be measured and insignificant. Who is at the receiving end or who is committing the crime divides the Muslim world.

Leaving aside these issues, which transcend national boundaries, the issue of globalization as understood universally in terms of economic liberalization, cultural interface, technological spread and massive influence of IT and transport communication, carry a different meaning to the Islamic world. It needs to be understood that globalization is neither uniform nor is it a unipolar expression of market expansion and economic *laissez-faire*. In the Islamic world, it is viewed as Western invasion of the cultural and religious frontiers of Islam. While some believe that globalization will adversely affect the existing diversities within Islam, others hold that it will not only consolidate diversities in Islam but also is likely to promote diversity within the religion.[10]

Islam as the religion of majority acts as a legitimizing force in all Muslim dominated countries in the world. From Algeria to Indonesia, there has been a conscious attempt to use Islam to legitimize in all political actions. For last three decades since the Iranian Islamic revolution in 1979, Islam has remained as the guiding principle in the political life of many of the Muslim dominated countries. The dissolution of the former Soviet Union and the dismantling of East European communism have created a vacuum in international politics. This has offered the Islamists an idea to fill up the vacuum and polarize the world on religious lines.[11] The negative and erroneous concept of 'clash of civilizations' offered an opportunity to debate as to whether Islam is a threat to the non-Muslim world. The public discourse on the issue leads one to assume that traditional Islamic societies, scattered all over the world, suffer from a threat perception that their culture and religion which have survived through ages, are in danger of being challenged and elimination. Like other societies, the Muslim society too feels threatened by the "tidal wave of globalization".[12] The Muslim societies alone have not faced the negative consequences of globalization. Others too are worried about its association with "panic culture" stemmed out of uncertain future. There are hosts of people including social activists who would share the views of Anthony Giddens when he writes that globalization "creates a world of winners and losers, a few on the fast tract to prosperity, the majority condemned to life of misery and disparity."[13] The threat perception of a considerable section of the Muslims that globalization will eventually wipe out a billion people of their faith may not have solid foundation but it is enough to garner support for a violent response.

Bangladesh has passed through a period when the call of back to basics and tradition became strong enough to threaten the existing order. The country which has been depending heavily on foreign trade, in terms of both export of its garment products and import of almost all items of daily life, and whose trade deficit had reached to an alarming point, could not afford to project itself as a hub of Islamic extremists. Hundreds of thousands of the Bangladeshi workers abroad have been sending their earning to back to the country. The foreign remittance constitutes a strong component of Bangladesh's national budget. Globalization has a role in this regard. The foreign dependency is too heavy a compulsion to be ignored while conniving Islamic militancy, which does not sell. The Bali bombing of 2002 also had an overbearing impact on Indonesian economy. The government crackdown including the recent execution of the three Bali bombing accused is a pointer to that direction. Mahathir had the foresight to crush the militants in 1985, for, a developing country like Malaysia, which had enormous potentialities, could not pamper the backward-looking militants.

Indonesian intellectual environment stands for a middle path or a third path which rejects the call for Islamic militancy, but at the same time also says no to westernization of culture which might eventually damage, if not eliminate, the national tradition and culture shaped by the experience of several centuries. The Malaysian leadership was busy with rationalizing the concept of 'civilizational Islam' (Islam Hadhari) for some time which is said to have an impact on the society and polity of the country. And Bangladesh, after the 2008 elections, is engrossed in consolidation of Bengali nationalism so that the foundational ideology does not get lost. The interconnectedness of ethnicity (may it be Bengali, Javanese or Malay) with religion Islam is in the process of finding an essence of national identity. Both are equally important and have their own domains and spheres of influence; one cannot subsume the other in a zero-sum dynamic. The contradictions between them are non-antagonistic and the apocalyptic view in taking recourse to the middle path is based on compassion, wisdom and a rational understanding that a national identity is not always expected to be uni-dimensional and monolithic. A nation does not stand by its religious character alone. It has other historical, cultural, traditional and societal compulsions, which cannot be sidelined. In each of the three countries, like any other, the nation had already found a shape and identity, much before the advent of the religion.

Yet, politicians in the newly emerging countries find religion as one of the most convenient tools that could be used to achieve their political objectives. The Muslim world has been no exception to this. Being Muslim majority countries in South and Southeast Asia, Bangladesh, Indonesia and Malaysia are vulnerable to religion-based politics. The political elite are aware of it, and therefore, tend to use religion to legitimize political actions on contentious issues or to retain its political position. Two generals in Bangladesh – Ziaur Rahman and Hossain Mohammad Ershad, and General Soeharto of Indonesia, who rose to power not by means of ballots but by military coup, used Islam in varied degrees to remain in power. While Ziaur Rahman fell to the gun of his own army, Ershad and Soeharto had to bow down to the popular movement in which the Islamic groups also joined. Religion could not come to rescue them. Mahathir Mohamad used Islam to counter an Islamic party, the PAS, but as an astute politician he knew how far he could go and was also aware of the limits of his religious card in a multi-cultural country, which has an image in the international community, as representative of liberal Islam.

Ethnicity extends a soothing touch in a multi-religious state. It has a wider coverage cutting across religious boundaries. Its inclusiveness to provide space to language, culture and tradition, facilitates a process of frequent interface among people having diverse primordial affiliations. Bangladesh is a Bengali nation-state. Its Bengalis constitute 98 per cent of the total population. Whereas its Muslim population is 89 per cent. This means that Bengali ethnicity has a wider coverage compared to Islam. Indonesia's Muslim population is overwhelming (88 per cent) which are divided into three categories – *abangon*, *santri* and *priyayi*. Nonetheless, it is the Javanese ethnicity that sways the socio-political life of the country. Malaysia has compartmentalized ethnic divisions – the Malays, the Chinese and the Indians. The recent post-2008 election developments have opened up a debate whether communal division has helped the nation-building process in the country. UMNO's internal debate to have a shift from exclusiveness to an inclusive and accommodative arrangement might broaden the base of Malay national identity. Mahathir's Bangsa Malaysia gained importance, but the new concept of '1 Malaysia' might replace it and the original concept of Malaysian nation-state is likely to gain wider currency.

In all these three countries of our study, the Muslims have distinct identities, which are distinguishable from that of the place of the origin of Islam – the Middle East. The physical appearance, culture, language and tradition of the people of these three countries are different from those in middle east. It is due to the process of Islamization in these countries. Islam arrived in all these Hindu and Buddhist dominated areas of South and Southeast Asia through the traders and then through the missionary activities of the Sufi saints. Naturally, a process of accommodation, adjustment and assimilation took place among three religions – Buddhism, Hinduism and Islam. In this way ethnicity and religion became two sides of the same coin.

As already stated, in the era of globalization, market alone does not preoccupy international public domain. A host of other issues, such as, environment, ecology, gender, human rights, poverty and hunger, peace and conflict resolution, sharing of knowledge and technology, exploration of outer space and so on, have kept policy makers, academia and social activists busy. The world has seen fast changing concepts and notion, and ways of life. The 21st century is likely to experience paradigm changes in all spheres of life. Change is an essence of adaptability and at the same time advancement. In keeping pace with the rhythms of changes, Islamic world has no option but to follow the course of *ijtihad*. A nation-state cannot rest entirely on religious foundation. The very matrix of nationality may not always be religion-centric. The ethnic and social components have a role to play in shaping the dynamics of a nation-state. In the era of globalization, the informed citizens, living far away from the Arab world, cannot afford to retreat to a life of the seventh century. The Arab world itself has changed dramatically over the centuries. This realization is evident in all these three Muslim majority countries. There is no opposition to the call for a pious and honest life, without hindrance to the pace of civilization and modernization, not in terms of Westernization, but in terms of scientific education, better health and social security, gender equality, good and responsive governance, democracy, liberal and tolerant approach to life, ecological protection and respect for diversity. A wind of change in this direction has touched all the three countries under study. It is a direction to the fourth wave of democracy.[14] This has inspired the people of the Muslim countries in different parts of the world to proceed in search of a resolution of the tangled issue of ethnicity and religion as the foundation of their nation-states. The resolution of the foundational crises, as to whether puritan and political Islam is the monolithic basis of the state, has become possible through ballots, and not by a cycle of violence using bombs and bullets. Bangladesh elections of December 2008, Malaysia's electoral verdict of March 2008 and all the three Indonesian polls of 1999, 2004 and 2009 have given a resounding mandate to the effect that religion might be a matter of great importance in the national life of the majority, but it does not constitute the core of political ideology of the state.

NOTES AND REFERENCES

1. For some discussion on this line see Susan Strange, *The Retreat of the State: The Diffusion of Power in the World Economy* (New York: Cambridge University, 1996).
2. For such an eloquent definition see R. Robertson, "Globalization Theory and Civilizational Analysis", *Comparative Civilizations Review*, Vo. 17, 1987, pp. 20-30.

3. Jagdish Bhagwati would prefer to remain absorbed and focused exclusively on economic globalization, see his *In Defense of Globalization* (New Delhi: Oxford University Press, 2006).

4. Johan Meuleman, "South-East Asian Islam and the Globalization Process" in his (ed), *Islam in the Era of Globalization: Muslim Attitudes towards Modernity and Identity* (Jakarta: INIS, 2001), pp. 13-30.

5. The common masses of Bangladesh, who are illiterate and politically least aware, could be swayed away by religious appeal. See Zayadul Ahsan, "Islam being used for political gains again", *The Daily Star*, August 24, 2006.

6. J.S. Furnivall, *Netherlands India: A Study of Plural Economy* (New York: Macmillan, 1944), p. 446.

7. Ummah is a global concept, for it encompasses the entire community of Muslims all over the world, see Peter G. Mandeville, "Reimagining the Ummah? Information technology and the changing boundaries of political Islam" in Ali Mohammadi (ed), *Islam Encountering Globalization* (London: RoutledgeCurzon, 2002), pp. 61-90.

8. For an analytical discussion see Natana J. Delong-Bas, *Wahhabi Islam: From Revival and Reform to Global Jihad* (London: Oxford University Press, 2004).

9. John Obert Voll, *Islam: Continuity and Change in the Modern World* (Boulder: Westview Press, 1982).

10. For a detailed discussion on globalization and its impact on Islam see Johan Meuleman (ed), *Islam in the Era of Globalization*, n. 3.

11. Samuel P. Huntington's erroneous thesis of clash of civilization emerges from this development. See his "The Clash of Civilization?" *Foreign Affairs*, Vo. 71, No. 3, Summer, 1993, pp. 22-49. The concept was fully developed subsequently in his book entitled *The Clash of Civilization and the Remaking of the World Order* (New York: Simon and Schuster, 1996).

12. Akbar Ahmed, *Journey into Islam: The Crisis of Globalization* (New Delhi: Penguin, 2007), p. 26, also his *Islam Under Seize: Living Dangerously in a Post-Honor World* (Cambridge: Polity, 2003).

13. Anthony Giddens, *Runaway World: How Globalization Is Reshaping Our Lives* (New York: Routledge, 2000), p. 33.
14. Samuel P. Huntington has argued that the third wave of democracy, which started in Portugal in 1974 swept different parts of the world. See his *The Third Wave: Democratization in the Later Twentieth Century* (Norman: University of Oklahoma Press, 1993). However, another phase of democratic movement has changed the political culture of a number of South and Southeast Asian countries, such as Bangladesh, Bhutan, Indonesia, Malaysia, Maldives, Nepal and Pakistan.

BIBLIOGRAPHY

DOCUMENTS

Bangladesh Documents (New Delhi: Ministry of External Affairs, 1971).

Beverly, Henry, *Reports on the Census of Bengal, 1872* (Calcutta: Secretariat Press, 1872).

Bureau of Public Relations and Protocol, Bali Province Secretariat, *Bali Bombing, 2003.*

Government of People's Republic of Bangladesh, *Speeches of Sheikh Mujib* (Dhaka: External Publicity Division, Ministry of Foreign Affairs, 1972).

Government of Pakistan, *Constituent Assembly Debates*, Vol. 1. No. 51, January 28, 1956.

Economic Intelligence Unit, *Country Report, Bangladesh, March 2008*

Economist Intelligence Unit, *Country Report, Indonesia, February 2008*

Economist Intelligence Unit, *Country Report, Malaysia, 2008*

Indonesia Official Handbook 2004.

Information Malaysia: 2005 (Kuala Lumpur: Berita Publishing, 2005).

Human Development Report, 2005 and 2006.

Mid-term Review of the Second Malaysia Plan 1971-1975 (Kuala Lumpur: Government Press, 1973).

Parliament Debates, October 1972 (Dhaka: Government of Bangladesh, 1972)

Quaid-I-Azam Mohamed Ali Jinnah's Speeches as Governor General 1947-48 (Karachi: Pakistan Publication, n.d.)

Statistik Indonesia, 2007, Statistical Yearbook of Indonesia

Yearbook of Statistics: Malaysia, 2005

Vital Statistics: Malaysia, 2003

Books

Abdillah, Masyukri, *Responses of Indonesian Muslim Intellectuals to the Concept of Democracy (1966-1930)* (Hamburg: Abera Berlag Meyer Co, 1997).

Abdulllah, Kamarulnizam, *The Politics of Islam in Contemporary Malaysia* (Bangi: Penerbit Universiti Kebangsaan, Malaysia, 2003).

Abdullah, Taufiq and Sharon Siddique (ed), *Islam in Southeast Asia* (Singapore: ISEAS, 1986).

Abu Bakar, Ibrahim bin, *Islamic Modernism in Malaysia: The Life and Thought of Sayid Syekh al-Hadi 1867-1934* (Kuala Lumpur: University of Malaya Press, 1994).

Abuza, Zachary, *How Jemaah Islamiyah Terrorist Network Operates*, Asia Report No. 43, December 11, 2002.

Abuza, Zachary, *Militant Islam in Southeast Asia: Crucible of Terror* (Boulder, London: Lynne Rienner Publishers, 2003).

Abuza Zachary, *Funding Terrorism in Southeast Asia: The Financial Network of Al-Qaeda and Jemaah Islamiyah*, NBR Analysis, Vol. 14, No. 5, (Eatle: National Bureau of Asian Research, December 2003).

Abuza, Zachary, *Political Islam and Violence in Indonesia* (London: Routledge, 2007).

Ackerman, Susan E. and Raymond L.M. Lee, *Heaven in Transition: Non-Muslim Religious Innovations and Ethnic Identity in Malaysia* (Honolulu: University of Hawaii Press, 1988).

Ahamed Emajuddin, *Foreign Policy of Bangladesh: A Small State's Imperatives* (Dhaka: University Press Limited, 1984).

Ahamed, Emajuddin, *Military Rule and the Myth of Democracy* (Dhaka: University Press Limited, 1988).

Ahamed, Emajuddin and Mushfiqur Rahman (eds), *Khaleda Zia: Rajnaitik Adarsha O Karmashusi* (Khaleda Zia: Political Ideology and Agenda) (Dhaka: Asia Publications, 2001)

Ahmed, Abu Nasar Saied, *Fundamentalism in Bangladesh* (New Delhi: Akansha Publishing House, 2008).

Ahmed, Akbar, *Journey into Islam: The Crisis of Globalization* (New Delhi: Penguin, 2007).

Ahmed, Akbar S. and Hastings Donnan, *IsIam, Globalization and Postmodernity* (London: Routledge, 1994)

al-Ahsan, Abdullah, *Ummah or Nation? Identity Crisis in Contemporary Muslim Society* (Leisester: The Islamic Foundation, 1992).

Ahmad, Khurshid and Zafar Ishaq Ansari, *Islamic Perspectives: Studies in Honour of Mawlana Sayyied Abul A'la Mawdudi* (Jeddah: Saudi Publishing House, 1979).

Ahmed, Kamaruddin, *Social History of East Pakistan* (Dacca: Orient Longman, 1969).

Ahmed, Moudud, *Era of Sheikh Mujbur Rahman* (Dhaka: University Press Limited, 1983).

Ahmed, Rafiuddin, *The Bengal Muslim 1871-1906: A Quest for Identity* (New Delhi: Oxford University Press, 1981).

Ahmed, Rafiuddin (ed), *Islam in Bangladesh: Society, Culture and Politics* (Dhaka: Bangladesh Itihas Samiti, 1983).

Ahmed, Rafiuddin (ed), *Religion, Nationalism and Politics in Bangladesh* (New Delhi: South Asia Publishers, 1990).

Ahmed, Rafiuddin (ed), *Understanding the Bengal Muslims: interpretative Essays* (New Delhi: Oxford University Press, 2001).

Ahmed, Siraj-udddin, *Bangabandhu Sheikh Mujibur Rahman* (Dhaka: Bhaskar Prakashini, 2001).

Ahmed, Sufia, *Muslim Community in Bengal: 1884-1912* (Dacca: Oxford University Press, 1974).

Akbarzadeh, Shahram and Abdullah Saeed (eds), *Islam and Political Legitimacy* (London: Routledge Curzon, 2003).

Akhtar Banu, UAB Razia, *Islam in Bangladesh* (Leiden: E.J. Brill, 1992).

Al-Attas, Naguib, *Some Aspects of Sufism as Understood and Practiced among the Malays* (Singapore: No Press, 1963).

Albar, Syed Hamid, *Selected Foreign Policy Speeches* (Kuala Lumpur: Institute of Diplomacy and Foreign Relations, 2005).

AlHabshi, Syed Othman and Syed Omar Syed Agil, (eds), *The Role and Influence of Religion in Society* (Kuala Lumpur, Institute of Islamic Understanding Malaysia, 1994).

Ali, A.M.M. Shawkat, *Faces of Terrorism in Bangladesh* (Dhaka: University Press Limited, 2006).

Alfian, *Muhammadiyah: The Political Behavior of a Muslim Modernist Organization under Dutch Colonialism* (Yogyakarta: Gadjah Mada University Press, 1989).

Andaya, Barbara Watson and Leonard Y. Andaya, *A History of Malaysia* (London: Palgrave, 2001).

Anderson, Benedict R., *Methodology and Tolerance of the Javanese* (Ithaca: Cornell University Press, 1965).

Anderson, Benedict R. *et al., Religion and Social Ethos in Indonesia* (Clayton: Monash University, 1977).

Anderson, Benedict R, *Imagined Communities: Reflections on the Origins and Spread of Nationalism* (London: New York, Verso, 1991).

Anderson, Benedict and Theodore Friend, *Indonesian Destinies* (London, Cambridge: Belknap Press of Harvard University, 2003).

Anggraeni, *Who Did This to Our Bali*? (Victoria, Australia: Indra Publishing, 2003).

Anshari, Saifuddin, *The Jakarta Charter 1945: Struggle for an Islamic Constitution in Indonesia* (Kuala Lumpur: Muslim Youth Movement of Malaysia, 1979).

Anwar, Zainah, *Islamic Revivalism in Malaysia: Dakwah among the Students* (Selangor Darul Ehsan: Penaduk Publication, 1987).

Appleby, R. Scott, Samuel C. Heilman, James Piscatory *et. al., Accounting for Fundamentalism: Dynamic Character of Movements* (Chicago: University of Chicago Press, 1994).

Aqsha, Darul *et.al. Islam in Indonesia: A Survey of Events and Developments from 1988 to March 1993* (Jakarta: INIS, 1995).

Arendt, W. and Hall Hill, *South East Asia's Economic Crisis: Origins, Lessons and the Way Forward* (Singapore: ISEAS, 2000).

Ariff, Mohammad, *Islamic Banking in Southeast Asia* (Singapore: ISEAS, 1988)

Ayoob, Mohammad, *et al., Bangladesh: A Struggle for Nationhood* (Delhi: Vikas Publications, 1971).

Ayoob, Mohammed (ed), *The Politics of Islamic Reassertion* (London: Croom Helm, 1981).

Azam, Ghulam, *Jamaate Islamir Karmaniti* (Policies of the Jamaat-i-Islami) (Dhaka: Publication Division of Jamaat-i-Islami, 1990).

Azra, Azyumardi, *The Origins of the Islamic Reformism in Southeast Asia* (Honolulu: Allen and Unwin and University of Hawaii Press, 2004).

Azimi, Hamzah *et.al.*, *Muslim Religiosity Personality Assessment* (Universiti Putra Malaysia: Institute for Social Science Studies, 2007).

Backman, Arnold C., *Communist Collapse in Indonesia* (New York: Norton, 1969).

Badawi, Abdullah Ahmed, *Islam Hadhari: A Model Approach for Development and Progress* (Kuala Lumpur: MPH Publishing, 2006).

Baginda, Abdul Razak (ed), *Malaysia and the Islamic World* (London: Asean Academic Press, , 2004).

Baginda, Abdul Razak and Peter Schier, *Is Malaysia an Islamic State? A Study of the Malaysian Constitution* (Kuala Lumpur: Malaysian Strategic Research Centre and Konrad-Adenauer Foundation, 2005).

Bahtiar, Effendy, *Islam and the State in Indonesia* (Singapore: ISEAS, 2003).

Baker, Jim, *Crossroads: A Popular History of Malaysia* (Singapore: Times Book International, 1999).

Baker, Richard W., *et.al* (eds), *Indonesia: The Challenge of Change* (Singapore: ISEAS, 1999).

Bakti, Andi M. Faisal, "Islam and Nation Formation" [microform] (National Library of Canada, 1993).

Barlow, Colin (ed), *Modern Malaysia in the Global Economy: Political and Social Change into the 21st Century* (Northampton: Edward Elgar, Cheltenham, 2001).

Barton, Greg, *Abdurrahman Wahid, Muslim Democrat, Indonesian President* (Honolulu, Hawaii: University of Hawaii Press, 2002).

Barton, Gerg, *Gus Dur: The Authorized Biography of Abdurrahman Wahid* (Jakarta: Equinox Publishing, 2002).

Barton, Greg, *Jemaah Islamiyah: Radical Islamization in Indonesia* (Singapore: Ridge Books, 2005).

Baxter, Craig, *Bangladesh: A New Nation in an Old Setting* (Boulder, Colorado: Westview Press, 1984).

Baxter, Craig, *Bangladesh: From a Nation to a State* (Boulder: Westview, 1997)

Beker, Judith O., *Gamelan Stories, Tantrism, Islam and Aesthetics in Central Java* (Arizona, Arizona State University: Programme for Southeast Asian Studies, 1993).

Bellwood, Peter, *The Pre-history of the Indo-Malaysian Archipelago,* Revised edition (Honolulu: University of Hawaii Press, 1997).

Benda, Harry J., *Crescent and the Rising Sun* (The Hague: Van Hoeve, 1958).

Beng, Ooi Kee, *Era of Transition: Malaysia after Mahathir* (Singapore: ISEAS, 2006).

Beverley, Henry, *Report on Census of Bengal, 1872* (Calcutta: Secretariat Press, 1872).

Beyer, Peter, *Religion and Globalization* (London: Sage, 1994).

Bhagwati, Jagdish, *In Defense of Globalization* (New Delhi: Oxford University Press, 2006).

Bhasin, Avtar Singh (ed), *India Bangladesh Relations: Documents – 1971-2002*, Vols. I-V (New Delhi: Geetika Publishers, 2003).

Biers, Dan, *Crash of '97* (Hong Kong: Review Publishing Company, 1998).

Black, Anthony, *The History of Islamic Political Thought: From the Prophet to the Present* (Edinburgh: Edinburgh University Press, 2001).

Booth, Anne (ed), *The Oil Boom and After: Indonesian*

Economic Policy in Soeharto Era (Kuala Lumpur: Oxford University Press, 1995).

Boland, B.J., *The Struggle of Islam in Modern Indonesia* (Hague: Martinus Nijhoff, 1982).

Bourchier, David and Vedi R. Hariz (ed), *Indonesian Politics and Society: A Reader* (London: Routledge, 2003).

Bowen, John R., *Muslims Through Discourse* (Princeton: Princeton University Press, 1993).

Brass, Paul R. and Marcus F. Franda (eds), *Radical Politics in South Asia* (Cambridge: MIT Press, 1973).

Bradley-Birt, Dacca: *The Romance of an Eastern Capital, First Published in 1914* (Guwahati: Spectrum Publication, 1992).

Budiman, Arief (ed), *State and Civil Society in Indonesia* (Melbourne: Centre for Southeast Asian Study, 1990).

Butterworth, Charles E. and I. William Zartman, *Political Islam* (Newbury Park, California: Sage Publications, 1992).

Chakma, Sudhin Kumar, *Prosongo: Parbattya Chattagram* (Context: Chattagong Hill Tracts) (Calcutta: Nath Bros, 1986).

Chakrabarti, Ratan Lal, *Bhasha Andolaner Dalilpatra* (Documents of Language Movement (Dhaka: Bangla Academy, 2000).

Chakravarty, S.R. (ed) *Society, Polity and Economy of Bangladesh* (New Delhi: Har-Anand Publications, 1994).

Chan, Chai Hon, *The Development of British Malaysia* (Kuala Lumpur: Oxford University Press, 1967).

Chapman, F. Spencer, *The Jungle is Neutral* (London: Chatto and Windu, 1949).

Chapra, M. Umer, *Islam and the Economic Challenge* (Leicester: The Islamic Foundation and The International

Institute of Islamic Thought, 1992).

Chatterjee, Basant, *Inside Bangladesh Today: An Eye-witness Account* (New Delhi: S. Chand & Co., 1979).

Cho, George, *The Malaysian Economy: Spatial Perspective* (London, New York: Routledge, 1990).

Chong, Terence (ed), *Globalization and its Counter Forces in Southeast Asia* (Singapore: ISEAS, 2008).

Chowdhury, A.M. and Fakrul Alam, *Bangladesh: On the Threshold of the Twenty-first Century* (Dhaka: Asiatic Society of Bangaldesh,2002).

Choudhury, Masudul Alam and Uzir Abdul Malik, *The Foundations of Islamic Political Economy* (London: Macmillan, 1992).

Cole, Fay-Cooper, *The Peoples of Malaysia* (Princeton, NJ.: Van Nostrant, 1945).

Cowan, C.D. and O.W. Wolters, *Nineteenth Century Malay: Origins of British Political Control* (London: Oxford University Press, 1961).

Cribb, Robert, *The Indonesian Killings, 1965-1966: Studies for Java and Bali*, Monash Papers on Southeast Asia, No. 21 (Clayton, Australia: Centre for Southeast Asian Studies, Monash University, 1990).

Crouch, Harold, *Government and Society in Malaysia* (Allen and Unwin, Cornell University Press, 1996).

Cutterbuck, Richard, *The Long War: Emergency in Malaysia, 1948-1960* (London: Oxford University Press, 1975).

Datuk, Musa Hitam, *Islam and State in Malaysia* (Singapore: ISEAS, 2001).

Daula, Aman-ud, *Ghulam Azamer Nagarikatta Mamla* (About Ghulam Azam's Citizenship) (Dhaka: Dibya Prakash, 1993).

Davidson, Lawrence, *Islamic Fundamentalism* (London: Greenwood Press, 1998).

Delong-Bas, Natan J., *Wahhabi Movement: From Revivalism and Reform to Global Jihad* (New York: Oxford University Press, 2004).

Denny, Frederick, *An Introduction to Islam* (London: Macmillan, 1994).

Dentan, Robert Knox *et.al.*, *Malaysia and the 'Original People'; A Case Study of the Impact of Development on Indigenous Peoples* (Boston: Allyn and Bacon, 1997).

Desker, Barry H.P., *Islam and Society in Southeast Asia after September 11* (Singapore: Institute of Defence and Strategic Studies, 2002).

Deutsch, Karl W., *Nationalism and Social Communication: An Inquiry into the Foundations of Nationality* (Cambridge, Mass: MIT Press, and New York: John Wiley and Sons, 1953).

Djiik, C. van, *Rebellion under the Banner of Islam: The Darul Islam in Indonesia* (The Hague: Martinus Nijhoff, 1971).

Dijk, C. van and A.H. de Groot (eds), *State and Islam* (Leiden: Research School CNWS, 1995).

Eaton, Richard M., *The Rise of Islam in and the Bengal Frontier, 1204-1760* (Berkeley: University of California Press, 1993).

Effendy, Bahtiar, *Islam and the State of Indonesia* (Singapore: ISEAS, 1998).

Eickelman, Dale F. and James Piscatori, *Muslim Politics* (Princeton, New Jersey: Princeton University Press, 1996).

Ellings, Richard J. and Aron L. Friedberg (eds), *Strategic Asia 2003-04: Fragility and Crisis* (Seattle: National Bureau of Asian Research, 2003).

Emerson, Rupert, *Malaysia: A Study in Direct and Indirect Rule* (New York: Macmillan, 1937).

Emerson, Rupert, *From Empire to Nation* (Cambridge, Mass: Harvard University Press, 1960).

Emmerson, Donald K., (ed), *Indonesia Beyond Suharto: Polity, Economy, Society, Transition* (New York: M.E. Shape, 1999).

Esposito, John L., *Voices of Resurgent Islam* (New York: Oxford University Press, 1983).

Esposito, John L., *Islam and Politics* (Syracuse: Syracuse University Press, 1984).

Esposito, John L. (ed), *Islam in Asia: Religion, Politics and Society* (New York: Oxford University Press, 1987).

Esposito, John L., *Iranian Revolution: Its Global Impact* (Miami: Florida International University Press, 1990).

Esposito, John L. (ed), *Political Islam: Revolution, Radicalism, or Reform?* (Boulder: Lynne Reinner Publishers, 1997),

Esposito, John L., *The Islamic Threat: Myth or Reality* (New York: Oxford University Press, 1999).

Esposito, John L. and Dalia Mogahed, *Who Speaks for Islam? What a Billion Muslims Really Think* (New Delhi: Gullup Publication, 2007).

Faaland, Just *et al.*, *Growth and Ethnic Inequality: Malaysia's New Economic Policy* (Kuala Lumpur: Utsan Publications, 2003).

Franda, Marcus, *Bangladesh: The First Decade* (New Delhi: South Asia Publishers, 1982).

Fealy, Greg and Greg Barton (ed), *Nahdlatul Ulama: Traditional Islam and Modernity in Indonesia* (Monas Asia Institute, 1996).

Fealy, Greg and Virginia Hooker, *Voices of Islam in Southeast Asia: A Contemporary Sourcebook* (Singapore: ISEAS, 2006).

Federspiel, Howard M., *A Dictionary of Indonesian Islam* (Monograph in International Studies South Asia)

Federspiel, Howard M., *Muslim Intellectuals and National Development in Indonesia* (New York: Nova Science Publications, 1992).

Federspiel, Howard M. and Nur Fadhil Lubis, *Islam and Development: A Politico-Religious Response* (Montreal: Permika-Montreal and LPMI, 1997).

Federspiel, Howard M., *Indonesia in Transition: Muslim Intellectuals and National Development* (Commack, New York: Nova Science Publishers, 1998).

Federspiel, Howard M., *Islam and Ideology in the Emerging Indonesian State: the Persatuan Islam (PERSIS), 1923-1957* (Boston: Brill Press, 2001).

Fieldhouse, D.K., *Economic and Empire 1830-1914* (London: Macmillan, 1973).

Fieldhouse, D.K., *The Colonial Empires: A comparative Survey from the Eighteenth Century* (Basingstoke and London: Macmillan, 1982).

Forrester, Geoff (ed), *Post-Soeharto Indonesia: Renewal or Chaos* (Singapore: ISEAS, 1999).

Frith, Tabitha, *Constructing Malay Muslim Womanhood in Malaysia* (Monas University: Monas Asia Institute, 2002).

Fuller, E Graham, *The Future of Political Islam* (New York: Palgrave, 2003).

Furnivall, J.S., *Netherlands India: A Study of Plural Economy* (New York: Macmillan, 1944).

Furnivall, J.S., *Colonial Policy and Practice* (New York: New York University Press, 1956).

Funston, John (ed), *Government and Politics in Southeast Asia* (Singapore: ISEAS, 2001).

Geertz, Clifford, *Religion of Java* (Chicago: University Chicago Press, 1976).

Geertz, Clifford, *Islam Observed: Religious Development in Morocco and Indonesia* (Chicago: University of Chicago Press, 1971).

Gibbs, H.A.R., *Modern Trends in Islam* (Chicago: University of Chicago Press, 1949).

Gomez, Edmund Terence and Jomo K.S., *Malaysia's Political Economy: Politics, Patronage and Profit* (London; Cambridge, 2001).

Gordon, Alijah (ed), *The Propagation of Islam in the Indonesian-Malay Archipelago* (KL: Malaysian Sociological Research Institute, 2001).

Grant, Bruce, *Indonesia* (Parkville: Melbourne University Press, 1964).

Guhathakurta, Basanti, *Ekattaorer Smriti* (Memories of Seventy One) (Dhaka: University Press Limited, 2000).

Gungwu, Wang (ed), *Nation-Building: Five Southeast Asian Histories* (Singapore: ISEAS, 2005).

Hafiz, M. Abdul and Rob Khan (eds), *Nation Building in Bangladesh: Retrospect and Prospect* (Dhaka: BISS, 1982).

Hall, D.G.E, *A History of Southeast Asia* (New York: Macmillan, 1966).

Hamid, Ahmad Sarji Abdul,(ed), *Malaysia's Vision 2020: Understanding the Concept, Implications and Challenges* (Petaling Jaya: Pelanduk Publications, 1993).

Haq, Mohammad Enamul, *A History of Sufism in Bengal* (Dhaka: Asiatic Society of Bangladesh, 1975).

Hardjono, Joan, *Indonesia: Resources, Ecology and Environment* (Singapore: Oxford University Press, 1991).

Hashmi, Sohail (ed), *Islamic Political Ethics: Civil Society, Pluralism and Conflict* (Princeton; Princeton University Press, 2002).

Hassan, Mohd. Affandi, *The Tawhidic Approach in Management and Public Administration: Concepts, Principles and An Alternative Model* (Kuala Lumpur: National Institute of Public Administration, 1992).

Hefner, Robert W., *Democratic Civility: The History and Cross-cultural Possibility of a Modern Political Ideal* (New Brunswick: Transaction, 1998).

Hefner, Robert W. (ed), *Market Cultures: Society and Morality in the New Asian Capitalism* (Boulder: Westview, 1998).

Hefner, Robert W., *Civil Islam: Muslims and Democratization in Indonesia* (New Jersey, Princeton University Press, 2000).

Hefner, Robert W., *The Politics of Multiculturalism: Pluralism and Citizenship in Malaysia, Singapore and Indonesia* (Honolulu: University of Hawaii Press, 2001).

Hefner, Robert W. and Petricia Horvatich (eds), *Islam in the Era of Nation-States: Politics and Religious Renewal in Muslim South East Asia* (Honolulu: University of Hawaii Press, 1997).

Hill, Hal (ed), *Unity and Diversity: Regional Economic Development in Indonesia since 1970* (Singapore: Oxford University Press, 1991).

Hindley, Donald, *Communist Party of Indonesia 1951-1963* (Berkeley: University of California Press, 1964)

Hilley, John, *Malaysia: Mahathirism, Hegemony and the New Opposition* (London: Zed Nooks, 2001).

Hitam, Tan Sri Musa, *Islam and State in Malaysia* (Singapore: ISEAS, 2001)

Hoa, Trans Van (ed), *The Asian Recovery: Issues and Aspects of Development, Growth, Trade and Investment* (Chelternhan: Edward Elgar, 2001).

Hooker, M.B. (ed), *Islam in South-East Asia* (Leiden: E.J. Brill, 1983).

Hooker, M.B., *Indonesian Islam: Social Change through Contemporary Fatawa* (Honolulu: Alen and Unwin and University of Hawaii Press, 2003).

Hooker, Virginia and Norani Othman, *Malaysia: Islam, Society and Politics* (Singapore: ISEAS, 2003).

Hooker, Virginia Matheson, *A Short History of Malaysia: Linking East and West* (Crows Nest: Allen and Unwin, 2003).

Hooker, Virginia and Amin Saikal (eds), *Islamic Perspective on the New Millennium* (Singapore: ISEAS, 2004).

Hosen, Nadirsyah, *Shari'a and Constitutional Reform in Indonesia* (Singapore: ISEAS, 2007).

Hossain, Golam, *General Ziaur Rahman and the BNP: Political Transformation of a Military Regime* (Dhaka: University Press Limited, 1988).

Hunter, Shireen T. (ed), *The Politics of Islamic Revivalism* (Bloomington and Indianapolis: Indiana University Press, 1988).

Huntington, Samuel P., *The Clash of Civilization and the Remaking of the World Order* (New York: Simon & Schuster, 1996).

Hussain, Muhammad Delwar (ed), *Bangladesher Rajnitite Dharma O Dharma Niropekdhata* (Religion and Secularism in the Politics of Bangladesh (Dhaka: Prerona Prokashan, 1993).

Hussain, Mohd Yusof, *Media and Muslim Society* (Kuala Lumpur: International Islamic University Malaysia, 2006).

Hwang, In-Wan, *Personalized Politics: The Malaysian State under Mahathir* (Singapore: ISEAS, 2003).

Ibrahim, Ahmad *et. al.*, (ed), *Readings on Islam in Southeast Asia* (Singapore: ISEAS, 1985).

Ibrahim, Anwar, *The Asian Renaissance* (Singapore: Times Books International, 1996).

Ilias, Khandakar Mohammad (ed), *Bangladesher Samaj Biplobe Bangabandhur Darshan* (Bangabandhu's Philosophy for Social Revolution) (Dhaka: Bangladesh Parishad, 1979).

Indonesia Publications, *The Petition of 50 Group and the Tanjung Priok Incident* (Lanham-Seabrook: Indonesia Publications, 1989).

Indonesia Publications, *Political Islam in Indonesia* (Lanham-Seabrook MD,: Indonesia Publications, 1989).

Isaacson, Jascon F. and Colin Ruberstein (eds), *Islam in Asia: Changing Political Realities* (New Brunswick: Transaction Publishers, 2002).

ISEAS, Regional Outlook forum 2008, *Summary Report* (Singapore: ISEAS, 2008

Ishida, Masami (ed), *Economic Crisis in Indonesia* (Chiba: Institute of Developing Economies, 2000).

Ismail, Faisal, *Islamic Traditionalism in Indonesia: A Study of Nahdlatul Ulama's Early History and Religious Ideology (1926-1950)* (Jakarta: KDT, 2003).

Ismail, Rose, *Hudud in Malaysia: The Issues at Stake* (Kuala Lumpur: SIS Forum (Malaysia) Berhad, 1995).

Islam, Sirajul, (ed), *History of Bengal 1704-1971* (Dhaka: Asiatic Society of Bangladesh, 1998).

Islam, Syed Sirajul, *The Politics of Islamic Identity in Southeast Asia* (Singapore: Thomson, 2005).

Jackson, Karl D., *Traditional Authority, Islam and Rebellion: A Study of Indonesian Political Behavior* (Berkeley: University of California Press, 1980).

Jahan, Rounaq, *Pakistan: Failure in National Integration* (New York: Colombia University Press, 1972).

Jahangir, Borhanuddin Khan, *Bangladeshe Jatiyotabad Ebong Moulabad* (Nationalism and Fundamentalism in Bangladesh) (Dhaka: Agami Prakashini, 1993).

Jalaluddin, Abul Khair Mohd., *The Role of Government in an Islamic Economy* (Kuala Lumpur, A.S. Noorden, 1991).

Johns, Anthony and Nally Lahoud (eds), *Islam in World Politics* (New York: Routledge, 2005).

Johnstone, Ronald L., *Religion in Society: A Sociology of Religion* (New Jersey: Prentice-Hall, 2007).

Kabir, Muhammad Ghulam, *Changing Face of Nationalism: The Case of Bangladesh* (New Delhi: South Asia Publishers, 1994).

Kahin, Audrey, *Regional Dynamics of the Indonesian Revolution: Unity from Diversity* (Honolulu: Hawaii University Press, 1985).

Kahin, George McTurnan, *Nationalism and Revolution in Indonesia* (Ithaca: Cornell University Press, 1952).

Kahn, Joe S. and Francis Loh Kok Wah (eds), *Fragmented Vision: Culture and Politics in Contemporary Malaysia* (Sydney: Allen and Unwin, 1992).

Kahn, Joel S., *Southeast Asian Identities: Culture and Politics of Representation* (Singapore: ISEAS, 1998).

Karaskiewicz, Peter, *National Unity in a Multi-ethnic State: Malaysia* (Bielefeld: University of Bielefed, 1996).

Karim, Muhammad Abdul, *Social History of the Muslims of Bengal* (Dacca: Asiatic Society of Pakistan, 1959).

Karlekar, Hirenmay, *Bangladesh: Next Afghanistan* (New Delhi: Sage, 2005).

Kausar, Zeenath, *Contemporary Islamic Thought: A Study of Eleven Islamic Thinkers* (Kuala Lumpur, International Islamic University Malaysia, 2005).

Kessler, Clive, *Islam and Politics in a Malay State: Kelantan, 1838-1960* (Ithaca: Cornell University Press, 1978).

Khan, Mohammad Ayub, *Friends, Not Masters: A Political Autobiography* (Karachi: Oxford University, Press, 1969).

Khan, Muin-ud-din Ahmad (ed), *Selection from Bengal Government Records on Wahhabi Trials, 1863-1870* (Dacca: Asiatic Society of Pakistan, 1961).

Khan, Muin-uddin Ahmed, *History of Fariadi Movement in Bengal* (Dhaka: Islamic Foundation, 1984).

Khan, Zillur R., *Martial Law to Martial Law: Leadership Crises in Bangladesh* (Dhaka: University Press Limited, 1984).

Kheng, Cheah Boon, *Malaysia: The making of a Nation* (Singapore: ISEAS,2002).

Kim, Khoo Kay (ed), *The History of Southeast, South and East Asia* (Kuala Lumpur: Oxford University Press, 1977).

Kipp, Rita Smith and Susan Rodgers (eds), *Indonesian Religions in Transition* (Tueson: University of Arizona Press, 1987).

Koon, Tan Chee, *Without Fear and Favour* (Singapore: Eastern Universities Press, 1984).

Kratoska, Paul H., *The Japanese Occupation of Malaya: A Social and Economic History* (London: Hurst and Co. 1998).

Kratoska, Paul H., *South East Asia: Colonial History*, Vol. VI, (London: Routledge, 2001).

Kurzman, Charles, *Liberal Islam: A Sourcebook* (New York: Oxford University Press, 1998).

Landon, Kenneth P., *Southeast Asia: Crossroads of Culture* (Chicago: University of Chicago Press, 1948).

Lapidus, Ira Marvin, *A History of Islamic Societies* (London: Cambridge, 2002).

Lau-Fong, Mak, *Islamization in Southeast Asia* (Taipei: Asia-Pacific Research Program, 2002).

Lawrence, Bruce, *Shattering the Myth: Islam Beyond Violence* (Princeton: Princeton University Press, 1998).

Lee, Raymond L. M. and Susan E. Ackerman, *Sacred Tensions: Modernity and Religious Transformation in Malaysia* (Colombia SC: University of South Carolina Press, 1997).

Lev, Daniel S., *Islamic Courts in Indonesia* (Berkeley: University of California, 1972).

Levtzion, Nehemia (ed), *Conversion to Islam* (New York: Honmes and Meier Publishers, 1979).

Limaye, Satu P. *et al., Religious Radicalism and Security in South Asia* (Honolulu, Hawaii: Asia-Pacific Center for Security Studies, 2004).

Lloyd, Grayson, Shannon Smith, *Indonesia Today: Challenges of History* (Singapore: ISEAS, 2001).

Mackie, J.A.C. (ed), *The Chinese in Indonesia* (Hong Kong: Heinemann Educational Books, 1976).

Mahdzan, Ahmad (ed), *Southeast Asia on the Growth Path* (Serdong: UPM, 1997).

Majumdar, Gayatri Sen, *Buddhism in Ancient Bengal* (Calcutta: Navana, 1983).

Mandeville, Peter G., *Transnational Muslim Politics: Reimagining the Umma* (London: Routledge, 2004)

Mandeville, Peter G., *Global Political Islam* (London: Routledge, 2007).

Manikas, Peter M. and Laur L. Thornton, *Political Parties in Asia* (Makati, the Philippines: National Democratic Institution for International Affairs, 2002).

Maniruzzaman, Talukdar, *The Bangladesh Revolution and Its Aftermath* (Dhaka: university Press Limited, 1988)

Manning, Chris and Peter Van Dierman, *Indonesia in*

Transition: Soviet Aspects of Reformasi and Crisis (Singapore: ISEAS, 1999).

Mansbeach, Richard W. and Edward Rhodes, *Global Politics in a Changing World* (Boston: Houghton Miffin Company, 2003).

Marr, David E. and A.C. Milner (eds), *Southeast Asia in the 9th and 14th Centuries* (Singapore: ISEAS, 1985).

May, Brian, *The Indonesian Tragedy* (London: Routledge, 1978).

McGlynn, John H. *et.al., Indonesia in the Soeharto Years: Issues, Incidents and Images* (Lontar, 2005).

McVey, Ruth T., *The Rise of Indonesian Communism* (Ithaca: Cornell University Press, 1968).

Mehden, Fred R. Von der, *Religion and Nationalism in Southeast Asia* (Madison: University of Wisconsin, 1963).

Meuleman, Johan, *Islam in the Era of Globalization: Muslim Attitude towards Modernity and Identity* (Jakarta: INIS, 2001).

Milne, R.S. and Diane K. Mauzy, *Malaysian Politics under Mahathir* (London: Routledge, 1999).

Millard, Mike, *Jihad in Paradise* (London, New York: M.K. Shape, 2004).

Milley, John, *Malaysia: Mahathirism, Hegemony and the New Opposition* (London: Zed Books, 2001).

Milner, Anthony, *The Invention of Politics in Colonial Malaya: Contesting Nationalism and the Expansion of the Public Sphere* (Cambridge: Cambridge University Press, 1995).

Milton-Edwards, Beverley, *Islam and Politics in the Contemporary World* (Cambridge: Polity Press, 2004).

Mohamad, Mahathir, *The Malay Dilemma* (Singapore: Donald Moore, 1970).

Mohamad, Mahathir, *The Challenge* (Petling Jaya: Pelanduk Publications, 1986).

Mohamad, Mahathir, *The Way Forward* (London: Weidenfeld and Nicolson, 1998).

Mohamad, Mahathir, *The Early Years 1947-1972* (Kuala Lumpur: Berita Publication, 1995).

Mohammadi, Ali (ed), *Islam Encountering Globalization* (London: RoutledgeCurzon, 2002).

Mohsin, Amena, *The Politics of Nationalism: The Case of the Chittagong Hill Tracts, Bangladesh* (Dhaka: University Press Limited, 2002).

Morais, J.V., *Mahathir: A Profile in Courage* (Singapore: Eastern Universities Press, 1982).

Mortimer, Rex, *Indonesian Communism under Sukarno: Ideology and Policies, 1959-1965* (Ithaca: Cornell University Press, 1974).

Moussalli, Ahmad S., *Moderate and Radical Islamic Fundamentalism: The Quest for Modernity, Legitimacy and the Islamic State* (Gainesville: University of Florida, 1999).

Mudzhar, Mohamad Atho, *Islam and Islamic Law in Indonesia: A socio-Historical Approach* (Jakarta: Ministry of Religious Affairs, 2003).

Munawir, Sjadzali, *Islam and Governmental System: Teachings, History and Reflections* (Jakarta: INIS, 1991).

Murshid, Tazeen M., *The Sacred and the Secular: Bengal Muslim Discourses, 1871-1977* (Calcutta: Oxford University Press, 1995).

Mutalib, Hussin, *Islam and Ethnicity in Malay Politics* (Singapore: Oxford University Press, 1990).

Mutalib, Hussin, *Islam in Malaysia: From Revivalism to Islamic State* (Singapore: Singapore University Press, 1993).

Mutalib, Hussin, *Islam in Malaysia: From Revivalism to*

Islamic State? (Singapore: National University of Singapore, 1993).

Mutalib, Hussin, *Islam in Southeast Asia* (Singapore: ISEAS, 2008).

Mutalib, Hussin and Taj ul-Islam Hashmi (eds), *Islam, Muslims and the Modern State: Case-studies of Muslims in Thirteen Countries* (New York: St Martin's Press, 1994).

Mutalib, Hussin (ed), *Islam and Democracy: The Southeast Asia Experience* (Singapore: Centre for Contemporary Islamic Studies and Konrad Adenauer Foundation, 2004).

Muzaffar, Chandra, *Protector?* (Penang: Aliran, 1979).

Muzaffar, Chandra, I*slamic Resurgence in Malaysia* (Petaling Jaya: Penerbit Fajar Bakti, 1987).

Myung-Seok, Oh and Kim Hyung-Jun, *Religion, Ethnicity and Modernity in Southeast Asia* (Seoul: Seoul University Press, 1998).

Nair, Shanti, *Islam in Malaysian Foreign Policy* (London: Routledge, 1997).

Nakamura, Mitsuo, *The Crescent Arises over the Banyan Tree: A Study of the Muhammadiyah Movement in a Javanese Town* (Yogyakarta: Gadjah Mada University Press, 1983).

Nakamura, Mitsuo, *Islam and Democracy in Indonesia: Observations on the 2004 General and Presidential Elections* (Harvard Law School, Occasional Publications 6, December 2005).

Nasr, Syyed Vali Reza, *Islamic Leviathan and making of State Power* (New York: Oxford University Press, 2001).

Nathan, K.S. and Mohammad Hashim Kamali (eds), *Islam in Southeast Asia: Political, Social and Strategic Challenges for the 21 Century* (Singapore: ISEAS, 2006).

Navarathan, Raman V., *Malaysia's Socio-economic Challenges* (Selangor Darul Ahsan: Pelanduk Publications, 2003).

Neelsen John P. and Dipok Malik (eds), *Crisis of State and Nation: South Asian States between Nation-Building and Fragmentation* (New Delhi: Monohar, 2007).

Nicholas, Colin, *The Orang Asli and the Contest for Resources: Indigenous Politics, Development and Identity in Peninsular Malaysia* (Copenhagen: International Working Group for Indigenous Affairs and Centre for Orang Asli Concerns, 2000).

Nicholson, Reynold Alleyne, *Studies in Islamic Mysticism* (Delhi: Adam Publishers and Distributors, 1998).

Noer Deliar, The Modernist Muslim Movement in Indonesia: 1900-1942 (London: Oxford University Press, 1973).

Noer, Deliar, *The Modernist Muslim Movement in Indonesia:1900-1942* (London: Oxford University Press, 1973)

Noor, Ismail, *Passing the Baton: From Dr. Mahathir to Abdullah Badawi* (Kuala Lumpur: Thinker's Library, 2004).

Noor, Farish A., *The Other Malaysia: Writings on Malaysia's Subaltern History* (Kuala Lumpur: Silverfishbooks, 2002).

Noor, Farish A., *Islam Embedded: The Historical Development of the Pan-Malaysian Islamic Party PAS (1951-2003)*, Vol. I and II (Kuala Lumpur, Malaysian Sociological Research Institute, 2004).

Okposin, Samuel Bassey, *et.al., The Changing Phases of Malaysian Economy* (Selangor Darul Ehsan: Pelanduk Publications, 2005).

Omar, Ariffin, *Bansa Melayu: Malay Concepts of Democracy and Community, 1945-1950* (Kuala Lumpur: Oxford University Press, 1993).

Omar, Raziah, *State Islam and Malay Reproduction* (Canberra: Australian National University, 1996).

Ongkili, James P., *Nation-building in Malaysia 1946-1974* (Singapore; Oxford University Press, 1985).

Osman, Mohd. Taib (ed), *Islamic Civilization in the Malay World* (Kuala Lumpur: Dewan Bhasa dan Pustak, 1997).

Owen, Norman G. (ed), *The Emergence of Modern Southeast Asia* (Singapore: Singapore University Press, 2005).

Peacock, James L., *Muslim Puritans: Reformist Psychology in Southeast Asian Islam* (Berkeley: University of California Press, 1978).

Peacock, James L., *Purifying Faith: The Muhammadiyah Movement in Indonesian Islam* (California: The Benjamin/Cummings Publishing Company, 1978).

Perkinson, C.N., *British Intervention in the Malay States 1867-77* (Kuala Lumpur: Oxford University Press, 1960).

Perwita, Anak Agung Banyu, *Indonesia and the Muslim World: Between Islam and Secularism in the Foreign Policy of Soeharto and Beyond* (Copenhagen: NIAS, 2007).

Phadnis, Urmila, *Ethnicity and Nation-building in South Asia* (New Delhi: Sage, 1989).

Porter, Donald J. *Managing Politics and Islam in Indonesia* (London: RoutledgeCurzon, 2005).

Purcell, Victor, *The Chinese in Southeast Asia* (Kuala Lumpur: Oxford University Press, 1980).

Puthucheary, Mavis and Norani Othman, *Elections and Democracy in Malaysia* (Bangi: Universiti Kebangsaan Malaysia, 2005).

Qureshi, Ishtaq Husain, *Ulema in Politics* (Karachi: Ma'aref Limited, 1974).

Qwek, Kim, *Where to, Malaysia: A Future with Anwar's Reformasi or Back to Mahathirsm?* (Petaling Jaya: SIRD, 2005).

Rahman, Fazlur, *Islam* (New York: Halt, Rinehart, and Winston, 1966).

Rahman, Siti Fathimah Abdul (ed), *The Impact of Globalization on Social and Cultural Life: An Islamic Response* (Kuala Lumpur: Institute of Islamic Understanding Malaysia, 2002).

Rahim, Rohani Binti Abdul, *Muslims in Indonesia and the Notion of an Islamic State* (Selangor Darul Ehsan; Dewan Pustaka Islam, 1991).

Ramage, Douglas E., *Politics in Indonesia: Democracy, Islam and the Ideology of Tolerance* (London: Routledge, 1995).

Rashid, Harun Or, *The Foreshadowing of Bangladesh: Bengal Muslim League and Muslim Politics 1906-1947* (Dhaka: University Press Limited, 2003).

Razak, Mohd Najib Abdul, *Globalising Malaysia: Towards Building a Developed Nation* (Selangor: MPH Group Publishing, 2006).

Reid, Anthony (ed), *Southeast Asia in the Early Modern Era: Trade, Power and Belief* (Ithaca: Cornell University Press, 1993).

Resosudarmo, Budy P. (ed), *The Politics and Economics of Indonesia's Natural Resources* (Singapore: ISEAS, 2007).

Reeve, David, *Golkar of Indonesia: An Alternative to the Party System* (Singapore: Oxford University Press, 1985).

Riaz, Ali, God Willing: *The Politics of Islamism in Bangladesh* (New York: Rowman and Littlefield, 2004).

Ricklefs, M.C., *A History of Indonesia Since C1200 to the Present* (London: Macmillan, 1981).

Rinkes, D.A., *Nine Saints of Java* (Kuala Lumpur: Malaysian Sociological Research Institute, 1996).

Rizvi, S.A.A., *A History of Sufism in India* (Delhi: Munshiram Manoharilal, 1978).

Robinson, Francis, *Atlas of the Islamic World since 1500* (Oxford: Phaidon Press, 1982).

Robinson, Francis, *Atlas of the Islamic World since 1500* (Oxford: Phaidon Press, 1982).

Robinson, Richard R. and Vedi R. Hadiz, *Reorganising Power in Indonesia: Politics of Oligarchy in an Age of Market* (London: Routledge, 2004).

Roff, William R. *The Origins of Malay Nationalism* (Kuala Lumpur, Oxford University Press, 1994).

Rose, Leo E., *War and Succession: Pakistan, India and the Creation of Bangladesh* (Berkeley: University of California, 1990).

Rosen, Nadirasyah, *Shari'a and Constitutional Reform in Indonesia* (Singapore: ISEAS, 2007).

Roy, Asim, *The Islamic Syncretistic Tradition in Bengal* (Princeton: Princeton University Press, 1983).

Roy, Oliver, *Globalised Islam: The Search for New Ummah* (London: Hurt and Company, 2002).

Ruthven, Malise, *Fundamentalism: The Search for Meaning* (New York: Oxford University Press, 2004).

Ryan, N.J., *The Cultural Background of the Peoples of Malaysia* (Kuala Lumpur: Longman, 1962).

Sadka, Enila, *The Protected Malay States 1874-1895* (Kuala Lumpur: University Press, 1968).

Saklayen, G., *Bangladeser Sufi Sadhak* (The Sufi Austere of Bangladesh) (Dhaka: Islamic Foundation, 1982).

Saleh, Fauzan, *Modern Trends in Islamic Theological Discourse in 20th Century Indonesia: A Critical Study* (Leiden, Boston: Brill, 2001).

Salim, Arskal and Azymardi Azra (ed), *Shari'a and Politics in Modern Indonesia* (Singapore: ISEAS, 2003).

Sandhu, K.S. and Paul Weatley (eds), *Melaka: The*

Transformation of a Malay Capital, 1400-1980, Vol. I and II (Singapore: ISEAS, 1983).

Sato, Yuri, *Indonesia Entering a New Era: Abdurrahman Wahid Government and its Challenge* (Chiba: Institute of Developing Economies, 2000).

Searle, Peter, *Politics in Sarawk 1970-1976: The Iban Perspective* (Kuala Lumpur: Oxford University Press, 1983).

Sen, Krishna and David T. Hill, *Media, Culture and Politics in Indonesia* (New York: Oxford University Press, 2000).

Sen, Rangalal, *Political Elite in Bangladesh* (Dhaka: University Press Limited, 1986).

Seng, Philip Loh Fook, *The Malay State 1877-1895: Political Change and Social Policy* (London: Oxford University Press, 1969).

Shah, Ibrahim Abu (ed), *Islam, Democracy and Good Governance: The Malaysian Experience: Essays in Honour of Tun Dr. Mahathir Mohammad* (Shah Alam, Selangor: Pusat Penerbitan Universiti, 2004).

Shihab, Alwi [Abdurrahman], *The Muhammadiya Movement and its Controversy with Christian Mission in Indonesia* (Ann Arbor, Michigan: UMI Dissertation Services, 2001).

Shirasishi, Takashi, *An Age in Motion: Popular Racialism in Java, 1912-1926* (Ithaca: Cornell University Press, 1990).

Sihahmed, Abdel Salam and Anoushiravan Ehteshami (ed), *Islamic Fundamentalism* (Boulder: Westview Press, 1996).

Siddiqi, Mazharuddin, *Modern Reformist Thought in Muslim World* (Islamabad: Islamic Research Institute, 1982).

Siddiqi, Muhammad Nejatullah, *Muslim Economic Thinking: A Survey of Contemporary Literature* (Jeddah: International Centre for Research in Islamic Economics, nd)

Siddiquee, Noore Alam, *Islam in Bangladesh Politics: The Role of Ghulam Azam* (London: Routledge, 2004).

Sidel, John Thayer, *The Islamist Threat in Southeast Asia* (Washington: East-West Center, 2007).

Sisson, Richard and Leo E. Rose, *War and Succession: Pakistan, India and the Creation of Bangladesh (Berkeley: University of California Press, 1990).*

Sivan, Emmanuel, *Radical Islam: Medieval Theology and Modern Politics* (New York: Yale University Press, 1988).

Sjadzali, Munwir, *Muslim Interests are Better Served in the Absence of Muslim Parties: Indonesian Experience* (Jakarta: Ministry of Religious Affairs, 1992).

Smith, Paul J. (ed), *Terrorism and Violence in Southeast Asia* (London, New York: M.E. Shape, 2005).

Snarr, Michael T. and D. Neil Snarr, *Introducing Global Issues* (London: Boulder, 1998).

Sobhan, Rehman, *Bangladesh: The Problems of Governance* (Dhaka: University Press, Limited, 1993).

Soong, Kua Kia, *Malaysian Critical Issues* (Selangor: SIRD, 2002).

Stauth, Georg, *Politics and Cultures of Islamization in Southeast Asia* (New Brunswick, Transition Publishers, 2002).

Steenbrink, Karel A., *Dutch Colonialism and Indonesian Islam: Contacts and Conflict 1596-1950*, translated by Jan Steenbrink and Henry Jansen (Amsterdam: Rodopi, 1993).

Steward, Brian, *Smashing Terrorism in the Malayan Emergency* (Selangor: Pelanduk Publication, 2004).

Stewark, Ian, *The Mahathir Legacy: A Nation Divided, A Region at Risk* (Sydney: Allen and Unwin, 2003).

Stibbe,D.G. and H. Colijin, *Netherlands Indies* (Amsterdam: N.V. Elsevier, 1935).

Strange, Susan, *The Retreat of the State: The Diffusion of Power in the World Economy* (London: Cambridge University, 1996).

Sukma, Rizal, *Islam in Indonesian Foreign Policy* (London: Routledge, 2003).

Sukma, Rizal and Clara Joewono (eds), *Islamic Thought and Movements in Contemporary Indonesia* (Jakarta: CSIS, 2007).

Suryadinata, Leo, *Ethnic Chinese as Southeast Asians* (Singapore: ISEAS, 1997).

Suryadinata, Leo, *Military Ascendancy and Political Culture: A Study of Indonesia's Golkar* (Ohio: Southeast Asia Series 85, 1989).

Suryadinata, Leo, *Elections and Politics in Indonesia* (Singapore: ISEAS, 2002).

Swatos Jr., William H., *A Future for Religion: New Paradigms for Social Analysis* (Newbury Park: Sage, 1993).

Taher, Tarmizi H., *Aspiring for the Middle Path: Religious Harmony in Indonesia* (Jakarta: Center fro the Study of Islam and Society, 1997).

Taher, Tarmizi H., *Islam Across Boundaries: Prospects and Problems of Islam in the Future of Indonesia* (Jakarta: Penerbit Republika, 2003).

Teik, Khoo Boo, *Paradoxes of Mahathir: An Intellectual Biography of Mahathir Mohammad* (Kuala Lumpur: Oxford University Press, 1995).

Thaib, Lukman, *Islamic Political Representation in Malaysia* (Kuala Lumpur: University of Malay Press, 2005).

Tahir, Hailani Muji, *Revenue and Fiscal Policy of an Islamic State* (Bandar Baru Bangi: Fatha Publishers, 1999).

Thaib, Lukman, *The Islamic Polity and Leadership* (Petaling Jaya : Delta Publishing, 1995).

Tan, Andrew T.H. (ed), *A Handbook of Terrorism and Insurgency in Southeast Asia* (Cheltenham, UK: Edward Elgar, 2007).

Tarling, Nicholas, *Imperialism in Southeast Asia* (London: Routledge, 2001).

Teik, Khoo Boo, *Paradoxes of Mahathirism: An Intellectual Biography of Mahathir Mohamad* (Kuala Lumpur: Oxford University Press, 1995).

Tibi, Bassam, *The Challenge of Fundamentalism: Political Islam and the New World Disorder* (Berkeley: University of California Press, 1998).

Trengonning, K.G., *A History of Modern Malaya* (Singapore: Eastern University Press, 1964).

Trimingham, J. Spencer, *The Sufi Orders in Islam* (London: Oxford University Press, 1971).

Truna, Dody S., *Islam and Politics under the 'New Order' Government in Indonesia 1966-1990* (Michigan: Michigan University film International, 1995).

Uddin, Sufia M., *Construction Bangladesh: Religion, Ethnicity and Language in an Islamic Nation* (New Delhi: Vistaar Publication, 2006).

Umar, Badaruddin, *Juddhotor Bangladesh* (Post-War Bangladesh) (Dhaka: Muktadhara, 1975).

Umar, Badaruddin, *The Emergence of Bangladesh*, Volume 2, *The Rise of Bengali Nationalism, 1958-1971* (New York: Oxford University Press, 2006).

Yunanto, S. et.al. *Militant Islamic Movement in Indonesia and Southeast Asia* (Jakarta: Friedrich-Ebert-Stiftung: Ridep Institute, 2003).

Varshney, Ashutosh *et.al., Pattern of Collective Violence in Indonesia (1990-2003)*: A UNISFIR Working Paper – 04/03 (Jakarta: United Nations Support Faculty for Indonesian Recovery, July 2004).

Vatikiotis, Panayiotis J., *Islam and the State* (London: Routledge, 1991).

Venardos, Angelo M., *Islamic Banking and Finance in South-East Asia: Its Development and Future* (Singapore: World Scientific Press, 2006)

Verma, Vidhu, *Malaysia: State and Civil Society in Transition* (Boulder: Lynne Rienner, 2002).

Vlekke, Bernhard H.M., *Nusantara: A History of Indonesia* (Bandung: W.Van Hoeve, 1959).

Voll, John Obert, *Islam: Continuity and Change in the Modern World* (Boulder: Westview Press, 1982).

Vorys, Karl Von, *Democracy without Consensus: Communalism and Political Stability in Malaysia* (Princeton: Princeton University Press, 1975).

Wah, Francis Loh Kok and Khoo Boo Teik, *Democracy in Malaysia: Discourses and Practices* (Surry: Curzon Press, 2002).

Wahid, Zainal Abidin A. (ed), *Glimpses of Malaysian History* (Kuala Lumpur: Dewan Bahasa Dan Pustak, 1970).

Wanandi, Jusuf, *Global, Regional and National: Strategic Issues and Linkages* (Jakarta: CSIS, 2006).

Weekes, Richard V., *Pakistan: Birth and Growth of a Muslim Nation* (Princeton: Van Nostrand Company, 1964).

Weekes, Richard V. (ed), *Muslim Peoples: A World of Ethnographic Survey* (London: Greenwood Press, 1978).

Winstedt, Richard O., *The Malays: A Cultural History* (London: Routledge and Kegan Paul, 1953).

Winstedt, Richard O., *A History of Malaya* (Kuala Lumpur: Marican and Sons, 1982).

Wolters, O.W., *The Fall of Sriwijaya in Malay History* (Kuala Lumpur: Oxford University Press, 1970).

Woodward, Mark R. (ed), *Towards a New Paradigm: Recent*

Development in Islamic Thought (Arizona: Arizona State University, 1995).

Zakaria, Rafiq, *The Struggle within Islam* (New Delhi: Penguin Books, 1989).

Ziring, Lawrence, *Bangladesh: From Mujib to Ershad: An Interpretative Study* (Dhaka: University Press Limited, 1984).

Articles

Abuza, Zachary, "Tentacles of Terror: Al-Qaeda's Southeast Asian Network", *Contemporary Southeast Asia*, Vol. 24, No. 3, 2002, pp. 427-465.

Anjum, Tanvir, "Sufism in History and its Relationship with Power", *Islamic Studies*, Vol. 45, No. 2, 2006, pp. 221-268.

Akhtar Banu, U.A.B. Razia, "The Fall of the Sheikh Mujib Regime: An Analysis", *Indian Political Science Review*, Vol. XV, No. 1, January 1981, pp. 1-19.

Bandoro, Bantarto, "Bali Bombing and Fight against Terrorism", *The Indonesian Quarterly*, Vol. 33. No. 4, 2005, pp. 324-328.

Bandoro, Bantarto, "Indonesian Foreign Policy in 2008 and Beyond", *The Indonesian Quarterly*, Vol. 35, No. 4, 2007, pp. 327-334.

Baswedan, Anies, "Indonesian Politics in 2007: The Presidency, Local Elections and the Future of Democracy", *BIES* (Bulletin of Indonesian Economic Studies), Vol. 43, No. 3, December 2007, pp. 323-340.

Berg, C.C., "The Islamization of Java", *Studia Islamika*, Vol. IV, No. 2, 1950, pp. 111-142.

Camroux, D., "State Responses to Islamic Resurgence in Malaysia: Accommodation, Co-option and Confrontation", *Asian Survey*, Vol. XXXVI, No. 9, 1996 pp. 861-866.

Chakma, Sugata, "Chakma" in *Indigenous Communities*, Vol. 5 (Dhaka: Asiatic Society of Bangladesh, 2007) pp. 36-83.

Cheek, Shabery, "The Politics of Malaysia's Islamic Resurgence, *Third World Quarterly*, Vol. 10, No. 2, April 1988, pp. 843-868.

Crouch, Harold, "Authoritarian Trends, the UMNO Split and the Limits to the State Poere" in Joel S. Kahin and Francis Loh Kok Wah (eds), *Fragmented Vision: Culture and Politics in Contemporary Malaysia* (Sydney: Allen and Unwin, 1992).

Custers, Peter, "Islamisation and More Aids for the Generals", *Economic and Political Weekly*, June 25, 1998, pp. 1317-1318.

Elson, R.E., "Islam, Islamization, the Nation and the Early Indonesian Nationalist Movement", *Journal of Indonesian Islam*, Vol. 1, No. 2, December 2007, pp. 231-266.

Feith, Herbert and Danial S. Lev, "The End of Indonesian Rebellion", *Pacific Affairs*, Vol. 36, No. 1, Spring 1963.

Fukuyama, Francis, "Development and Limits of Institutional Design", keynote address, 7th Annual Conference of the Global Development Network (GDN), St. Petersburg, January 20, 2006.

Grant, Ronald M., Indonesia 1978: A Third Term for President Suharto, *Asian Survey*, Vol. XIX, No. 2 February 1979, pp. 141-146.

Gersham, John, "Is Southeast Asia the Second Front, *Foreign Affairs*, Vol. 81. No. 4, 2002, pp. 20-74.

Hooker, M.B., "Introduction: Islamic Law in South-East Asia, *Studia Islamika*, Vol. 10, No. 1, Special Issue, 2003, pp. 1-22.

Hooker, M.B. and Tim Lindsey, "Public Faces of Shariah in Contemporary Indonesia: Towards National Madhhab", *Studia Islamika*, Vol. 10, No. 1, 2003, pp. 23-64.

Indorf, Hans H., "Malaysia 1978: Communal Coalitions Continue", *Asian Survey*, Vol. XIX, No. 2, February, 1979, pp 115-140.

Jomo, K.S. and Ahmad Shabery Cheek, "Malaysia's Islamic Movements" in Jeo S. Kahn and Francis Loh Kok Wah (eds), *Fragmented Vision: Culture and Politics in Contemporary Malaysia* (Sydney: Allen and Unwin, 1992) pp. 79-106.

Kroef, Yusuf. M. Van der, "The Term Indonesia: Its Origin and Usage" *Journal of American Oriental Society*, Vol. 70, No. 3, 1951, pp. 166-17.

Lee, Alex, "The Chinese and Malay Dilemmas in Malaysia", *Pacific Community*, Vol. 3, 1971-1972, pp. 561-572.

Liddle, R. William, "The Islamic Turn in Indonesia: A Political Explanation", *Journal of Asian Studies*, Vol. 55, No. 3, August 1996, pp. 613-634.

Locher-Scholten, Elsbeth, "Dutch Expansion in the Indonesian Archipelago around 1900 and the Imperialism Debate", *Journal of Southeast Asian Studies*, 25 No. 1 March 1994, pp. 91-111.

Mauzy, Diane K. and R.S. Milne, "The Mahathir Administration in Malaysia: Discipline through Islam", *Pacific Affairs*, Vol. 56, No. 4 (Winter 1983-84) pp. 617-648.

Milne, R.S., "The Politics if Malaysia's New Economic Policy", *Pacific Affairs*, Vol. 49, No. 2 (Summer 1976) pp. 235-262.

Milner, A.C., "Islam in the Muslim State" in M.B. Hooker (ed), *Islam in Southeast Asia* (Leiden: E.J. Brill, 1983).

Ramage, Douglas E., "Indonesia: Democracy First, Good Governance Later" in Daljit Singh and Lorraine C. Salazar (eds), *Southeast Asian Affairs: 2007* (Singapore: ISEAS, 2007), pp. 135-160.

Samsul, A.B., "Identity construction, nation formation and Islamic revivalism in Malaysia' in Robert W. Hefner and Particia Horvatich (eds), *Islam in an Era of Nation States* (Honolulu: University of Hawaii Press, 1997).

Shari, Ishak and Ragayah Mat Zin, "Economic Growth and Equality in Malaysia: Performance and Prospects in Ahmad Mahdzan (ed), *Southeast Asia on the Growth Path* (Serdong: UPM, 1997), pp. 89-103.

Soesastro, Hadi, "Political Transition and Economic Development: What Do We Know, What are the Key Issues, and What is the Main Agenda Ahead?" in *Political Transition and Economic Development in East Asia* (Jakarta: CSIS, 2007), pp. 1-30.

Wahid, Zainul Abidin, "Malaysian Economic Development: A Historical Perspective" in Ahmad Mahdzan (ed), *Southeast Asia on the Growth Path* (Serdong: UPM, 1997), pp. 1-13.

Wahid-uz-Zaman, "Editor's Note" in *The Quest for Identity* (Proceedings of the First Congress on the History and Culture of Pakistan held at the University of Islamabad, April 1973, Islamabad: University of Islamabad Press, 1974), p. iv.

Newspapers

The Daily Star, Dhaka

Protom Alo, Dhaka

Ittefaq, Dhaka

The Straits Times, Kuala Lumpur

The Star, Kuala Lumpur

The Malay Mail, Kuala Lumpur

The Jakarta Post, Jakarta

Index

□□□